Lessons from the Heartland

Lessons from the Heartland

A TURBULENT HALF-CENTURY OF
PUBLIC EDUCATION IN AN ICONIC AMERICAN CITY

Barbara J. Miner

THE NEW PRESS

NEW YORK
LONDON

Requests for permission to reproduce selections from this book should be mailed to: Permissions Department, The New Press, 38 Greene Street, New York, NY 10013.

The publisher is grateful for permission to reprint the following copyrighted material:

"Glory Days" by Bruce Springsteen. Copyright © 1984 Bruce Springsteen (ASCAP). Reprinted by permission. International copyright secured. All right reserved.

"As I Grew Older" and "Let America Be America Again" from THE COLLECTED POEMS OF LANGSTON HUGHES by Langston Hughes, edited by Arnold Rampersad with David Roessel, Associate Editor, copyright © 1994 by the Estate of Langston Hughes. Used by permission of Alfred A. Knopf, a division of Random House, Inc. Reprinted by permission of Harold Ober Associates.

Money (That's What I Want)
Words and Music by Berry Gordy and Janie Bradford
© 1959 (Renewed 1987) JOBETE MUSIC CO., INC.
All Rights Controlled and Administered by EMI APRIL MUSIC INC. and EMI BLACKWOOD MUSIC INC. on behalf of JOBETE MUSIC CO., INC. and STONE AGATE MUSIC (A Division of JOBETE MUSIC CO., INC.)
All Rights Reserved   International Copyright Secured   Used by Permission
Reprinted by Permission of Hal Leonard Corporation

Published in the United States by The New Press, New York, 2013
Distributed by Perseus Distribution

LIBRARY OF CONGRESS CATALOGING-IN-PUBLICATION DATA

Miner, Barbara.
  Lessons from the heartland : a turbulent half-century of public education in an iconic American city / Barbara Miner.
    p.   cm.
  Includes bibliographical references and index.
  ISBN 978-1-59558-829-6 (hardback)
  ISBN 978-1-59558-864-7 (e-book)
  1. Public schools—Wisconsin—Milwaukee—History.   I. Title.
  LA390.M5M56 2013
  371.010977595—dc23

                                                          2012018151

The New Press publishes books that promote and enrich public discussion and understanding of the issues vital to our democracy and to a more equitable world. These books are made possible by the enthusiasm of our readers; the support of a committed group of donors, large and small; the collaboration of our many partners in the independent media and the not-for-profit sector; booksellers, who often hand-sell New Press books; librarians; and above all by our authors.

www.thenewpress.com

Composition by Westchester Book Composition
This book was set in Minion

Printed in the United States of America

10   9   8   7   6   5   4   3   2   1

To my mother, who never questioned—and understood—why I sent my children to the Milwaukee Public Schools

CONTENTS

ACKNOWLEDGMENTS

Any book reflects the many influences on one's life. There are several people, however, who provided essential advice on this particular project. Thanks to Doug, Martha, and Terri for their writing advice. Thanks to Fred for his feedback as a journalist, and to Larry, Kathy, Rita, Nicki, Caitlin, Mahalia, and Bob for their school-based and community perspectives. Specific thank-yous to Bob Lowe for his feedback as an educational historian, and to Mary Bills for her encouragement, enthusiasm, and financial support that made this project possible.

Most of all, thanks to Bob Peterson. Among his many contributions, he exemplifies how quality teaching and social justice activism can instill in children both civic courage and a love of learning.

INTRODUCTION:
MILWAUKEE, PUBLIC SCHOOLS, AND THE FIGHT FOR AMERICA'S FUTURE

The past is never dead. It's not even past.

—William Faulkner

In the grip of a national recession that hit rust belt states especially hard, Milwaukee was used to bad news in the spring of 2010. Home foreclosures continued unabated. Decent-paying manufacturing jobs kept disappearing. The public schools were battered by one dismal report after another, from truancy to dropouts and test scores.

On Wednesday, March 24, a report in the *Milwaukee Journal Sentinel* shocked even the most cynical. The state's African American fourth graders were at a lower reading level than their peers anywhere in the country. Lower than black students in Missouri, Arkansas, Tennessee, Oklahoma, and the District of Columbia. Worst of all, lower than Mississippi, a state that in the Wisconsin psyche was forever trapped in a stereotype of outhouses and illiteracy.[1]

Although the results were statewide, they were an indictment of Milwaukee in general and its public schools in particular. Milwaukee, Wisconsin's largest city, is home to about three-quarters of the state's African American population, and about 60 percent of the city's public school students are African American.

A few months earlier, Wisconsin had earned another "worst in the nation" recognition, this time for black joblessness. Although driven by Milwaukee-area figures, the news failed to make major headlines in Milwaukee. It was left to the *Washington Post* to do a Christmas Eve feature on how Wisconsin's official unemployment rate for African Americans "surpassed that of every other state, reaching an average of 22 percent for the past 12 months."[2] The jobless rate was even worse. Looking at those not in the labor force for various reasons (including incarceration), 53.3 percent of working-age black men in Milwaukee did not have a job in 2009. At the time, it was the highest rate ever recorded in the city. A year later, the rate was 55.3 percent.[3]

In March 2011, meanwhile, Milwaukee gained notoriety as the most segregated metropolitan region in the country. The designation, based on U.S. Census data and compiled by social scientists from the University of Michigan, was reported on Salon.com.[4] Milwaukee's mainstream media chose not to report the findings.

A half century earlier, in the 1950s, Milwaukee was a symbol of industrial power and a promised land of family-supporting jobs. Even as late as 1970, the black male employment rate was about 85 percent, just a shade lower than the white percentage.[5] No one would have predicted that within a generation, Milwaukee would become a national symbol of joblessness, decline, and racial disparity.

What's more, few would have foreseen that the nation's urban centers would become synonymous with "failing schools" surrounded by equally hard-pressed neighborhoods. Or that at the beginning of the twenty-first century the most segregated schools would be outside the South, with the fifteen most segregated metropolitan regions in the Northeast and Midwest.[6]

Above all, no one would have predicted that Milwaukee's educational claim to fame would be its school voucher program, the country's oldest and largest and a conservative model for similar initiatives. An unabashed abandonment of public education, Milwaukee's voucher program has funneled more than $1 billion in public money into private and religious schools since 1990.

What happened? How did Milwaukee, the working-class but ever-optimistic setting for *Happy Days* and *Laverne & Shirley*, fall so far from its idealized 1950s image?

In this era of standardized tests, the tendency is to look for a single "correct" answer. But the lessons of Milwaukee cannot be approached as a multiple-choice quiz. Milwaukee's plight—as is true in so many other American cities—is rooted in complex and interdependent issues of housing, jobs, and schools, all of which are shaped by race and class. One issue may dominate at a particular moment: Milwaukee's most sustained civil rights protests, for instance, focused on housing discrimination. But over time, housing, jobs, and schools have worked together as the most important mechanisms for reproducing inequality, in particular racial inequities.

Among those issues, public education plays a unique role. It is fundamental not only to the individual hopes and dreams of students and their families but also to this country's vision of an informed citizenry and a vibrant democracy. As Justice William J. Brennan wrote in the 1982 *Plyler v. Doe* decision upholding public schooling for undocumented children, public education is not merely "some governmental 'benefit' indistinguishable from other forms of social welfare legislation. Both the importance of education in maintaining our basic institutions and the lasting impact of its deprivation on the life of the child mark the distinction."[7]

Milwaukee and Wisconsin are symbols of middle America, and not just because of their geographic location in the heartland. Wisconsin has long been recognized as a political swing state, neither firmly Republican nor Democratic. Like Milwaukee, it embodies working-class pride and values. Like Milwaukee, it faces an uncertain future in the postindustrial world.

I began working on this book in 2009, disturbed by Milwaukee's glaring disparities and concerned by what passed for policy debate. Throughout Wisconsin, meanwhile, power brokers had taken advantage of racial stereotypes to foster the illusion that the state could prosper even as Milwaukee, its largest city, declined. As for education, private voucher schools and semiprivate charter schools seemed to be the only reform that policy makers wanted to talk about.

In February 2011, newly elected Republican governor Scott Walker made clear his willingness to abandon public schools and the public sector across the state, not just in Milwaukee. Walker's first assault involved unprecedented legislation that eliminated collective bargaining rights for most public sector workers in Wisconsin—ironically, the first state to allow collective bargaining by public sector unions. In Wisconsin, elementary, secondary, and higher education employees account for the majority of those employed in the public sector. Teachers and students soon were in the forefront opposing Walker's antiunion agenda.[8]

A few weeks later, Walker cut $840 million from funding of public elementary and secondary schools, $250 million from the state university system, and $72 million from the technical colleges—the biggest education cuts in Wisconsin's history.[9] At the same time, Walker significantly expanded the private school voucher program.

In response to Walker's proposals in the spring of 2011, Wisconsin became the scene of massive, round-the-clock protests unlike anything that had ever happened in the state. Every day, for almost a month, demonstrations at the state capitol in Madison linked the attack on the public sector with a defense of democracy. Wisconsin's sleeping giant of populist outrage awakened.

Walker's conservative agenda in Wisconsin was part of a national strategy. The nation's eyes were soon on Wisconsin, and "We Are Wisconsin" became a national battle cry in the growing movement to defend the middle class and rebuild our country's democracy. In the fall of 2011, taking a cue from the Arab Spring and the round-the-clock sleepovers during the Madison uprising, the Occupy Wall Street protests began in New York City. A new chapter in the nation's history unfolded.

All politics is local, but with national repercussions. The Milwaukee story is the Wisconsin story is the nation's story. And I keep returning to the question: what happened?

How did Milwaukee fall so far from grace? Will it find redemption in the twenty-first century? More important, what does this iconic city in America's heartland tell us about the future of public education in the United States and our vision of democracy in our multicultural society?

Part I

Segregation, Prosperity, and Protests: 1950s and 1960s

1.

THE GLORY DAYS OF 1957

Glory days, well, they'll pass you by
Glory days, in the wink of a young girl's eye
Glory days, glory days

—Bruce Springsteen, "Glory Days"

Henry Aaron was well established as a baseball legend when, at the age of forty, he beat Babe Ruth's career home run record on April 8, 1974, and reached what some consider the pinnacle of accomplishment. But it is 1957 that Aaron recalls as his most memorable year. Just twenty-three years old at the time, he helped the Milwaukee Braves win the National League pennant and go on to defeat the seemingly invincible Yankees and capture the 1957 World Series. His lightning-fast wrists, impeccable eyesight, and ability to understand pitchers were in top form that year. Even Casey Stengel, manager of the New York Yankees, was forced to admit so—especially after game four of the World Series at Milwaukee's County Stadium.

With temperatures in the fifties, gusty winds were blowing off Lake Michigan on that Sunday. It was the fourth inning and the Yankees had led 1–0 since the first inning. But suddenly they were in trouble: there was a walk, then a double by Milwaukee's ever-popular third baseman, Eddie Mathews. Henry Aaron stepped up to the plate. Yankee pitcher Tom Sturdivant, knowing Aaron's ability, wanted to walk him. Stengel disagreed. "No, pitch to him," Stengel said during a huddle at the pitcher's mound. "With this wind, Babe Ruth couldn't get one out of here."

Sturdivant did as he was told, and Aaron hit a three-run homer. By the inning's end, the Braves were ahead 4–1, winning the game 7–5. The Yankees, who had hoped to wrap up a third win and destroy the Braves' confidence, instead found the series even at two games apiece. Sturdivant entered the dugout after that fourth inning and said to Stengel, "I thought you said Babe Ruth couldn't get one out of here." To which Stengel reportedly replied, "Well, that wasn't Babe Ruth you were facing."[1]

It was the pennant race, however, where Aaron found the most glory, with an extra-innings homer that clinched the pennant for a city not yet fully accustomed to playing in the major leagues. *Time* magazine explained Aaron's feat by referencing the Israelites' journey into the Promised Land. Quoting from Exodus 8:17, *Time* wrote: "For Aaron stretched out his hand with his rod, and smote the dust of the earth."[2]

In his autobiography, Aaron recalls both the World Series and being named Most Valuable Player of the National League that year: "All of those things made 1957 the best year of my baseball life, and it went along with the best year of baseball that any city ever had. It doesn't get any better than Milwaukee in 1957."

A surprising number of Milwaukeeans, even today, would agree with that assessment. Beneath the surface of 1957, however, two separate and unequal realities existed—as Aaron himself realized.

The morning after his home run won the pennant, the *Milwaukee Sentinel* printed a front-page photo of Aaron being carried off the field by his jubilant teammates, under a banner headline: "We're the Champs! Bring on the Yankees." To the left of that photo, relegated to second-place coverage, a modest headline noted: "I'll Send U.S. Army, Ike Warns." In Little Rock, Arkansas, white mobs were beating on black students attempting to integrate Central High School.[3]

In his autobiography, *I Had a Hammer*, Aaron speaks of his conflicted feelings on seeing that day's newspaper. "The morning after, there was a picture in the paper of me on the shoulders of my teammates," he writes. "Most of them, naturally, were white. On the same front page was a picture of a riot in Little Rock, Arkansas. It seemed that Little Rock, like much of the South, wasn't leaping into the spirit of Brown vs. Board of Education."[4]

Little Rock became a symbol of southern resistance to school desegregation. Its historical significance was amplified by the media attention that zoomed in on what was a little-known southern city, foreshadowing the nonstop news cycles of the future. With a population of just over

100,000 people in 1957, Little Rock was a small city that became a big story.

Ernest Green never considered Little Rock, Arkansas, as part of the Deep South, where opposition to desegregation was the strongest and not a single black student attended school with whites during the 1955 school year.[5] When Green was a junior in the spring of 1957, he put his name in as a student interested in integrating Central. He didn't anticipate the raw racism that would greet him the following September. After all, he recounts, "the year before we went to Central, both the city buses in Little Rock and the public libraries were integrated without any problems."[6]

Although he attended the all-black high school Horace Mann, Green was familiar with Central. Horace Mann students often got Central's hand-me-down textbooks, with the names of the students still inside. He knew that the all-white Central had better facilities, a better curriculum, and better science labs. Shortly before school started he was told he wouldn't be able to be in the band, play football, or go to the prom. But he figured helping to integrate Central was more important than continuing to play tenor sax, as he had done for five years.

Green, the only senior among the black students who came to be known as the Little Rock Nine, never made it to Central on the first day of school. The night before, Arkansas Governor Orval Faubus warned that "blood will run in the streets" if black students entered Central. When the school doors opened on September 4, 1957, troops from the state's National Guard were on hand—not to protect the nine black students but to stand guard, bayonets and all, to keep them out.[7]

Faubus had thrown down the gauntlet. He made clear he was not about to obey the U.S. Supreme Court and its decision three years earlier in *Brown v. Board* that separate schools were inherently unequal and violated the U.S. Constitution. And he was backing up his defiance with National Guard troops under his command.

The drama of the Little Rock Nine seized the nation's attention. "The prolonged duration and the military drama of the siege made Little Rock the first on-site news extravaganza of the modern television era," Taylor Branch writes in his seminal work, *Parting the Waters: America in the King*

Years 1954–63.[8] There were important legal issues as well. Faubus was using armed forces to oppose the federal government, creating what some considered the most severe test of the Constitution since the Civil War.[9]

President Dwight Eisenhower, never a strong supporter of civil rights, hemmed and hawed. For weeks the crisis went unresolved. On September 23, Faubus seemed to comply with White House demands and withdrew the National Guard—only to leave the Little Rock Nine at the mercy of white mobs. "By mid-morning," Branch writes, "angry whites had beaten at least two Negro reporters, broken many of the schools' windows and doors, and come so close to capturing the Negro students that the Little Rock police evacuated them in desperation."[10]

Eisenhower was furious. A military man, he decided to send in his own troops, and enough of them to crush any thought of defiance. Forget U.S. marshals, he told the Pentagon. Call up riot-trained units of the 101st Airborne Division. By the end of the day, fifty-two planeloads had brought more than one thousand federal paratroopers to Little Rock.[11] The next morning, the Little Rock Nine were transported via military convoy to Central High and protected by federal troops. Once inside, the paratroopers transferred the nine students to military personnel who would accompany each student to their classroom so that they were never alone.

The troops were gradually withdrawn, and by the second semester they were gone. For Green, those were the roughest months, as hostility from white students increased. That spring, he became the first black ever to graduate from Central. During the graduation ceremony, he had a space on both sides of him inside the auditorium "because nobody wanted to sit next to me."[12]

History, however, embraced the Little Rock Nine, and they became a beacon of courage for generations to come. It was a young senator from Illinois who acknowledged his debt to the nine on the fiftieth anniversary of Little Rock, saying: "They proved that *Brown* could work, signaling the beginning of the end of Jim Crow, and making a life of hope and opportunity possible for someone like me."[13] Barack Obama again recognized his gratitude in January 2009, inviting the Little Rock Nine to Washington for the inauguration of the first African American as president of the United States.

At the time of the Little Rock crisis, Milwaukee media coverage was overshadowed by what was deemed a more important event: the World Series. After all, Little Rock was a faraway place, a minor-league town somewhere down south.

Located on the shores of Lake Michigan in a state known for its lush farmlands and bucolic landscape, Milwaukee has always been a blue-collar city. If you had the good fortune in the 1950s to be on the top floor of one of downtown's tall buildings (what remains the tallest skyscraper, at forty-two stories, was not built until 1973), to the east was a never-ending line of blue water. City residents bragged Lake Michigan was better than the ocean because it was fresh water. In all other directions, the skyline would have been dominated by symbols of the city's foundational institutions—the belching smoke of factories, well-maintained multistory schools, and church steeples reaching to the heavens. Nearby would have been another Milwaukee trademark, the neighborhood tavern, where the typical order was a draft beer and a shot of bourbon.

The population of Milwaukee, Wisconsin's largest city, has hovered around 600,000 in recent decades. For generations, the city has lived in the shadow of Chicago, ninety miles to the south. As a result, Milwaukee has developed a personality that both resents and boasts of its image as a small-town big city. Spend a day strolling along Milwaukee's lakefront or go to one of its many summer festivals where strangers may treat you as a long-lost friend, and the small-town description is easy to understand. But it has always been difficult for Milwaukee to claim that it is a big city able to compete with the big boys. Over the years, Milwaukee has consistently resorted to one surefire way to bolster its big-city ambitions: host a major-league baseball team.

Milwaukee briefly had such a team, back in 1901, known as the Milwaukee Brewers (a name also used by the city's current National League team). But that moment of glory didn't last, and after one season the team moved to St. Louis. For the next fifty years, the city's team was still called the Milwaukee Brewers, but it was a minor-league team. Which meant that Milwaukee was a minor-league town. It stung. The term "minor-league" became an enduring source of shame, hauled out by critics to describe not just Milwaukee's status as a baseball town, but also the city's shortcomings in every imaginable sphere.

Even Cleveland and St. Louis were major-league towns. But not Milwaukee. "It was fun to go to Borchert Field on a hot afternoon and sit on the wooden bleachers, pulling out splinters and drinking beer and yelling for the Brewers," Robert W. Wells recounts in his book *This Is Milwaukee*. "But when the game was over, Milwaukee was still in the minor leagues."[14]

In the 1950s, Major League Baseball mirrored the nation's mood and was eager to expand. Although no team had relocated since 1903, Milwaukee believed that its fantasy of a major-league team could become a reality. The city had such faith that in 1950 it decided to build Milwaukee County Stadium, three years before it was even sure it could woo a major-league team. "The decision to build County Stadium was a staggering leap of faith for a community that no one has ever mistaken for impetuous," notes historian John Gurda in his book *The Making of Milwaukee*.[15]

With a stadium in place, deals and dreams were bandied about. On Thursday, March 19, 1953, it all came together: league owners okayed the transfer of the Boston Braves to Milwaukee. At the time, the Boston Braves were playing a spring training game in Bradenton, Florida. It was the fifth inning, the game more than half over. Suddenly the scoreboard was changed: the home team switched from BOS to MIL. The Braves were now officially from Milwaukee.[16]

Milwaukee was ecstatic. The following Sunday, three days after the transfer—while the team was still in Florida—ten thousand people showed up at County Stadium just to sit in the stands and imagine the future. There was no team, just an empty field, and it was raining. But the crowd didn't mind. It basked in the glory that Milwaukee was no longer a minor-league town.[17]

Not all the slurs ended, however. Four years later, when the Yankees arrived in Milwaukee for game three of the World Series, Milwaukee tried to extend a hand of friendship. Prominent civic leaders and hundreds of people formed a welcoming committee to greet the Yankees' train as the players arrived and transferred to a chartered bus. But the Yankees gave them the cold shoulder, a slight reported on the front page of the *Milwaukee Journal* on Friday, October 4: " 'This,' said an unidentified Yankee spokesman, shoving a group of reporters and photographers off a chartered bus, 'is strictly bush league.'" The paper did not need to translate. Everyone knew that "bush league" was a synonym for "minor league."

Milwaukee rubbed the snub back in the Yankees' nose. When the Braves won the World Series, deliriously happy fans unfurled a banner that read, "Bushville Wins." Back in Milwaukee, dancing broke out on the streets of downtown. "No single event in the community's history—not V-J Day or the end of World War I or even the return of legal beer—has ever caused such a spontaneous outpouring of joy," Gurda notes.[18]

Milwaukee's attention in 1957 was on the World Series, but the world was not standing still. Joe McCarthy, the anticommunist demagogue from Appleton, Wisconsin, died that year. Osama bin Laden was born. Sputnik, the world's first artificial satellite, was launched by the Soviet Union, ushering in a cold war "space race" and fostering demands for better math and science education. On the pop charts, Elvis Presley ("All Shook Up") and Pat Boone ("Love Letters in the Sand") had the year's top songs. John Lennon, meanwhile, was a teenager forming his first band.

Television started the decade as an upstart challenge to radio but soon came to dominate the nation's living rooms. The share of U.S. households with TV sets rose from about 10 percent in 1950 to 90 percent by the decade's end—what social scientist Robert Putnam calls "probably the fastest diffusion of a technological innovation ever recorded."[19] It was television that, two decades later, crowned Milwaukee as the quintessential 1950s all-American city of hard-working, everyday people.

Milwaukee was chosen as the locale for the *Happy Days* sitcom, followed by the spin-off *Laverne & Shirley*. The shows, surviving for decades through reruns, featured a romanticized 1950s that specialized in saccharine scenes from a white working-class perspective, complete with ice cream floats and sock hops. The Fonz—sporting a leather jacket and greased pompadour but otherwise reduced to a cardboard caricature of James Dean or Marlon Brando—was as edgy as the characters would get. (More than thirty years later, many Milwaukeeans still bask in the glow of such TV-based reality. In 2008, the city's tourism booster organization sponsored a bronze statue of the Fonz in downtown, even convincing the actor who portrayed the character, Henry Winkler, to attend the dedication. The statue became an instant hit, scene of many a tourist photo.)

*   *   *

Milwaukee was rebounding in the 1950s from the combined effects of a depression followed by a world war. Its spirits were high, the economy was booming, and support for the public schools was strong.

From buildings to staff and students to extracurricular offerings, the city's public schools expanded and never once seemed to doubt what had been commonly accepted wisdom for large-city districts since the 1920s: they were unquestionably superior to small-town or rural schools.[20] Forty-four major school district building projects were completed in the 1950s, from new high schools and junior highs to eighteen new elementary schools and sixteen major elementary additions.[21] Three citywide votes were held in the 1950s and two more in the 1960s to approve necessary bonds for school construction. In every instance, the voters approved by a significant majority.[22]

The only significant pall was the 1950s' concern with "civil defense" and fears of a nuclear attack from the Soviet Union. It was an era when students were taught the "duck and cover" method of surviving a nuclear attack by hiding under a desk and assuming a fetal position. Families, meanwhile, were encouraged to build fallout shelters in their basements, complete with food, cooking supplies, flashlights, and blankets. The schools enthusiastically took part in civil defense initiatives. In 1956, the Milwaukee school board unanimously passed a policy outlining school evacuation procedures and embracing a "bracelet tagging program." Across the city, in public and private schools alike, families were encouraged to spend 50 cents and buy stainless steel bracelets with a child's name, next of kin, address, birth date, and religious preference. "A sturdy clasp prevents the child from removing the bracelet easily," the *Milwaukee CD News Notes* noted in a March 1956 article. The bracelets, the newsletter said, would help establish a child's identity in case of a traffic accident, evacuation, or enemy attack.

The student population, meanwhile, was growing dramatically, from 68,607 students in 1950 to 101,242 by June 1960, in large part fueled by the city's annexation of neighboring towns.[23] And the district was adding not only students but also programs. Behind-the-wheel driver's ed was added to the curriculum in 1956, starting with a modest eleven teachers and eleven cars. The school board, arguing that paying for sports through gate receipts would disadvantage many schools, assumed financing of interscholastic

sports in 1956, with ten officially sponsored sports.[24] The Wisconsin legislature did its part to support the schools, raising ceilings on local school
revenues for day-to-day operations.[25]

The structure of the school day was not that different from practices
fifty years later. Then as now, most high school students changed classes
when loud, insistent bells started ringing. Elementary students sat in desks
lined up row by row. School plays, athletics, prom, and yearbooks were
more important to high school students than their lecture-style classes.
Most high schools were comprehensive, offering both academic and a broad
array of vocational courses, with a capacity of twelve hundred to two thousand students.[26]

Academic requirements were not as intense as today's. Expectations
were changing, however. In 1958, the district strengthened graduation requirements. In what would nevertheless today be considered low standards,
it required three years (six semesters) of English and a year (two semesters)
each of math, science, and U.S. history.[27] More important, a high school
diploma was quickly becoming the societal norm. In the 1920s, roughly 65
percent of high-school-age youth in Milwaukee were not in high school,
having left in order to work full-time. By the late 1950s, only 25 percent were
dropping out.

Harold Vincent, as was generally true of superintendents till the later
decades of the century, enjoyed good relations with the school board, serving for seventeen years until 1967. Like his predecessors, Vincent was committed to a strongly centralized system, and there was a public consensus
about educational goals and structure. As one historical overview of the
district noted, "The administrative apparatus which was erected in the decades of the 1940s and 1950s represented the crowning achievement of the
bureaucratic model of school reform."[28]

Milwaukee's public schools, perhaps because of the city's strong German heritage and a belief that strong bodies lead to strong minds, enjoyed
a national reputation for a pioneering recreation department, serving not
only students but also adults. Many programs, including weaving and knit-
ting classes, dated back to the turn of the century. In the 1950s, the Department of Municipal Recreation and Adult Education further blossomed,
adding programs that included year-round outdoor education, a softball
spring training camp for girls, a traveling playground theater, Saturday arts

programs, and a family camping association. The programs were funded by a separate tax levy, and increases were approved in 1955 and 1965 to support the expanded programs.[29]

In line with the city's reliance on manufacturing and industrial businesses, Milwaukee had a strong program in vocational education, with both a Boys Trade and Technical High School and a separate trade and tech school for girls. Offerings at Boys Tech included specialties ranging from auto mechanics to electricity, machining, printing, and toolmaking.

In general, schools were organized by neighborhood, with students walking to the closest school. This was before expressways, and before disease wiped out the city's majestic Dutch elm trees, which for decades had provided a comforting canopy over city streets. Crime was low on people's list of concerns, and city residents, black and white alike, reminisce that they rarely locked their doors back in the 1950s. Except during the city's long winter, the walks were generally pleasant. Many students even had the convenience of walking home for lunch.

The school system did not gather racial statistics, but the African American student population, while growing, was still relatively small. Given the housing segregation in Milwaukee, African Americans were confined to a few specific neighborhoods and a few specific schools, many of them overcrowded.

There was also a thriving system of private schools in Milwaukee in the 1950s, with private school enrollment accounting for about a third of all students throughout the decade.[30] Catholic and Lutheran schools were particularly vibrant. It was common in the 1950s for Catholics to identify themselves not by neighborhood but by parish.

Economically, World War II was good to Milwaukee, and the city emerged as a still-strong industrial powerhouse. Even before the war Milwaukee had been known as "the machine shop of the world," and defense industries turned to the city to produce materials for the war effort. Manufacturers, in turn, willingly converted to wartime production. Froemming Brothers, a highway contractor, opened a shipyard. Allis-Chalmers, the city's largest employer and best known for its tractors, built a number of armaments, including key components for the atomic bomb.

In the 1950s, jobs were plentiful, even for those without a high school diploma. The work was often hard and dirty, especially in the foundries and tanneries, but it paid well. A typical job meant working in a factory—at A.O. Smith, Allis-Chalmers, Allen-Bradley, Globe-Union, or Harley-Davidson, or perhaps at one of the city's many machine shops or steel plants, pounding metal. Not to be outdone, the city's breweries were economic powerhouses in the 1950s—from Miller to Blatz, Pabst, and Schlitz (the last of these was once the world's largest producer of beer and was known for decades as "The Beer that Made Milwaukee Famous").

As the decade began, the city's unemployment rate was 2.8 percent, essentially full employment.[31] Some 40 percent of the city's labor force was in manufacturing, one of the highest proportions in the country. The blue-collar jobs wouldn't make one rich, but they made it possible to buy a home and raise a family. What's more, prices of everyday items were cheap: gas was 25 cents a gallon, a first-class postage stamp was 3 cents, and a case of a local beer was $3.13. It was even inexpensive to be fashionable: "full-fashioned nylon stockings" were only 59 cents a pair at Gimbels, Milwaukee's most popular department store.[32]

More than the economy was flourishing. The city itself was on a growth spurt, increasing in size by more than 50 percent in the 1950s. Gobbling up nearby towns and unincorporated areas, Milwaukee annexed huge swaths of land, with farmland and cow pastures soon to become bustling housing developments to accommodate the city's growing population. By 1960 the city had grown to its largest size ever: 741,324 people. Some Milwaukeeans boast that for a brief time in the early 1960s, the city made it to the top ten of U.S. cities.

With the car becoming the country's preferred mode of transportation, Milwaukee began buildings its system of freeways, four-lane roads, and easy-to-drive-to shopping malls, each new one bigger than the last. Major public projects were either completed or in the works—a new art museum, a new zoo, a new conservatory, a new post office, a new airport terminal, a new center for the performing arts. Civic pride was high.

For more than half a century, a handful of terms have routinely been used to describe Milwaukee: "blue-collar," "frugal," "friendly," "down-to-earth."

These well-deserved descriptions coexist with another reality, one that is rarely discussed. Milwaukee is one of the most segregated cities in the country.

Hank Aaron rarely talked of the discrimination he faced. Over time, however, details came out—not just about the problems common to any black player integrating major-league baseball, but also the difficulties Aaron and his family faced in Milwaukee. For instance, the Milwaukee Athletic Club, a downtown gathering spot for the city's rich and powerful, had a policy against allowing in blacks, and members would sometimes make a stink about Aaron attending events.[33] Even the Braves' locker room was unofficially segregated, with Aaron and the other black players often taking their showers and getting dressed after their white teammates had finished.[34]

Matters of housing and schools were more complicated. When Aaron and his family broke the color line in Mequon, a suburb to the north of Milwaukee known for its rural ambience and large lots, the builder was worried that word might get out he sold a house to a Negro. He insisted that he be able to sell the house to a friend of Aaron's who was a realtor, and then the real estate company could resell it to Aaron.[35] But buying the house was just one of several obstacles. Aaron's new neighbors were not used to nonwhites. Most were friendly, but a few were hostile. One man, Aaron recalls, "called all the neighborhood women and made filthy suggestions to them, identifying himself as me."[36] Aaron took personal slights in stride and overall got along well with his neighbors. The most disturbing incidents had to do with school and Aaron's younger sister, Alfredia.

When Alfredia was eleven years old and living at the family home in Mobile, the offer came to live with her brother in Milwaukee. Alfredia was excited. To pressure her mother, Alfredia sent half her clothes up in a trunk. Her mother agreed, and Alfredia moved to Milwaukee. But Alfredia was unprepared for how she was to be treated at school, where she was the only black.[37] Some of the incidents seemed minor—boys who referred to her "going back home to Africa," parents who would pick up their kids at school so they wouldn't walk home with Alfredia. But the slights and insensitivities added up. As Alfredia relates in a first-person account in Aaron's biography, one day she burst out crying at the breakfast table. "Finally, Henry and [his wife] Barbara took me into the principal's office to talk about what was happening," Alfredia writes. "The principal looked Henry right in the face and said, 'There wouldn't be a problem if you hadn't brought her to this school.'"[38]

Before long Alfredia moved back to Mobile.

Hank Aaron was the most famous African American in Milwaukee. If he and his family had problems with discrimination, what did that mean for others in Milwaukee's black community? How deep were Milwaukee's separate and unequal realities?

2.

THE 1950S: MILWAUKEE'S BLACK COMMUNITY
COMES OF AGE

We've danced the NAACP Waltz: Two steps forward, a side step, and one step backward. Which means, of course, that you haven't gone real far.

— Vel Phillips, commenting on racial progress in Milwaukee[1]

Even as a child, Vel Phillips had big dreams. She wanted to be a lawyer. While growing up in the late 1930s, she would eavesdrop on her parents' conversations with James Dorsey, a black man who unsuccessfully ran for alderman. One day, she was baking oatmeal-raisin cookies with her mother and her mother asked what she might like to be when she grew up. "And I said, 'I want to be a lawyer like Mr. Dorsey. Can I be a lawyer?'" Phillips recollects. "And my mother would say, 'Of course you can, honey, but it will be hard, because there aren't many women lawyers.'"

When Phillips got to Roosevelt Junior High, she was not encouraged to excel academically. When she tried to sign up for a college prep class, a faculty adviser said the course wasn't open to her. "She then proceeded to tell me that Negro women were best prepared to train for cooks and maids and not to take college courses," Phillips recounts.[2]

Phillips ignored her adviser and went on to become the most celebrated African American woman in Milwaukee history. Her string of many firsts began when she was the first African American woman to graduate from the University of Wisconsin Law School in 1951. In 1956, she was the first woman and first African American elected to the Common Council, Milwaukee's legislative body. In 1971, she became the first woman in Milwaukee and the first African American in the state to be a judge. In 1978, she was the first woman and first African American elected Wisconsin secretary of state. (As late as 2011 she remained the only African American to have been elected to statewide office in Wisconsin.)

But Phillips is known for more than the formal accomplishments that shattered myths of black inferiority. She is a mentor and role model for the younger generation. In an often divided city, she spans communities not only of race but also of generations and gender. It's hard to think of any other contemporary person, white or black, man or woman, whose life has intersected with so much of the city's political history.

In Milwaukee, Vel, like Oprah, invariably goes by her first name. (Even her paperboy used to call her Vel.)[3] She was born in Milwaukee on February 18, 1924, the second of three daughters to established members of Milwaukee's small but tight-knit African American community. She attended two Milwaukee schools that would become synonymous with the black community—Roosevelt and then North Division High School. She won a nationally sponsored oratory scholarship (also won two years later by Martin Luther King Jr.) that helped finance her way to Howard University in Washington, D.C.

Milwaukee's black population was relatively small in 1950, about 22,000 people, accounting for only 3.4 percent of the city's population. But throughout the decade, the black community was growing fast as southern immigrants poured into the city. By 1960, the black population had almost tripled, to about 62,500, accounting for 8.4 percent of city residents. Within that decade, the racial composition of entire neighborhoods changed as the black community expanded from just north of downtown to areas further north and west. In Census Tract 37, just northwest of downtown, blacks were less than 2 percent of the population in 1950; by 1960, they were more than 78 percent of the population. Other central-city census tracts had similar changes.[4]

In 1956, Milwaukee was reapportioned and the African American community believed its time had come to win representation on the Common Council. The original idea was for Phillips's husband, Dale, a lawyer who was president of the local NAACP chapter, to run for the aldermanic seat. One day, however, Dale told her, "Honey, this is not my cup of tea. But you have the same credentials I have." Phillips didn't take much convincing.

Phillips's 1956 breakthrough marked an important coming-of-age both for Milwaukee's African American community and for women. It would be twelve years before another African American would be elected to the Common Council and sixteen years before another woman would. (Milwaukee has yet to elect an African American mayor. Women also have had minimal representation, with only one woman on the council in 2010, after years in which no woman served.)

Phillips often says she has felt more obstinate discrimination as a woman than as an African American. It's not that being African American didn't present as many obstacles, Phillips explains. But after the obstacles were overcome, after she was admitted to law school or elected to the Common Council, she felt the burden and stereotypes of her gender more strongly. "We are a very racist country, unfortunately," Phillips says. "But once you're there, they [whites] will realize you're just like everybody else. But the men never forget that you are a woman. Never ever ever."

A story Phillips tells about then mayor Henry Maier is particularly revealing about gender politics in the 1960s. Phillips says that Maier personally liked her but was angry with her for pushing a city ordinance prohibiting discriminatory housing practices. "Henry felt I had let him down," Phillips recollects. "He'd call me into his office and read the riot act and swear like a sailor. . . . I'd sit there and listen and then tell him, 'If all you are going to do is get mad at me, don't call me in anymore.' That's when he'd say, 'You are sassy and Dale ought to give you a good beating.'"

Phillips has not been shy about expressing her feelings—always clearly, often bluntly, and occasionally with biting sarcasm. When an alderman, for instance, she publicly labeled her opponents "examples of stupidity on the council floor" when they voted against public funds for a birth control program. And she has always been known for her lightning-quick verbal skills. In one exchange during the 1960s, a fellow alderman asked Phillips why she didn't "keep your people in line."

"She looked down at a newspaper which had front page stories about the sentencing of two white men," the Milwaukee Journal recounts. "One was accused of a mass murder in Chicago and another of attempted murder here.

"'Why don't you keep your people in line?' she responded, pointing to the newspaper stories."[5]

Phillips says Thurgood Marshall, whom she and her husband met during an NAACP conference in the early 1950s, is the public figure who left the most lasting impression on her. She still remembers his advice at that conference: all lawyers, especially African American lawyers, have a special responsibility to make the world a better place. "From then on," Phillips says, "that became my goal, to somehow make a difference."

Like many activists of that era, Phillips focused on an interconnected tripod of concerns: housing, jobs, and schools. In fact, her first attempt at political office was in 1953 when she unsuccessfully ran for the school board. At the time she was also working with the League of Women Voters on door-to-door voter registration in the African American community, including some of the most impoverished areas. She realized the depth of the housing crisis. "The homes, especially the ones in the rear, there'd be no real heat, just space heaters," Phillips recalls. "The homes were run down, with rickety porches. . . . That was my first experience with true poverty and my heart just turned over."

For much of the era after World War II, the Milwaukee power structure and media had a specific name for the city's black neighborhood: the Inner Core. The term fit in well with Milwaukee's self-image as a defender of polite civic discourse. When someone referred to the Inner Core, everyone knew what was meant without needing to bring race into the discussion.

The name nominally derived from a description of neighborhoods closest to downtown and therefore at the city's core. Interestingly, however, there was another neighborhood close to downtown, one that was overwhelmingly white. That neighborhood was not described as part of the Inner Core but was called the South Side, and became Milwaukee's code for a lower-income neighborhood of ethnic whites, in particular Polish immigrants. Thus in Milwaukee there were two distinct names given to two working-class neighborhoods near downtown. Only one neighborhood, where African Americans lived, was called the Inner Core and had negative connotations. A 1963 academic report on Milwaukee's Negro community noted the somewhat peculiar labeling and said: "It should be mentioned that if a city's inner core is older, deteriorating and less desirable, characterized by high unemployment, lower incomes and other social problems, then Milwaukee has at least two such areas: one on the south side, in addition to parts of the north side area generally referred to as the inner core. . . . For all practical purposes this [the Inner Core] is Milwaukee's Negro ghetto."[6]

(As the black population grew in the 1950s and 1960s, "Inner Core" described those areas closest to downtown, and "the Core" described the broader and expanding black neighborhood.)

The Inner Core did not develop by happenstance. It was the result of restrictive covenants prohibiting selling or renting to anyone other than Caucasians, and of a "gentlemen's agreement" among realtors not to sell or rent to blacks or Jews except in the central city.[7] The most explicit covenant involved the Washington Highlands, an affluent neighborhood in a suburb bordering Milwaukee. The Highlands were one of the area's first planned subdivisions, and the homeowner's deed in 1919 explicitly said: "At no time shall the land included in Washington Highlands or any part thereof, or any buildings thereon, be purchased, owned, leased or occupied by any person other than that of the white race. . . . This prohibition is not intended to include domestic servants while employed by the owner or occupant of any land included in the tract."[8]

Few homes were built in Milwaukee during the Depression, and when construction began again after World War II, the Inner Core was left behind. A study by the Citizens' Governmental Research Bureau in 1946 found that 67 percent of the city's African Americans lived in homes that were either "unfit for use" or "in need of major repair," compared to about 6.5 percent of units occupied by whites. In Detroit and Buffalo, two other northern cities with growing African American populations, percentages were about half that. A *Milwaukee Journal* article a few years later described Milwaukee's Core as a "dilapidated, overcrowded tinder box."[9]

Milwaukee has long prided itself on its multiethnic immigrant heritage. In 1890, immigrants and their children made up 86.4 percent of the city's population (Germans in particular), and Milwaukee was known as the most "foreign" city in the country. Twenty years later, the percentage had dipped only slightly. But those various ethnic immigrant groups, from Germans to Poles, Italians, Irish, and Serbians, all had one thing in common: they were white. African Americans, meanwhile, were viewed as "gate crashers" to the *gemütlich* ideal that was Milwaukee.[10] And these "gate crashers," whether common laborer or renowned physician, were confined to the Inner Core. As a 1955 city report described the practice, "The Negro middle and upper classes, regardless of their education, skills, professional accomplishments—if their skin is dark—must reside in the slum."[11]

Inferior housing stock was part of a larger disparity. According to the city's 1958 vital statistics, for instance, the premature infant mortality rate per 100,000 was more than three times higher for nonwhites than for whites.[12] (Milwaukee's nonwhite community at the time was overwhelmingly African American.)

In 1960, Mayor Frank Zeidler issued an assessment designed to spur the city to action. Although sidestepping the racism and discrimination that bred many of the problems described, Zeidler's report noted: "The problems of the core include the physical deterioration of this core, excessive traffic, overcrowding of people, littered streets and alleys, lack of adequate play space and green spots, concentration of low-income families, presence of problem families, large numbers of aged families, presence of fragmented families, presence of bad forms of recreation, high rates of crime, insecurity of people on the streets, and group resistance to the police in their performance of their duties."[13]

In the 1950s, the city's black community was segregated, but it was intact. Freeway construction had not yet torn apart Milwaukee's neighborhoods, the suburbs did not yet dominate, and the black middle and professional class lived in the same neighborhood as workers. The name "Bronzeville" recently has been used to brand the heart of the black community, in line with other midwestern cities referring to historic black neighborhoods. At the time, however, regular people—the barbers, store owners, newspaper deliverers—called the neighborhood "Chocolate City," according to Clayborn Benson, head of the Wisconsin Black Historical Society and Museum. It was an era when, for blacks and whites alike, neighborhoods were vibrant. Malls, big-box stores, and distant multiplex theaters had not yet supplanted neighborhood-based shopping and recreation. The Zeidler report, for instance, notes that in one area of the Inner Core alone, there were seven movie theaters, five billiard parlors, and twelve bowling alleys. A half century later, there were only a handful of movie theaters in the entire city.

Most important, there were family-supporting jobs. "It wasn't the best job, and it was the hardest," notes Benson. "But it was enough to bring income in, when they couldn't do that in the South, coming off of being a sharecropper."

Thanks in part to the organizing of A. Philip Randolph, a pioneer in African American unionism and civil rights, blacks in Milwaukee bene-fited economically from World War II. In 1941, Randolph threatened a march on Washington to pressure the U.S. government into prohibiting discrimination in defense industries. In order to head off the march, Presi-dent Franklin D. Roosevelt issued such an executive order in 1941. Com-bined with efforts by the Milwaukee Urban League, the order meant that blacks who previously had been shut out of major manufacturers now found work as the factories retooled for defense work and increased their employ-ment. "You could quit one job in the morning and get another in the after-noon," one Milwaukee black worker boasted.[14]

Having gained a foothold in manufacturing, Milwaukee's blacks moved up. "Once World War Two ended, there would be no large-scale loss of these jobs as there had been after World War One," notes historian Paul Greib.[15] With unemployment low and the economy humming, there was demand for black labor. In the coming decades, a disproportionately high percentage of blacks in Milwaukee were employed in manufacturing, com-pared to national trends.

At the same time, there were limitations. In 1960, there were only 22 blacks out of 1,869 members of the police force. At the fire department, there were only 5 out of more than 1,000.[16] And while blacks were welcome to take on manufacturing's backbreaking jobs, they were too often kept out of the craft unions. The International Association of Machinists (IAM), for instance, had a national policy against allowing black members, and Mil-waukee IAM Lodge 66 did not accept any black members until after World War II. In 1957, the NAACP was forced to take the Milwaukee Bricklayers Union to court when it denied membership to two African Americans.[17]

Discriminatory practices went beyond craft unions. There were no Af-rican Americans in the large-scale printing industry, or in white-collar jobs at banks or insurance companies, and black real estate agents were not admitted to the Milwaukee Board of Realtors until 1965.[18] Black women, meanwhile, were by and large employed in light industry or in service jobs, especially as nurses' aides, maids, or cleaning ladies. From 1960 to 1963, a short-lived but influential group known as the Milwaukee Negro Ameri-can Labor Council focused on increasing jobs for blacks. In a confrontational approach not yet common in Milwaukee's civil rights community, it picketed local stores, called for an economic boycott, and linked issues of joblessness and police/community relations.

Despite clear problems of discrimination, however, many black Milwaukeeans who grew up in the 1950s remember it as an era of good jobs and high hopes. "People had jobs and families were more intact," notes Annette "Polly" Williams, who served in the Wisconsin legislature for thirty years and whose father worked at a tannery. "The industries were there—you could get a job at A.O. Smith or Allis-Chalmers. And as soon as the young men graduated from high school, the father took them to the factory and they started working."[19]

In the schools, the civil rights focus in the 1950s was on jobs for African American teachers, not on the segregation of students.

The first black teachers in Milwaukee's public schools were not hired until 1931, when two women were hired as substitutes at predominantly black elementary schools; by the mid-1930s, when jobs were tight, the women lost their jobs. By 1940, no black held a regular teaching position in the schools. It wasn't until 1951 that the district assigned a black teacher to a high school. Thomas Cheeks was sent to Lincoln High School, where 15 percent of the students were black and the principal asked that he be sent "a colored man."[20]

Cheeks's assignment was the result of behind-the-scenes organizing, in particular by William Kelley of the Milwaukee Urban League. Kelley had targeted the hiring of black teachers as the main education reform in the black community. While the number of black teachers increased, the increase was slow, and there were still only nine by 1950.[21] Furthermore, they were assigned to predominantly black schools. In the fall of 1953, the NAACP met with officials of the Milwaukee Public Schools and demanded that black teachers be allowed to teach at predominantly white schools, and that white teachers hold higher expectations for black students. Summarizing the meeting, the *Milwaukee Journal* led its story by asking: "Should Negro teachers teach in schools that have mostly non-Negro pupils? Should Negro pupils be encouraged to enter college and head toward professions which they may have difficulty entering?"

Overall, however, public discussion on black-white relations in the 1950s centered on housing. Large numbers of blacks were moving into the city, and many whites were not ready to share their neighborhoods with these newcomers. The home, not the school, was their first line of defense.

Frank Zeidler, mayor from 1948 to 1960, was a proponent of public housing to replace homes in the central city and to provide homes for returning GIs, both black and white. He was a member of the Socialist Party. Back in 1910 Milwaukee became the first major city to elect a Socialist mayor. For most of the next fifty years Milwaukee had a Socialist mayor, a unique accomplishment in twentieth-century U.S. politics. When Zeidler left office in 1960, he was the last Socialist to oversee a major city in the United States.

Milwaukee's Socialists were a far cry from the stereotype of rabble-rousing troublemakers eager to throw a stick of dynamite or organize a wildcat strike. In fact, Milwaukee's brand of socialism earned the nickname "sewer socialism" because the Socialists were so identified with developing publicly financed and controlled services such as parks, cultural centers, zoos, and sewers. They believed in using government to promote a strong and vibrant public sector, and their commitment to the common good was perhaps outdone only by their fiscal conservatism and integrity. No one ever accused the Socialists of financial or political corruption; they were scrupulously honest, with their frugality bordering on being downright cheap.

After World War II, when Zeidler pushed for low-income housing and urban renewal in the central city, he was met with stiff resistance from realtors and businessmen who believed the free market and not the government should solve housing problems. Race was a quiet but ever-present subtext, with concerns about integrated housing projects as the number of African Americans in the city increased. When African Americans were just a small community and provided a much-needed pool of porters, servants, cooks, and common laborers, the city's power structure didn't worry too much about the African American community. When numbers started increasing, when the housing crisis grew worse, and when African Americans started seeking better-paying jobs, tensions escalated.

As noted, Zeidler was a Socialist, and the racial controversies around public housing overlapped with anticommunist invectives that were common in the 1950s, especially in Wisconsin, the home state of Senator Joe McCarthy. It all came to a head in 1956—the year my uncle Mac ran for mayor against Frank Zeidler.

Uncle Mac was my favorite uncle. He always had a smile on his face, played the ukulele, knew wondrous card tricks, and was capable of amazing feats such as winning a bet on a lazy summer's evening to eat a dozen ears of corn on the cob. He also had a log cabin "up north" along a river, complete with woodstove and water pumped by hand. If we behaved, we were rewarded with being able to shoot a .22 rifle under careful supervision, or visit the one-room general store and buy penny candy.

I didn't know what Uncle Mac did before he married Aunt Dorothy, the third-oldest of my mother's eight siblings. All I remember is that he was from a faraway place called Escanaba, so far up north that it was in Michigan, and that he came to Milwaukee during the Depression in search of work. And that my aunt Dorothy, ten years younger, didn't like him at all when they first met—he was too brash. I also knew he was Irish Catholic, like my mother's family, and that was a big plus.

Uncle Mac was involved in politics. I wasn't sure what that meant, only that he worked at this important building called city hall and had friends whose names were often in the newspaper. Most glorious to me as a young child, one year he recruited me and my younger brother to be in the city's Christmas parade, dressed up as Santa's helpers and waving from a float that traveled through downtown. For one splendid day, we believed we were famous.

I was only six years old when Uncle Mac ran for mayor, so I have no firsthand knowledge of that infamous campaign. Even today, as I stare at newspaper articles in unforgiving black and white print, I find it hard to link my uncle's quotes with the man I knew as a child. It is a personally disturbing reminder that good people can be involved in bad politics.

To Milwaukee voters, my Uncle Mac was Milton J. McGuire, the fifty-year-old president of the Common Council and, in the words of the *Milwaukee Journal*, "a rough and tumble political fighter."[22] For twenty years, since 1936, he had been alderman, and for twelve years his fellow aldermen had elected him president of the Common Council. From that position, he led opposition to Zeidler's policies. City offices in Milwaukee were nonpartisan, as they remain, but everyone knew McGuire was a conservative Democrat.

McGuire was alderman of the old Third Ward, an area just south of downtown that was home to Irish and then later Italian immigrants. By the mid-1950s, the homes were run down and many residents had moved to better neighborhoods. As part of an urban renewal plan, in 1954 Zeidler proposed to make room for light industry and small businesses in the Third Ward by razing a number of dilapidated homes and the Blessed Virgin of Pompeii Catholic Church. The pastor, Father Anthony Cogo, was a staunch anticommunist and successfully led an attack against the plan, calling Zeidler a "church burner."[23] In hindsight, it seems obvious that Zeidler's plan for McGuire's ward was a factor in the 1956 campaign's animosity. (Blessed Virgin of Pompeii was named Milwaukee's first architectural landmark, in 1967, but soon after was torn down so a freeway could be built.)

McGuire focused his anti-Zeidler comments on the need to defend the American free enterprise system against an avowed Socialist. Among his supporters, a consistent fixation was the need to stand firm against "Negro lovers," although such assessments were not voiced publicly.

One knows a campaign is poisonous when *Time* magazine, hardly soft on communism or overly sensitive to racism, described the 1956 mayoral campaign under the headline "The Shame of Milwaukee." The article outlined the "vicious rumor campaign against Zeidler." False allegations included claims that Zeidler was plastering the South with billboards inviting Negroes to Milwaukee. And that Zeidler's sister "is married to a Negro." And that McGuire's aides "sneered at Zeidler workers for associating with a 'nigger lover.'"[24] The Uncle Mac I knew never would have used such a term.

McGuire the candidate publicly denounced the whispering campaign, but it continued. One political observer noted that the smears were being repeated "in 1,000 bar-rooms around the city."[25] In an attempt to squelch the rumors, the Milwaukee Federated Trades Council contacted labor federations in the South to see if there were billboards welcoming Negroes to Milwaukee. No one could find a single one.[26]

Who exactly was responsible for the whispering campaign may never be known. Just about everyone involved is either dead, including both mayoral candidates, or at a stage in life where their memories are unreliable. But Zeidler linked McGuire to the campaign. He left no doubt that he believed the anticommunism and racism were related, and that the racism was the more dangerous of the two: "If my opponent leaves any heritage to Milwaukee, whether he wins or loses, it will be racial tension where none existed before."[27]

It wasn't the only set of inflammatory allegations linked to McGuire's campaign. A few days before the election, a McGuire advertisement in the city's newspapers said, in part:

> Milwaukee Needs Action to Rid Itself of Moral Termites! These are youthful hoodlum mobs, often excited by marijuana and drinking parties, ranging Milwaukee with wolfpack viciousness, "dragging" our streets in danger ridden hot rods. . . . There are groups of teenagers, ogling magazine racks, eyes unnaturally bright, faces unhealthily excited . . . emotionally warped by row upon row of the salacious, suggestive or downright obscene covers and titles displayed.[28]

The police chief and district attorney roundly denounced the ad. McGuire said he had not seen it before it was printed, and immediately pulled it.

Publicly, McGuire stuck to anticommunism. A February 23, 1956, *Milwaukee Sentinel* report is typical, with McGuire denouncing Zeidler for "making un-American utterances" and "trying to sell us a foreign ideology." In contrast, McGuire emphasized his support for "free enterprise."

The ideologically based campaign was clearly linked to controversy over Zeidler's support of public housing projects and his concern with alleviating problems in the Inner Core. Because the public housing was financed and overseen by the government, it was seen as inherently socialistic. And given the planned location of the projects, with some not far from the Inner Core, they were seen as overly welcoming to black people. Thus, in the voters' minds, the issues were linked. The smear of socialism and anticommunism was powerful enough to be used on its own, allowing race to be an omnipresent but muted topic.[29]

The city's media also focused on anticommunism. The *Milwaukee Sentinel*, the more conservative of the city's two daily newspapers, felt so strongly that it initiated a front-page campaign series under the headline "Which Do YOU Want? Americanism or Socialism?" The editors called Zeidler a "longtime, dedicated, doctrinaire, Marxian socialist." McGuire, in contrast, was described as defending "the American system of free enterprise."

The *Milwaukee Sentinel* ran a number of anti-Zeidler editorials. It linked "socialism" quotes from Zeidler with quotes from Joseph Stalin and Nikita Khrushchev, followed by "Americanism" quotes from McGuire. The Milwaukee voters, however, did not see the race as a life-and-death struggle against communism: Zeidler won handily. But, as Zeidler predicted, the campaign's legacy continued and racial tensions increased. Before long, race—not anticommunism—became the dominant feature in the city's politics.

The 1960s, and Milwaukee's civil rights movements, were just around the corner. Vel Phillips, elected in 1956 as the city's first black alderman, was one of many activists who would soon become household names as Milwaukee earned a reputation as "the Selma of the North."[30]

3.

1964: FREEDOM SCHOOLS COME TO MILWAUKEE

I want you to think about this. There will be a Negro president of this country. But it will not be the country that we are sitting in now. But if you do say to yourself, "There never will be a Negro president of this country," then what you're doing is agreeing with white people who say you are inferior.

—James Baldwin, talking to San Francisco youth, 1963[1]

On May 18, 1964, ten-year-old Kathy Williams and her twelve-year-old brother stepped out their front door, walked down the porch steps, and headed to the corner. Once there, they stopped briefly. Williams took a deep breath. Instead of turning west to their elementary school three blocks away, she and her brother turned east and walked a block to Pilgrim Rest Baptist Church. Williams, pencil and notepaper in hand, wearing a skirt and a light jacket to keep her warm during the cool morning temperatures, was excited but unsure of what the day would bring. She was on her way to a Freedom School.

"I remember thinking, 'This day is really important,'" she recalls. "You just didn't miss school in those days unless you were really sick with mumps or measles or pneumonia or something."[2]

Milwaukee's school desegregation movement was on the offensive, organizing what became an unprecedented grassroots show of unity against racism and for opportunity.

The Freedom Schools were part of a one-day boycott of the Milwaukee Public Schools in the spring of 1964 (with a three-day boycott in October 1965). The recently formed Milwaukee United School Integration Committee (MUSIC) had organized the boycott to commemorate the tenth anniversary of the U.S. Supreme Court *Brown* decision and to "stand with

Milwaukee's civil rights' demand for integration of our schools and true equality of educational opportunities in the inner core."[3]

Estimates ranged from 11,125 boycotting students to almost 15,000, or roughly half of the nonwhite students in public schools. More than three hundred adults were mobilized to teach the students, and scores of churches and community buildings provided classroom space. The teachers were a mix of businessmen, retired teachers, clergy, blue-collar workers, and a few public school teachers. Churches included almost all the city's denominations; Baptist churches were most prominent, but Catholic, Episcopal, Presbyterian, and other Protestant denominations took part (there were no Lutheran churches involved in the boycott, however, and the archdiocese prohibited Catholic churches and clergy from taking part in a second boycott in October 1965).

The initial boycott had been unanimously approved on March 1 at a mass meeting of nine hundred people at St. Mark's AME Church, the city's oldest African American congregation. Following more than a year of demands that the school board take action against school segregation, the boycott upped the ante in terms of protest.

The boycott dominated the news for weeks as the school board remained intransigent and the city's media and power elite repeatedly decried the illegality of what they dismissed as mere truancy. County judge Christ Seraphim went so far as to call the boycott "a goofy stunt."[4] Although Catholic nuns and priests were involved, a prominent archdiocesan leader, Monsignor Franklyn Kennedy, asked organizers to call off the boycott. Frank A. Aukofer, a *Milwaukee Journal* reporter who covered many of the protests of that era, notes that the criticisms were typical of the white majority's response "to every civil rights protest before and since. Instead of focusing on the issue the boycott was intended to dramatize, the boycott itself became the issue."[5]

A few older and more conservative forces in the black community also criticized the boycott. James Dorsey, considered "an elder statesman" of Milwaukee's black leadership, made his criticism public, even reaching out to what was considered the white media. In a letter to the *Milwaukee Journal* he said that the boycott stirred up race hatred and he worried that the Milwaukee NAACP "had slipped into the rut of emotional rabble rousers." He subsequently resigned in protest from the Milwaukee NAACP.[6] Dorsey also helped organize an antiboycott rally in the black community the night before the boycott, working with a county judge and the president of the teachers union. Only seventy-five people showed up.

Despite the controversy and logistical complications, the boycott made clear the black community's widespread dismay at segregation and discriminatory practices. Vel Phillips, the city's lone black and woman official on its legislative Common Council, called the boycott "the greatest demonstration of Negro unity in the history of the city."[7]

Milwaukee's civil rights movement was also garnering significant national attention. Martin Luther King Jr.—after an intense year of organizing in Birmingham and just months after his famous "I Have a Dream" speech at the March on Washington—had visited Milwaukee that January. He spoke to an overflow crowd of more than six thousand people. During his stay, he publicly addressed the issue of Milwaukee's schools and agreed that residential segregation should not be used "as an excuse for perpetuating de facto segregation" in the schools. In a prescient comment, he noted that "honesty impels me to admit that the school problem cannot be solved permanently until the housing problem is solved."[8]

King endorsed efforts to pressure the school board, and called the Freedom School boycott "a creative way" to dramatize the issue. "Several months ago," he noted favorably, putting Milwaukee in a national context, "the Northern Negro rose from his apathetic slumber."[9]

The highly popular Dick Gregory—part of a new generation of black comedians who abandoned stereotypical images in the minstrel tradition and ventured into social satire—came to Milwaukee and took part in the 1964 boycott. He declared its importance "from one end of the country to the other, and all over the world."[10]

Kathy Williams came from a family of educators, and her mother and grandmother were teachers. (Williams went on to become an educator herself, working more than three decades for the Milwaukee Public Schools.)

Even as a child, Williams knew that school was serious business. The decision to take part in the boycott was not made lightly. Her mother, Classie Cox, at the time a fifth-grade teacher in the public schools, said that "of course" she supported her daughter's decision to attend a Freedom School. "You do whatever you need to make the system better," Cox recalls. "It was worth a try."[11]

Williams was in fifth grade at Twelfth Street School, one of the city's most segregated and overcrowded. On the day of the boycott, few students attended her public school. The next day, her teacher did not openly chastise those who had been absent. "I remember him saying how he believed in integration, but that people shouldn't miss school. In his own subtle way, he didn't say anything negative about the boycott, but he inferred that there are many ways to accomplish a goal."

She remembers more the significance of the boycott rather than particulars of what they were taught at the Freedom School. "I was only ten years old," she laughs. "But I remember it being a really big deal and thinking at the time it must have been a success because my Freedom School was packed."

Records from the time show that the Freedom Schools went beyond the traditional three Rs. Many buildings were given a new name for the day, such as the James Baldwin School, named after the writer; the Crispus Attucks school, named after an African American killed in the Boston Massacre in 1770 and the first martyr of the American Revolution; and Frederick Douglass Senior High, named after the brilliant orator and renowned abolitionist. Handouts to teachers noted that the general objective of the day was "to make the basic concepts of Freedom, Brotherhood, Justice and Equality an integral part of the children's learning experience in a democratic society."

One thing remained the same: the day started with students reciting the Pledge of Allegiance. After that, however, the curriculum had a far different flavor. History classes focused on "Negro history" and discussion questions included "When did the first Negroes first come to America?" Students talked of slavery, the Civil War, the Emancipation Proclamation, and the Thirteenth, Fourteenth, and Fifteenth Amendments. English class included writing essays on such topics as "Why did I come to the Freedom School?" Students wrote brief autobiographies, discussed the importance of family and community, and learned vocabulary such as "indentured servants" and "insurrection." Music class incorporated new lyrics to traditional songs. The curriculum for the primary grades suggested these lyrics for the tune "Are You Sleeping?":

Bells are ringing, bells are ringing

Freedom's song, Freedom's song

Waking up the country, waking up the country

Ding, ding, dong, ding, ding, dong.[12]

The high school curriculum, meanwhile, said that for "a lighter touch" teachers might want to work with the limerick form, with the following as an example:

Milwaukee's a silly old town

She thinks we don't care if we're down.

But boycott we will

Until she grows ill

Of frowning on those who are brown.

On a national level, Freedom Schools were first proposed in 1963 by the Student Nonviolent Coordinating Committee. They were being experimented with in places such as Boston, New York City, and Prince Edward County, Virginia, which had closed its schools rather than desegregate after the *Brown* decision. The most prominent example became the Mississippi Freedom Schools, part of the 1964 Freedom Summer, which focused on voter registration and educating citizens to defend their rights.

The spirit and politics of this national movement were on display in Milwaukee's Freedom Schools, both the initial boycott on May 18, 1964, and a follow-up boycott in October 1965. A teaching guide distributed to Milwaukee's Freedom School teachers captured the movement's philosophy:

What have we to learn from Freedom Schools? The politics of education. That our schools are political grounds in which our students begin to learn about society's rules. That, therefore, if we wish to alter our students and our society, we must alter our schools. That if we would have strong and creative minds we must remove chains both from bodies and spirits. . . .

The Freedom School students and teachers who heard Langston Hughes's "As I Grew Older" understood that Hughes's prayer was theirs too—for a strength and wisdom to break through all spiritual prisons of self and society and so to reach freedom:

My hands!

My dark hands!

Break through the wall!

Find my dream!

Help me to shatter this darkness,

To smash this night,

To break this shadow

Into a thousand lights of sun,

Into a thousand whirling dreams

Of sun![13]

The Freedom School boycott was a reflection of the frustration and anger and also the hope and vision among Milwaukee activists involved in civil rights issues. In the summer of 1963, Lloyd Barbee, as state president of the NAACP, had asked the Wisconsin state superintendent of public instruction to order an end to de facto school segregation throughout the state. The superintendent replied that he could not do so without proof of illegal segregation.

In December 1963, Barbee and other civil rights leaders presented a seventy-seven-page paper to the school board documenting policies and practices of school segregation. For example, the Milwaukee board had redrawn school boundaries in changing neighborhoods in a way that increased rather than decreased segregation. Board policies also led to fewer educational opportunities at majority-black schools. June Shagaloff, an expert from the national NAACP who had helped local activists gather data, called Milwaukee's schools among the most segregated in the nation.

For its part, the school board avoided taking action by appointing committees and commissions. It blamed the problem on housing patterns and hid its recalcitrance behind a defense of neighborhood schools as the bedrock of public education. School board member Harold Story, a white corporate lawyer with a history of antiunionism and resistance to integrated housing, became the spokesperson for the board's policies and headed up the board's Special Committee on Equality of Educational Opportunity. In December 1963, soon after being appointed to the new committee, Story said the demands for desegregation "would abolish the neighborhood schools system."

"From then on," *Milwaukee Journal* reporter Frank Aukofer notes in his history of Milwaukee's civil rights era, "preservation of the neighborhood school system at all costs became the guiding principle of the majority of the special committee and the majority of the school board . . . their minds were made up to preserve the status quo."[14]

Instead of desegregation the board emphasized "compensatory education." In essence, the approach assumed that low achievement was the result of deficiencies in black children's abilities, rather than the result of inferior educational opportunities. The approach focused on memorization and repetitive drills. In Milwaukee, it included special classes for black children newly arrived from the South. An April 23, 1962, *New York Times* feature on the Milwaukee program and its special classes captured the tenor of the approach and noted, "Tests show that, intellectually, the pupils in the classes range from 'defective' to above average. Their chief handicap is that they are remote from the ideas and experiences of the white middle-class world on which American education is built. . . . The Milwaukee project is also throwing new light on another problem: The lack of motivation among young Negroes to train themselves for job opportunities. Examples are plentiful."

The Milwaukee school board's resistance was such that it said it could not even consider integration proposals because that would require the board to openly consider race in setting policy. "It's almost sacred in our democratic concept of things that we do things without reference to race, religion and all the other things," argued Story.

Activists insisted that racism was the main factor in school segregation. As one of several examples, they cited a 1962 incident in which the president of the school board, Lorraine Radtke, complained at a Republican ward meeting that the inner city was changing, and that children who come from the South to Milwaukee "do not have the same cultural background." Predicating her comments by noting, "I possibly shouldn't say this," Radtke went on to say that the recently arrived Negro children sometimes "don't understand our plumbing. You have urination in water bubblers."[15] There is no record of any of the city's white political and business leaders publicly criticizing Radtke's remarks.

Teachers, meanwhile, carried their own stereotypes into the classroom. A 1965 board report, based on anonymous questionnaires to teachers in central-city schools, summarized problems among what it termed "the culturally deprived" students, such as boys and girls "in a state of hyper-activity, sexual stimulation and anger," many of whom "have never known maternal or paternal love." The report lists twenty different problems, all of them variations on such themes.[16]

Ironically, it was a white student who most succinctly summarized Milwaukee's separate and unequal school policies of that era. *U.S. News & World Report* ran a front-cover, first-person feature by a young woman in Milwaukee who watched both her neighborhood and her high school turn from predominantly white to predominantly black. ("The whole changing-over process takes approximately five years," the young woman notes.) Her matter-of-fact delineation of curricular changes is particularly striking. "Higher mathematics and science were falling by the wayside in favor of shop work or home economics," she writes. "When I was a freshman, four foreign languages were being taught. When I graduated, the program for the next year included only Spanish. In my last two years at the school the teaching staff changed every semester. The teachers who had been there for a few years transferred to other schools. Our new teachers generally came directly from the colleges."[17]

It was in this context that MUSIC formed in the spring of 1964, becoming the city's main civil rights organization for the next two years. MUSIC activists chafed at the less-militant stance of many of the city's established civil rights leaders and were eager to embrace a bold plan of action. Its founders were members of the state and local NAACP and recently organized groups such as the Northside Non-Partisan Conference (NNPC) and the Milwaukee Congress of Racial Equality (CORE).

MUSIC pressed for school desegregation, but members were involved in broader issues of housing, jobs, and police/community relations. Milwaukee's CORE, for instance, in 1963 initiated the first militant sit-ins in Milwaukee. The sit-ins called for the resignation of Fred Lins, a prominent business leader, from a governmental antipoverty agency. At the agency's first meeting, Lins said that Negroes look so much alike "that you can't identify the ones that committed the crime." He also said "an awful mess of them have an IQ of nothing."[18]

The fourteen top leaders of MUSIC's initial Freedom School boycott represented a broad cross section. They included a former nun, two attorneys, three ministers, a county supervisor, and a social worker, according to a report in the *Milwaukee Journal*. Marilyn Morheuser, a white former nun who was also editor of the black newsweekly the *Milwaukee Star*, played a particularly prominent role, as did Cecil Brown of NNPC and John Givens of CORE. But the essential person, a man who was the driving force in MUSIC and whose name became synonymous with Milwaukee's desegregation movement, was attorney, activist, and legislator Lloyd Barbee.

Born in Memphis, Tennessee, on August 17, 1925, Barbee was the youngest of three boys. His mother, Adlena, died when he was six months old. His father, Earnest, instilled in him not only a love of classical music and literature but also a lifelong passion for fighting for justice. He told the young Lloyd: "Be right or get right. And when you are right, go ahead."[19]

As a young man, Barbee was acutely aware of school segregation. He walked past several all-white schools each day to get to his all-black school. Jim Crow segregation also kept Barbee from taking advantage of the Memphis public library. When he was just twelve years old, he joined the NAACP.

It was during a three-year stint in the navy that Barbee first came to Wisconsin, visiting relatives in Milwaukee and Beloit while on leave. After graduating from LeMoyne College in Memphis, Barbee went on to receive a law degree from the University of Wisconsin–Madison in 1955, as part of a young generation of African American trailblazers at white-dominated universities. Degree in hand, he immediately became involved in civil rights issues, serving on both local and statewide commissions on human rights. He became president of the Madison chapter of the NAACP in 1955. In 1961, he was elected president of the state branch.

Barbee received widespread public attention in 1961 when he spearheaded a thirteen-day round-the-clock sit-in at the state capitol to promote housing and equal opportunity legislation—the first such Wisconsin protest since the Great Depression.[20] Shortly after, he successfully organized to rename Nigger Heel Lake, in northern Wisconsin, Freedom Lake.

While most well-known for his efforts to end school segregation, Barbee was a renaissance man both politically and culturally. His love of theater ranged from *A Raisin in the Sun* to *Othello*. He liked to cook, specializing in Greek omelets, bread, and dandelion wine. Opera, however, was the love of his life, and he was known to joyously (if not always harmoniously) sing along, thrusting his fist into the air. Politically, Barbee had a broad view of human rights that was ahead of its time. He did not suffer fools lightly, spoke his mind, and distrusted wealthy white liberals who were prone to viewing integration as a fashionable issue and to leaving unexamined their own unconscious racism.

Barbee had a well-honed ability to alienate people, and he was called bombastic, elitist, and outrageous. He often responded by being even more erudite in his vocabulary or more provocative in his positions. He once called for abolishing police forces altogether because the police "are taught violence and actively practice it." In 1967, he criticized whites who were abandoning civil rights issues and instead protesting the war in Vietnam, saying they "have a fascination about the east, about the plight of the Vietnamese that does not exist about the plight of the Negro."[21] During the desegregation movement, he called a bureaucratically minded school board member "the king of the pussyfooters."[22] Although suspicious of organized religion (he called churches "god boxes"), he regularly referred to the "evil" of segregation.

Controversy surrounded Barbee, but no one doubted his passion and commitment to equal opportunity for African Americans and to the belief that everyone—rich or poor, white or black, man or woman, gay or straight—has inalienable rights by virtue of belonging to the human race. "Lloyd laid the groundwork for a whole series of social and legal reform efforts," recalls former Wisconsin legislator David Clarenbach, a lifelong friend who briefly overlapped with Barbee's fourteen years in the Wisconsin assembly, from 1964 to 1977. "He felt an obligation to assume that groundbreaking role, because he was elected from a relatively safe district and one which provided him the freedom to do things that virtually no other legislator could do."[23]

Barbee opposed halfhearted reforms. Clarenbach recalls that in the mid-1970s, Clarenbach wanted to introduce a bill decriminalizing small amounts of marijuana, and he asked Barbee to co-author the bill. "And he looked at me with this eye of disgust that I will never forget," Clarenbach says. "He just shook his head and said, 'Yes, for you I will put my name on it.' But he thought it was a halfway measure. His point was, you legalize alcohol, so why not drugs?"

Both a staunch integrationist and a fierce opponent of white supremacy, Barbee explained his views this way in a 1969 interview: "I see myself as a human being, interested in humanity and fulfilling its maximum potentialities. I realize this will never happen as long as whites view themselves as being superior because of their whiteness—therefore I must fight racism. As a black human struggling in this period of utter madness, I consider myself almost like John the Baptist, alone at times, and I try to speak in the wilderness rather than cry."

The following account from the June 18, 1969, *Milwaukee Journal* provides a glimpse of Barbee's wide-ranging views:

> Assemblyman Lloyd Barbee, who represents one of the poorest districts in the state, is attempting this legislative session to meet the needs of his race and the poor in general with perhaps the most radical libertarian legislative proposals anyone has offered. . . .
>
> Barbee's views transcend the question of race and go to the basic question of man's nature. The Democratic assemblyman from Milwaukee's inner core has introduced bills that would:
>
> Permit sexual intercourse among consenting adults.
>
> Repeal the crime of abortion.
>
> Repeal state obscenity statutes.
>
> Permit prisoners to have sexual intercourse with visitors.
>
> Require inquests when requested into deaths caused by law enforcement officers.
>
> Expunge juvenile criminal records if there have been no convictions in three years.
>
> Give a defendant in a criminal action access to records and information.
>
> Grant the right of bail on appeals to the state and United States supreme courts.
>
> Prohibit physical and verbal abuse by law enforcement officers.
>
> Require psychological screening of applications for police jobs.

During his time as a legislator, Barbee also called for reparations to Wisconsin residents whose ancestors were slaves or "persecuted" Native Americans; eliminating "debtor's prison" arrests; making Malcolm X's birthday and the day of Martin Luther King Jr.'s assassination legal holidays; and setting a four-year term for the Milwaukee police chief (who at the time was police chief for life).

Despite his expansive views, Barbee remains almost exclusively re-membered in Milwaukee as the man who led the movement to desegregate the public schools. He died on December 29, 2002, at the age of seventy-seven. In death, as in life, he wanted people to remember his father's lesson: "Be right or get right." He told his children he did not want a public funeral with sobbing remembrances and insincere platitudes. Instead, he wanted people to use their time more productively.

"He felt like nobody lives forever, so instead of wasting time mourning, step up to the plate," his daughter Daphne explained. "Just do something."[24]

Milwaukee's Freedom Schools and one-day boycott weren't the only racial issue garnering national attention in the spring of 1964. History books cite Milwaukee for the reception given to Alabama governor George Wallace that April as he launched a presidential campaign. In a strategy later per-fected by the Republican Party, Wallace promoted his arch-segregationist message by fusing populist rhetoric and support for the workingman with a defense of states' rights against the Washington, D.C., elite. Wisconsin underscored the power of Wallace's approach.

4.

MILWAUKEE LOVES GEORGE WALLACE

If I ever had to leave Alabama, I'd want to live on the south
side of Milwaukee.

—George Wallace

The overflow crowd at Milwaukee's American Serb Memorial Hall on April
1, 1964, was boisterous, its enthusiasm edging toward unruliness. When
Bronco Gruber, the master of ceremonies, called out two African American protesters who had remained seated during the singing of "The Star
Spangled Banner," the white crowd's anger was barely contained. There were
boos, catcalls, and a shout of "Send 'em back to Africa." Gruber one-upped
the crowd's antagonism, launching into a tirade against Milwaukee Negroes who "beat up old ladies 83 years old. They rape our women folks."

Gruber calmed down a bit and continued with the main business at
hand: introducing George Wallace, the Alabama governor who was using
Wisconsin to launch a presidential campaign. When Wallace walked onto
the stage, he was given a standing ovation. His forty-minute speech was
interrupted thirty times by cheering and applause from the more than 550
people present.[1]

Wallace had won a landslide victory as governor a year and a half earlier and had used his January 11, 1963, inaugural speech to proclaim "segregation today, segregation tomorrow, segregation forever." Six months
later, on June 11, he stood at the door at the University of Alabama to block
two black students from enrolling. In little over a year, he had become a
national symbol of opposition to federal mandates dismantling Jim Crow.
He unexpectedly entered the 1964 presidential campaign with a message
that embraced lower taxes, lower spending, states' rights, and anticommunism but centered on highlighting northern opposition to the Civil Rights

Act then before the U.S. Senate—legislation that Wallace called "the civil wrongs bill." Wisconsin was the first test of his candidacy.

It had been a tumultuous year in U.S. politics. In the spring of 1963, Birmingham, Alabama's police chief, Bull Connor, used police dogs and fire hoses to attack civil rights marchers, including children. Medgar Evers, field director of the NAACP in Mississippi, was shot and killed at his home on June 12, 1963. On August 28, the March on Washington gathered an interracial crowd that was the largest civil rights demonstration in U.S. history. But the jubilation of that moment was soon overtaken by the events of Sunday, September 15. At 10:22 A.M., a bomb exploded at the Sixteenth Street Baptist Church in Birmingham, which had been a center for civil rights activities; four young African American girls were killed.

Some blamed Wallace for helping set the climate that allowed such a bombing, especially by his pronouncement ten days earlier when persuading the Birmingham school board to close schools scheduled for integration. "The society is coming apart at the seams," he said. "What good is it doing to force these situations when white people nowhere in the South want integration? What this country needs is a few first-class funerals, and some political funerals, too."[2]

A few months after the Birmingham bombing, on November 22, 1963, President John F. Kennedy was assassinated. Lyndon Johnson became president, proceeding with Kennedy's civil rights bills and in early 1964 declaring his "War on Poverty." Muhammad Ali, then known as Cassius Clay, won the world heavyweight championship on February 25, 1964, and announced his conversion to Islam the next day. Malcolm X, charismatic, articulate, and an ardent proponent of black pride and power, spoke to sellout crowds across the country.

With these events as a backdrop, in March 1964 Wallace entered the Wisconsin primary, which at the time was the country's second presidential primary, a few weeks after New Hampshire. His candidacy was initially dismissed as irrelevant. But over the next several weeks, he spoke to enthusiastic crowds throughout the state. His Wisconsin campaign swing culminated with his April 1 appearance at Serb Hall on Milwaukee's South Side, a stronghold of working-class whites, especially second-generation immigrants from Poland and Eastern Europe. "I went down to the Serbian hall last night and got the best reception I've ever gotten," he told the press.[3]

When the primary was held a week later, Wallace stunned political pundits. He won 23 percent of the total statewide vote in the three-way race, and a third of the Democratic votes. "Segregationists hailed Wisconsin as a victory, a demonstration of their contention that the North, as well as the South, was opposed to racial change," the *New York Times* reported.[4]

The press linked Wallace most closely with blue-collar ethnic whites, especially on the South Side of Milwaukee. But the actual results were complicated. Wallace did indeed run strongly on the South Side—and might have polled even better except that organized labor campaigned against Wallace based on his labor record as governor. Post-voting analysis showed that eight Milwaukee neighborhoods that were more than three-quarters blue collar had a lower percentage of votes for Wallace (33 percent) than eight neighborhoods that were almost half white collar (42 percent). Throughout the metropolitan area, Wallace's appeal crossed ethnic, class, and party lines as voters in Republican neighborhoods in Milwaukee, Waukesha, and Ozaukee counties more consistently voted for Wallace than voters in Democratic neighborhoods. Due to significant crossover voting, the affluent and Republican county of Waukesha led the state in the proportion of voters (33 percent) for Wallace. Within Milwaukee County, three white, affluent suburbs to the north and west of the city (Wauwatosa, Brown Deer, and Glendale) gave a plurality of their votes to Wallace.[5]

Wallace went on to win significant votes in other northern Democratic primaries before dropping out of the race. He was understandably fond of his reception in Wisconsin, which gave him his start and proved his claim of a northern "white backlash." As he told the Milwaukee press on election night: "If I ever had to leave Alabama, I'd want to live on the south side of Milwaukee."[6]

5.

MILWAUKEE'S GREAT MIGRATION #1: BLACKS MOVE FROM THE SOUTH TO THE INNER CORE

Winter is coming, and we can't make it.

—Willie Jude Sr., Mississippi Delta sharecropper,
shortly before his move to Milwaukee

On October 2, 1944, a crowd of three thousand people gathered at the Hopson plantation four miles south of Clarksdale, Mississippi, in Coahoma County. Eight machines quickly and efficiently picked a field of cotton in what was the first public demonstration of a commercially viable cotton picker.

A skilled field hand could pick twenty pounds of cotton in an hour. The machine picked a thousand pounds. The sharecropper system, which had provided the inexpensive labor sought by plantation owners after the end of slavery, and which was the dominant economic institution in the rural South for eighty years, was about to become obsolete. "Suddenly, cotton planters no longer needed large numbers of black people to pick their cotton, and inevitably the nature of black society and of race relations was going to have to change," writes Nicholas Lemann in *The Promised Land: The Great Black Migration and How It Changed America.*

The migration of blacks to the North and West lasted from roughly 1910 to 1970, with the first substantial wave following World War I. The Great Migration, as it is called, first impacted northern industrial powerhouses such as Detroit and Chicago, where blacks gained an early foothold and, unlike in Milwaukee, had the time to develop a significant middle class.

In 1940, according to Lemann, 77 percent of black Americans lived in the South, mostly in rural areas. But then migration increased dramatically. Five million of the 6.5 million blacks who took part in the Great Migration moved after 1940. By the time the migration ended in 1970, "black America was only half Southern, and less than a quarter rural; 'urban' had become a euphemism for 'black.'"[1]

Willie Jude has worked for almost forty years in education in Milwaukee, as a teacher, principal, and administrator. He thinks of retiring and returning to the South, where he was born. But retirement is a difficult concept for someone who has worked hard his whole life. And though Jude retains deep emotional ties to the South, Milwaukee is where he built a career, married, bought a home, and raised a family.

In 1947, a few years after the mechanical cotton picker's debut in Clarksdale, Willie Jude was the third generation in his family to be born on a plantation in Coahoma County. He was named after his father, and was the oldest of fifteen children at a time when big families were seen as essential to economic survival. "We were all sharecroppers," he explains. By the time he was six years old, the young Jude was chopping and picking cotton. By seven years old, he was picking fifty pounds a day. The larger and more well-off plantations in the Mississippi Delta had moved on to the cotton picker but, as with many revolutionary inventions, the pace of change was uneven. By 1958, 27 percent of the cotton crop of the Mississippi Delta was harvested by mechanical cotton pickers, with the number increasing to more than 84 percent by 1964.[2] Not yet realizing that their way of life soon would be gone forever, the Jude family held on.

For much of his youth, Jude's family moved from one plantation to another in search of work. In Tunica, the family (then numbering fifteen people) lived in a four-room house. At Dubbs, Mississippi, on a small plantation with only about fifty families, members of the Jude family would chop cotton for ten hours a day, each of them earning $2.50. The plantation owner wanted to drop the children's wages to $1.75 a day, and Jude's mother refused, figuring that at those wages the children might as well stay home and further their learning. "It was almost like slavery," Jude recalls of that plantation. "We only stayed one year."[3]

The Jude family experienced a period of relative stability from 1960 to 1966 at a small farm with only three families. But in the fall of 1966, new legislation prohibited schools from dismissing students from September till after Thanksgiving, as had been the custom so that children could help work the harvest. As a result of the legislation, the plantation owner refused to give Jude's father any crops. "He said that the kids wouldn't be able to harvest them," Jude recalls. Without a crop, the family was destitute.

"Winter is coming and we can't make it," Jude's father told the family.

Jude, young and resourceful, responded, "Well, your brother is in Milwaukee. Maybe he can get you a job in a packing house if you moved up there."

Jude drove his father to Memphis to catch a bus, not wanting to take the risk of seeing him off on a local bus because the family still owed the plantation owner money. The father arrived in Milwaukee in November, got a job at a meatpacking plant, and after six weeks sent for his wife and children. "That's how my family got to Milwaukee," Jude explains.

Change the names, modify the dates, tweak a few of the details, and multiply the story by thousands of people, and Willie Jude's story tells of Milwaukee's role in the Great Migration of southern blacks to northern industrial cities, one of the seminal developments in twentieth-century America.

Milwaukee's migration has been called the "Late Great Migration" because it occurred decades after the height of migration to cities such as Cleveland, Gary, Chicago, and Detroit. But it no less profoundly shaped the city.

In 1950, there were 21,772 blacks in Milwaukee, compared to almost 500,000 in Chicago and 300,000 in Detroit. Blacks accounted for only 3.4 percent of Milwaukee's population that year. Two decades later, by 1970, blacks were almost 15 percent of the population and their numbers had risen to 105,088.[4] (By the 2000 Census, Milwaukee had become what is called, in an odd twist of semantics, a "majority minority city." Whites accounted for just under 50 percent of city residents, African Americans for 37 percent, and Latinos for 12 percent.)

It is not uncommon for blacks in Milwaukee to name the city from which their ancestors left for Milwaukee and the year in which they did so. After one family member moved and was settled, brothers, sisters, or cousins often followed. Small-town networks were re-created. Milwaukee legislator Polly Williams, for instance, came to Milwaukee in 1946 from Belzoni, Mississippi, a Delta town an hour's drive from Coahoma County. Monroe Swan, her cousin who also went on to serve in the Wisconsin legislature, arrived about the same time. Both families were lured by the jobs in Milwau-kee's factories, foundries, tanneries, and meatpacking plants.

Mississippi was the most common state of origin for Milwaukee blacks during the height of the Great Migration. As late as 1960, roughly half of all African Americans in Milwaukee had been born in the South, and only about a third had been born in Wisconsin.[5]

In 1970, when the Great Migration formally ended, that enticing moni-ker given to Milwaukee and other northern cities—"the Promised Land"—had not yet been tarnished beyond redemption. While the black professional and middle classes remained relatively small in Milwaukee, the official black unemployment rate was only 5.3 percent. The black poverty rate was signifi-cantly lower than the comparable U.S. average, and black median income was significantly higher. The number of black owner-occupied homes had nota-bly increased.[6]

Black migrants to Milwaukee "seized upon the opportunity to shape a better life for themselves, and despite the odds against them, were remark-ably successful," writes historian Paul Geib. "Their collective experience represented a tantalizing moment in African-American history when it appeared that the model of mobility through industrial employment that had served the European immigrants might serve black migrants as well. It seems fair to conclude that at least in one place at one time—Milwaukee, 1940 to 1970—black Americans found it possible to go from peasant to proletarian to upwardly mobile blue-collar property owner all in one generation."[7]

6.

1965: DIRECT ACTION TARGETS "INTACT BUSING"

Let this MUSIC demonstration be a warning to the city that we will continue picketing, sit-ins, lay-ins, chain-ins and other kinds of "ins" until the intransigent school board caves in.

—Lloyd Barbee, describing a direct action campaign against school segregation

On July 30, 1957, in the middle of summer when few paid attention to school board meetings, Superintendent Harold Vincent outlined what he called a "rather unique" experiment for the new school year. Known as "intact busing," the initiative solved two interrelated problems: overcrowding in schools in the black community, and white fears of black students at their schools.

Under "intact busing," students at African American schools would report to their school at their regular time and then be bused to a white school with extra classroom space. Arriving after white students were already in their classrooms, the black students would be taken to separate, self-contained classrooms. In most cases, they would also have a separate recess period. At lunchtime, the black students would be bused back to their original school, fed lunch, and then bused once more to the white school. At the end of the day, the black students were returned to their original school.[1]

School board members saw no problem with the plan. Indeed, board member George Hampel Jr. stated at a Finance Committee meeting on August 28, 1957, that the proposal was "most generous" and "most appropriate" because "I know what kind of hackling" might otherwise result—apparently a reference to "heckling" from white parents who would object to black students being mixed in with students at the white schools.[2]

In the school board's eyes, that 1957 "experiment" was a success, and the policy of intact busing was formally adopted on September 2, 1958. With only slight modifications, it remained in effect until 1972. While Milwaukee's desegregation movement was grounded in a broad-based effort against both racism and segregated schools, black activists saw intact busing as a particularly disturbing practice, crystallizing the length to which some Milwaukee whites would go in order to keep apart black and white students. Over the years, there were hundreds of instances of intact busing involving tens of thousands of black students. While the school board argued it was a race-blind policy, there were only nine instances in which white students were bused to predominantly black schools.[3] The first instance in which blacks were allowed to eat lunch at the receiving school was not until 1964.[4]

Intact busing was to be a temporary measure to relieve overcrowding or school renovations, designed to last anywhere from a few months to a year. Some central-city schools, however, were subjected to intact busing for five years.[5] What's more, the school board stood by its policy of intact busing even when the practice undermined its stated preference for neighborhood schools. A 1967 report of the U.S. Commission on Civil Rights included an analysis of Milwaukee and noted that in one instance, "a number of Negro children lived closer to their white receiving school than to the Negro sending school where they were enrolled officially. They were nonetheless required to walk to the sending school to board the bus. If the boundary had been changed, these children could have been enrolled officially in the school to which they were bused as a group and then could have walked to their neighborhood school."[6]

Intact busing came to symbolize the Milwaukee school board's commitment to segregated and unequal schooling, and was a potent organizing tool. In February 1964, CORE and the NAACP picketed the district administration building to protest the policy. In the following months, energy was channeled into the Freedom Schools and boycott. After a period of relative calm and behind-the-scenes organizing, in the spring of 1965 Milwaukee's desegregation movement once again focused on intact busing. It embraced militant sit-ins, civil disobedience, and picketing of officials' homes to protest the policy—confrontational tactics that became a harbinger of things to come in Milwaukee.

Just after 8:00 A.M. on May 24, 1965, three yellow school buses showed up at Brown Street School in Milwaukee's Inner Core. It was to be a typical day, transporting roughly 150 black students from the overcrowded school to two different white schools several miles away.

On this particular Monday, however, eighty demonstrators picketed on the sidewalk and called for an end to intact busing. As the buses prepared to roll, nine people led by MUSIC chairman Lloyd Barbee walked in front of the lead bus, linked arms, sang "We Shall Overcome," and refused to move. All held placards in which a bright red stop sign was the graphic centerpiece of their slogan: "Stop Busing for Segregation."

Patrolman Jack Anthony, on duty at the school, approached the nine and asked each one, "Will you move?"

All refused.[7]

"Then, you are under arrest," Anthony said. He hailed a patrol wagon and told the protesters, "Ladies and gentlemen, you can walk in whenever you want."

The demonstrators didn't budge.

Two police officers walked up to Barbee and physically escorted him into the wagon. The officers then went back for the others. Using a tactic common at the time, under a philosophy of noncooperation that was an integral aspect of civil disobedience, the protesters went limp and had to be lifted into the wagon.

With the protesters inside, the police officers closed the wagon's doors and signaled the first school bus to take off. As it did so, two protesters left the picket line and placed themselves in front of the second bus. The process repeated itself as they were arrested.

In total, eleven people were arrested in what was a new tactic, a "human chain-in," that inaugurated weeks of direct action. "Let this MUSIC demonstration be a warning to the city that we will continue picketing, sit-ins, lay-ins, chain-ins and other kinds of 'ins' until the intransigent school board caves in," Barbee said.[8]

The night of the arrests, fourteen members of Milwaukee CORE held a sit-in at a school board committee meeting and called for an end to intact busing. Led by Reverend Leo Champion, CORE chairman, they prayed, marched, and sang. At one point, Champion knelt on the floor and invoked the Lord to "help Brother Vincent, help Sister Radtke." He was referring to Superintendent Vincent and to board president Lorraine Radtke, who had won notoriety three years earlier for her comment that Negro children coming from the South didn't understand modern plumbing and urinated in drinking fountains.

Milwaukee CORE had been holding sit-ins at Vincent's office since May 5 and, in a tactic not yet common in Milwaukee, had begun picketing the homes of school board members.[9] At the time of the protests, nineteen hundred students were being bused intact. The MUSIC and CORE protesters called the policy "worse than de facto segregation" and dismissed school board claims that such busing was temporary. They pointed to the Siefert School, which had been renovated, was still overcrowded, and was scheduled to have six classes bused intact the following fall. (Siefert was also one of the three schools affected when intact busing began eight years earlier in 1957.)

Less than two weeks after that first "human chain-in," the desegregation movement led to a new first in Milwaukee: the civil rights arrest of a Catholic priest.[10] The priest, Father James Groppi, was the white assistant pastor at St. Boniface in the central city, and he would go on to lead Milwaukee's Open Housing movement. It was during the protests against intact busing that Groppi crossed his point of no return, moving his locus of influence from the pulpit to the streets.

The catalyst for Groppi's heightened activism that summer was located 850 miles away, in Selma, Alabama, following what will forever be known in U.S. history books as "Bloody Sunday."

On March 7, 1965, six hundred civil rights marchers set off from Selma, Alabama, on a fifty-mile march to the state capital, Montgomery, to press for voting rights. Governor George Wallace had announced he would block the march. As the marchers crossed the Edmund Pettus Bridge just outside the Selma city limits, they were greeted by a wall of state troopers, sheriff's deputies, and white possemen. Fifteen were on horseback. Some had launching rifles for tear gas, others wide-nozzle tear gas spray guns or rubber hoses laced with spikes.

As the marchers crossed the bridge and headed down its slope there was an eerie silence, broken only by the sound of snorting horses. When they reached the other side, there was a new sound: "snapping noises that swept along the barrier line ahead as officers secured otherworldly gas masks of bug-eyed goggles and elongated rubber snouts," historian Taylor Branch recounts.[11]

The marchers stopped, and state trooper John Cloud stepped forward. He shouted through a bullhorn that the assembly was illegal and that marchers had two minutes to disperse. After one minute and five seconds Cloud told his advance unit, "Troopers, advance."

With nightsticks held high the troops did as they were told, "toppling marchers with accelerating speed as troops hurtled over and through them." Before long there was a clattering of horses' hooves, the launching of tear gas, the swinging of clubs. "The cloud of tear gas from canister and spray darkened toward the mouth of the bridge, obscuring all but the outlines of a half-dozen figures on the ground and scattered nightsticks in the air."

Horsemen chased marchers who tried to escape down along the riverbank. On the bridge—which at its crest was nearly a hundred feet above the cold, choppy waters of the Alabama River—protesters clung to the bridge railing, fearful of both the water below and the mounted horsemen rushing by. More than a hundred troopers, possemen, and sheriff's deputies pursued marchers the mile back to Selma, attacking stragglers "in a frenzy."[12]

The media named the attack "Bloody Sunday," its brutal images seared into the nation's mind by on-the-scene newspaper and television accounts. Martin Luther King Jr. issued a national call for "people of conscience" to join a new march to Montgomery. Clergy from across the country responded, both black and white. In Milwaukee, the NAACP and CORE sent Reverend Leo Champion as their representative, along with fourteen other African Americans. (The black community newspaper the *Milwaukee Star* complained, however, of "the pathetic attitude of the Negro ministry" and its "conspicuous absence" in heeding the Selma call.) Four white Catholic priests from Milwaukee also headed to Selma: Father Groppi, Patrick Flood, Matthew Gottschalk, and Austin Schlaefer. It marked a turning point not only for those four priests but also for the Catholic Church's relationship to the civil rights movement in Milwaukee and nationally. Unlike the civil rights movement in the South, Catholic clergy and laypeople played a pivotal role in the civil rights movement in the North, not just in Milwaukee but in other Catholic strongholds such as New York, Boston, Philadelphia, and Cleveland.[13]

In the 1960s, the Catholic Church was going through its own radical changes. In 1962, Pope John XXIII had convened the Second Vatican Council to reassess the church's role in the modern world, a reassessment that stressed a global and ecumenical vision, honored the role of laypeople and community, and reaffirmed the Catholic duty to the poor and downtrodden. The church's spirit of change affected far more than traditions such as the Latin Mass. "To reformers and liberals . . . the Second Vatican Council appeared to offer official sanction for their dissent," notes historian Patrick Jones. What that meant on the ground in Milwaukee, he added, "was that an increasing number of priests and nuns were sympathetic to the struggles of their parishioners and to issues of social justice generally."[14]

Church traditionalists resisted many of the changes, in particular what they perceived as a weakening of Rome's authority and its hierarchical chain of command. And they looked askance at the growing link between activist Catholic clergy and the civil rights movement.

Both social activists and conservative Catholics had a strong foothold in Milwaukee, often mirroring the city's geographic divisions. Local church officials in Milwaukee had prohibited local priests from attending the August 1963 March on Washington, saying it would be "rash and imprudent."[15] And in February 1965, just a month before Bloody Sunday, conservative Catholics had blocked an appearance from the author of *Black Like Me* at a Milwaukee youth convention, allegedly because of the book's "offensive language."[16]

Large institutions change slowly, and the spirit of the Second Vatican Council and Pope John XXIII prevailed in Milwaukee, even after John's death in 1962 and the council's end in 1965. Following Bloody Sunday, Catholic clergy, nuns, and parishioners were increasingly active in Milwaukee's two main civil rights causes at the time, school desegregation and open housing. It wasn't until after 1968, when Pope Paul VI issued his *Humanae Vitae* encyclical denouncing birth control, that conservative church leaders were able to reassert their views and change the church's direction. Downplaying social justice, the church increasingly focused on birth control, abortion, and sexuality issues.

Returning to Milwaukee after his trip to Selma, Groppi threw himself into the desegregation movement. Within weeks he was elected second vice president of MUSIC, helping to organize MUSIC's summer of protest. When Groppi was arrested on June 4, it was part of what MUSIC called a "clergymen's demonstration." Along with four other clerics and four nuns, Groppi formed a human chain in front of a bus at the Siefert School.

Groppi's arrest created a stir within the local Catholic community, which by and large subscribed to Milwaukee's dominant ethos of unquestioning respect for order and authority. This was, after all, a city that strictly enforced laws against jaywalking. The following Sunday, Groppi explained why he was willing to be arrested. "When the orderly procedures do not bring man his rights in society, then a man can go beyond those orderly procedures," he said. He went on to explain that "every means possible" had been used to move the school board to end intact busing, but to no avail. He ended by calling upon other clergy "to get involved in the temporal order, to struggle for the equality of man."[17]

By the time MUSIC's campaign of direct action against intact busing ended on June 17, 1965, there had been more than ten demonstrations and more than sixty people arrested as they formed human chains, sat, knelt, or stood in front of school buses, went limp, and were tossed into patrol wagons, all to the tune of freedom songs. Milwaukee's CORE, meanwhile, continued its picketing at school board meetings and at board members' homes, leading to additional arrests.

That August, on the anniversary of the 1963 March on Washington, an estimated six hundred people took part in the MUSIC-sponsored Milwaukee March Toward Freedom and Independence. Demands focused on the need for jobs and for an end to police brutality, inferior schools, lousy housing, and economic discrimination. Roughly half those in the march were Catholic clergy and activists.[18]

On October 18, 1965, MUSIC began a second boycott and Freedom School, following up on efforts in the spring of 1964 and this time vowing to stay out for an undetermined amount of time. Both Groppi and Barbee played leading public roles. Groppi, in what would become a signature of his organizing style, led some 250 young people for thirty-eight blocks in a march that evening to the home of school board president John Foley. The tactic compelled Mayor Henry Maier to label Groppi's march as "Ku Klux Klanism in reverse." Barbee, in turn, said that Maier's record on civil rights "ranges from a mere whisper to a whining whimper." Groppi responded by leading more than three hundred people on a march in front of the mayor's apartment building the next night.[19]

District attorney Hugh O'Connell, meanwhile, ruled that the boycott was illegal, and he threatened to prosecute boycott leaders. The Catholic archdiocese not only forbade the use of any parish facility for the boycott but also, on the second day of the boycott, gave Father Groppi direct orders to abstain from Freedom School activities. It was the first and last time that the archdiocese specifically forbade Groppi from taking part in a civil rights activity.[20]

The legal threats and escalating turn of events made it difficult to sustain the boycott. After three and a half days it was called off. At the time, it was the longest school boycott in a U.S. city.[21]

Despite the controversy, MUSIC continued organizing. That December MUSIC led two weeks of daily protests against the construction of a new school in the black community that protesters said made no allowances for promoting an integrated solution to overcrowding. The protests began with an all-night vigil and included a civil disobedience action on December 6 that led to twenty-two arrests, including a second arrest for Groppi. But as Milwaukee's long winter set in, street protests dwindled and MUSIC's campaign ended. As spring arrived, local and national developments coalesced in a way that shifted civil rights organizing.

Nationally, in August 1965, President Lyndon Johnson had signed the Voting Rights Act, a major goal of the civil rights movement. The year before, the Civil Rights Act had been enacted, prohibiting racial and sexual discrimination in public accommodations and in employment, from hiring and promoting to firing. The most important pieces of legislation striking down Jim Crow were now in place. The civil rights movement's focus moved to more difficult and complicated issues of institutionalized racism and de facto segregation, and to practices that had their roots in slavery and Jim Crow but were intertwined with issues of culture and class. The black power movement, meanwhile, would soon emerge as a growing force, especially in urban areas in the North and West.

Locally, on June 17, 1965, Barbee had filed a federal lawsuit to overturn segregated practices within Milwaukee's public schools. This moved the desegregation struggle into the federal courts, a venue that did not lend itself to direct action protests. In addition, Barbee had been elected to the state legislature in the fall of 1964, which limited the time he could devote to organizing in Milwaukee. The Milwaukee civil rights movement was on the cusp of a new era, with open housing demonstrations soon to take center stage. Protests against the Milwaukee Eagles Club—the local chapter of the nationwide Fraternal Order of Eagles, which had a whites-only membership policy—provided a transition.

My thirteen-year-old cousin Rosemary was caught up in the Eagles Club controversy. It changed her life.

Rosemary, a year younger than me and the only child of my mother's sister, Aunt Rose, remembers exactly when she first met Father Groppi. It was 1960, when she was a third grader at St. Veronica's on Milwaukee's South Side.

At the time, the newly ordained Father Groppi was the assistant priest at St. Veronica's, and he oversaw religious education. About once a week, he would come to talk to the students—a momentous event in Catholic elementary schools of that era, when priests held godlike status and it was unusual for children to directly converse with them except through the grates of the confessional.

Rosemary sat in the front row, and Groppi had a habit of casually perching himself on the edge of her desk as he addressed the class. "He always called me 'my angel,'" Rosemary fondly recalls.

Groppi didn't drill the children about the catechism or preach about mortal sin, but instead talked about how to treat each other. He had a gentle manner and a soft voice, so the class had to listen hard. And they did. "He always told us to treat people with respect, that's one of the things I remember most," Rosemary says from the perspective of forty years later. "He was an amazingly effective teacher."

Over the next few years Groppi grew increasingly influential with St. Veronica's schoolchildren, becoming a Milwaukee version of the charismatic young priest so effectively portrayed by Bing Crosby in *The Bells of St. Mary's*. When he left in 1963 to take up the new post he had sought at St. Boniface's in the central city, Rosemary was confused and upset. "I couldn't figure out why he would want to leave St. Veronica's," she remembers. "It was such a great school, and of course I was completely unaware of what was going on elsewhere in Milwaukee. And I really missed him when he left."

It would be two years before she would again see Groppi face-to-face, and under far different circumstances. It was in 1965, when issues overlapped as the civil rights movement segued from focusing on desegregation to discrimination at the Eagles Club. Rosemary's father, Milan Potter, was both on the Milwaukee school board and manager of the Eagles Club. He was in the crosshairs of both issues.

The evening started out like many a Friday night. Rosemary and her parents were heading out for a fish fry, a long-standing tradition in Milwaukee growing out of the pre–Second Vatican Council admonition that Catholics were not to eat meat on Fridays as an act of contrition and spiritual growth.

While driving to dinner, Rosemary's father turned on the radio. The news reported that two hundred Negroes were picketing the home of Milan Potter. "My father spun around the car and my mother became very, very upset," Rosemary recalls. "This was 1965, when stereotypes were strong, and my mother started worrying that our house could be looted."

Rosemary laughs as she recalls how her dad tried to make light of the matter. "He looks at my mother and says, 'Rose, maybe we should invite them all in for coffee.'"

Before long, they arrived back home, pulling up in front. "There were all these people, and I remember thinking, 'How are we going to get to the door?' And then I get out and the first person I see is Father Groppi. He raises his arms in welcome and yells out, 'Rosemary, angel!'

"I run to him, because I love him, he was my parish priest. And I hug him."

The next thing Rosemary remembers, her father grabbed her by the coat collar and yanked her away, telling her to get into the house immediately. Sheriff's deputies on the scene directed the family into the basement, worried that matters could perhaps turn violent because whites from the neighborhood were forming a counterpicket. After a while, the family was allowed to go back upstairs.

Rosemary's father and mother went to the living room, while Rosemary ran to the den with its large picture window. She looked outside and saw her neighbors picketing the picketers. Father Groppi was in the midst of it all.

All she could think about was how much she wanted to be with her parish priest. "I remember asking my dad, 'Why can't I go outside? It's Father Groppi, he's a friend.'

"I loved my father and trusted him," she continues. "But I loved Father Groppi and trusted him as well."

Rosemary's father insisted she stay inside. She didn't openly challenge that decision, but a threshold was crossed. "In that moment, I knew that issues were not black and white, and there were many shades of gray," she says. "I realized the world was far more complicated than I had been taught, and that I could no longer blindly listen to what my father had to say."

Rosemary credits the events as integral to future decisions to become involved in politics, including almost a decade as a Democrat in the Wisconsin assembly, where she supported a range of women's and human rights issues. "After that day, I never looked at the world the same way again," Rosemary recalls.

The protests at Rosemary's house foreshadowed similar demonstrations the following summer. Both the protests and white backlash escalated—this time in an upper-middle-class white neighborhood in the suburb of Wauwatosa.

The first demonstration against the Eagles Club was a Mother's Day march in 1965 organized by MUSIC. The action was both to protest the club's discriminatory policy against African Americans and to demand that Rosemary's father, the club manager, resign from the school board. It was Groppi and the NAACP Youth Council, however, who carried the Eagles Club protests to a new level.

The Youth Council had been active for several years in Milwaukee. Inspired by the role of youth in the South, it had picketed Big Boy restaurants in Milwaukee to protest job discrimination. When on a national level NAACP youth councils were allowed to separate from adult branches in 1965, the Milwaukee Youth Council quickly embraced a more militant stance. In the spring of 1965, the council asked Groppi to serve as its adviser. The request was unusual—a reflection of Groppi's ability to relate to young people and his proven commitment to direct action.[22] Under Groppi's leadership, the Youth Council later formed the Commandos, a group of African American young men who protected civil rights demonstrators during tense confrontations, maintained order on picket lines, and embraced a philosophy that combined nonviolent militancy with black pride and power.

In the spring of 1966, the Youth Council held a series of relatively quiet pickets at the Eagles Club, focusing on its discriminatory membership policies. With 5,400 members, the Milwaukee club was the second-largest Eagles chapter in the country. Its membership was a virtual who's who among Milwaukee's powerful, from labor union leaders to politicians, judges, and businessmen.

That summer in Milwaukee, tensions escalated. On August 9, 1966, three Ku Klux Klan members, two of them Milwaukee men who had worked for the George Wallace campaign in 1964, firebombed the headquarters of the Milwaukee NAACP.[23] The Youth Council soon changed tactics. It demanded that specific members of the Eagles Club resign and moved beyond peaceful picket lines on the edge of downtown. The first target of the new campaign was circuit judge Robert C. Cannon. Youth Council members and supporters decided to march from the central city out to Cannon's home in Wauwatosa. Residents of the relatively affluent community did not take kindly to the picketers.

The picketing at Judge Cannon's began in late August as a series of peaceful protests almost resembling a carnival. Enterprising street vendors even offered popcorn, ice cream, and soda. But after a few days the situation became increasingly tense as white counterdemonstrators started heckling the civil rights protesters. On Saturday, August 27, 1966, hundreds of white counterdemonstrators were on hand. They yelled slogans such as "We don't want the niggers in Wauwatosa," "Send them back to the Congo," and "Burn, Barbee, burn." Wauwatosa policemen protecting the civil rights picketers lost control until a dozen sheriff's deputies came to their rescue.[24] Governor Warren Knowles called out the National Guard to maintain order at the next day's protest. It was the first time the Guard had been mobilized for riot duty since a 1934 strike against the Kohler Company in Kohler, Wisconsin, and a 1933 farmer's milk strike.

Sunday's action began at 6:55 P.M. as civil rights protesters left the Youth Council's headquarters and began their march of eight miles to Cannon's neighborhood. As they crossed into Wauwatosa, counterdemonstrators lined the streets. Thousands of whites had mobilized, many cursing and screaming. About one-quarter of the civil rights protesters were white, and counterdemonstrators shouted, "Kill the white nigger-lovers." At another point, the counterprotesters yelled, "This is a white man's town. We don't want any cannibals in here."[25]

Nervous picketers arrived at Judge Cannon's home around 9:00 P.M., unsure if the white crowd could be contained. Unlike the night before, however, a solid wall of sheriff's deputies separated the civil rights picketers from the white counterdemonstrators. A squad of National Guardsmen stood nearby, carrying unloaded M1 rifles and carbines with fixed bayonets. Several hundred more Guardsmen lined nearby streets, holding back angry whites.

At 9:53 P.M., a brief prayer service was held to signal the end of the picketing at Judge Cannon's. It was time for the picketers to march back to the central city.

"A flying wedge of about 40 sheriff's deputies cleared a path for the demonstrators as they ended their prayer vigil," the *Milwaukee Journal* reported. "Steel helmeted guardsmen with bared bayonets walked along each side of the wedge—with the pickets in the middle—and other guardsmen held cursing spectators at bay on the sidewalks and lawns in the fashionable neighborhoods. . . . Wauwatosa police and guardsmen escorted them to the Milwaukee city limits."

The counterprotests exposed an underbelly of intolerance that Milwaukee's power structure had been unwilling to acknowledge. What's more, they were just a trial run for events the following summer, when Groppi and his Youth Council began their open housing marches.

7.

1967–68: OPEN HOUSING MOVES TO CENTER STAGE

A Good Groppi Is a Dead Groppi.

—White supremacist sign during Milwaukee's
open housing marches

June 14, 1967, was a typical day for open housing legislation in Milwaukee. Except for Alderman Vel Phillips, who had been raising the issue for five years, no alderman would even consider the topic. "Seventeen white Milwaukee aldermen listened silently for 30 minutes Tuesday while their lone Negro colleague urged them to consider the adoption of a city fair housing ordinance," the *Milwaukee Sentinel* wrote of the day's events. "Then, without a word of comment or criticism, they voted to reject the proposal."

That summer, Phillips got support from outside the council. Father James Groppi and the NAACP Youth Council launched their Open Housing campaign, demanding the city pass legislation prohibiting discrimination in the sale, lease, and rental of housing property in Milwaukee. The campaign began with picketing outside the homes of prominent aldermen. On July 30, however, the marches were interrupted by what in Milwaukee are known as the 1967 Riots, part of a national explosion of pent-up black rage.

In Milwaukee, as in other cities, anger in the black community had long simmered over police brutality, unemployment, housing discrimination, school segregation, political and economic disenfranchisement, and the refusal of the white power structure to acknowledge the pressing need for change. On July 12, 1967, disturbances broke out in Newark, New Jersey, sparked when two white policemen arrested a black cabdriver for improperly passing them. Rumors that the cabbie had been killed led to six days of rage, leaving twenty-six people dead. Less than a week after the end of

Newark's riots, Detroit was in flames. Police action—this time against an after-hours bar—once again lit the fire. Disturbances grew so intense that not only did the governor call out the Michigan National Guard, but President Lyndon B. Johnson sent in army troops equipped with machine guns and tanks. The riots lasted five days, leaving forty-three people dead and more than two thousand buildings destroyed.

Milwaukee's two-day upheaval began the night of July 30. By national standards, it was a relatively small disturbance. But it left whites in Milwaukee absolutely terrified, and it had a lasting impact on the city's psyche.

The outbreak was fueled by rumors that a white policeman had killed an African American boy. Before long, the central city was beset with arson, gunshots, and looting. At around 3:00 A.M., Mayor Henry Maier instituted a twenty-four-hour curfew and asked that the National Guard be called out. Only emergency and medical personnel were to leave their homes. Mail delivery and bus service were suspended. Those who violated the curfew were subject to immediate arrest.

The following morning, the city's freeways and streets were empty and still. Six armored personnel carriers, each mounted with a .50 caliber machine gun, were ordered into the Milwaukee area. In the central city, the *Milwaukee Journal* reported, "every pedestrian and civilian vehicle was challenged by troops armed with bayonet-tipped rifles." The riots left four people dead, almost a hundred injured, and 1,740 arrested.

Maier's show of force was widely praised as saving the city from even more devastating consequences. At the same time, nothing of substance was done to alleviate the conditions leading to the unrest and anger in the African American community.

Shortly after the riots, Father Groppi and the NAACP Youth Council again took up their demands for open housing. And, just as they had crossed into the suburb of Wauwatosa, the civil rights demonstrators were not afraid to venture into white supremacist strongholds of Milwaukee. The decision led to the now legendary marches across the Sixteenth Street Viaduct separating the city's downtown and Inner Core from the South Side.

On Monday, August 28, 1967, protesters gathered at St. Boniface in the central city. For the first time, they set out for the South Side, infamous as a stronghold of ethnic whites opposed to civil rights.

In a tribute to Father Groppi's reputation among his former South Side parishioners, a small group of supportive whites from St. Veronica's met the demonstrators at the beginning of their march across the bridge.[1] By the time the protesters walked the half mile across the bridge, however, matters had changed. Most of the three thousand whites on the other side were hostile, with signs that read "A Good Groppi Is a Dead Groppi." Some yelled *"Sieg heil,"* others "Go back to Africa." The marchers continued. Before long, counterdemonstrators along the march route were throwing bottles, stones, and chunks of wood at them. Another five thousand white counterdemonstrators were waiting when the civil rights protesters arrived at their destination, Kosciuszko Park in the heart of the South Side.

The next night, Groppi and the Youth Council once again headed to the South Side. This time, an estimated thirteen thousand counterdemonstrators challenged them. Once again, Groppi and the marchers continued. After their march, they returned to their Freedom House in the Inner Core. At about 9:30 P.M., the house was on fire. Groppi said the police started the fire with tear gas; the police said a firebomb had been tossed into the house by an unknown person. When fire trucks arrived, the police would not let them near, citing reports of gunshots and fears of a sniper. "Youth council members said the gunshots came from police weapons," writes journalist Frank Aukofer in his civil rights history of Milwaukee. "No arsonist or sniper ever was found."[2]

After the day's events, Mayor Maier banned nighttime demonstrations. On the night of August 30, however, Groppi held a rally at the burned-out Freedom House and led a march down city streets. Police ultimately arrested fifty-eight people.[3] The next night, declaring that Maier's ban violated their First Amendment rights of assembly, marchers headed toward city hall. Some 137 people were arrested, including Alderman Phillips and Father Groppi.

Within days, the mayor was forced to lift his ban. Keeping their promise to continue marching every day, Father Groppi and the Youth Council didn't stop even during the cold winter months, when temperatures sometimes dipped below zero.

On the South Side, white racists organized Milwaukee Citizens for Closed Housing, led by a white priest, Father Russell Witon. Decrying "forced open housing," Father Witon and his supporters organized counter-demonstrations at the Milwaukee archdiocesan chancery office and in the central city. The group, however, had more fury than staying power. Their efforts dwindled.

Open housing supporters, meanwhile, refused to give up. Beginning with the walk across the Sixteenth Street Viaduct on August 28, 1967, they continued with marches and protests for two hundred consecutive days.[4] Finally, propelled by national events, Milwaukee's power brokers realized they could no longer hold onto the past. On April 30, 1968, Milwaukee's Common Council finally passed the open housing bill. The vote occurred two weeks after Martin Luther King Jr. was assassinated during his campaign in support of striking sanitation workers in Memphis. Riots of rage broke out across the country. In Milwaukee, an estimated fifteen thousand to twenty thousand people marched somberly but peacefully through downtown.

The open housing legislation ended a long chapter in Milwaukee's civil rights struggles, spanning almost a decade and involving the city's seminal civil rights leaders and organizations. As early as 1961, Barbee helped organize a thirteen-day sit-in at the state capitol to ban discrimination in housing. In 1965, by that time a legislator, Barbee successfully co-sponsored statewide open housing legislation, but even supporters acknowledged it was a weak bill. In Milwaukee, meanwhile, Phillips and Groppi were pushing the more comprehensive local ordinance.

Barbee, Phillips, Groppi, and countless other activists easily moved between housing, school, and employment issues. They believed not only that the issues were inherently intertwined but also that they all had deep roots in overarching problems of racism and discrimination. Even the Milwaukee media saw the issues as part of an inseparable whole. As WTMJ television noted in a special report on school segregation in October 1965: "De facto segregation is caused by racial concentration in one area of the city. While there has been some outward migration from this ghetto, prejudice in housing has kept the number down. Even if this should be lifted, the economic position of most central city Negroes prohibits renting or buying in another part of the city. Negroes would have to have a better economic position, or would have a better economic position if they had better jobs. But better jobs require a better education. And here is the circle."[5]

For a variety of reasons, not the least of which was the continued domi-nance of racist attitudes and institutionalized practices, as the 1960s ended, the circle of problems remained intact in Milwaukee.

In the fall of 1969, Groppi led a weeklong march to Madison to protest cuts in the welfare budget. The effort, known as the Welfare Mothers March, galvanized a broad array of supporters, from welfare mothers to college students to low-income people of color, both African Americans and Lati-nos. But the march ended in an unplanned, chaotic occupation of the capitol that turned public opinion against the protesters—and resulted in a monthlong jail sentence for Groppi. Tactics aside, the march reflected the difficulties of organizing around complicated issues in an increasingly con-servative climate that viewed welfare and other social problems primarily as the result of individual irresponsibility, rather than grounded in structural problems of poverty, joblessness, and racism.

After years of struggle, meanwhile, many of the civil rights activists in Milwaukee moved on. Members of the Youth Council and Commandos took on full-time jobs, went to college, or started raising families. A num-ber of clergy involved in civil rights, including Groppi, left the priesthood or convent. Many remained active, but their activism took new directions as they found themselves looking for jobs and/or raising families.

Within Milwaukee's black community, nationalism was a growing force. Father Groppi and the Youth Council had developed a unique blend of black pride and power, but within the contexts of nonviolent resistance to segregation and an alliance between whites and blacks. That stance came under growing criticism from black nationalist forces who espoused sepa-ratism and emphasized empowering the black community over fighting segregation. When Groppi resigned in November 1968 as adviser to the Youth Council, both of Milwaukee's African American newspapers welcomed the priest's ouster.[6]

Milwaukee mayor Henry Maier, who had had a contentious relation-ship with the civil rights activists, perfected the skill of bringing his ene-mies close. In 1968, he appointed the first African American man as a mayoral assistant—John Givens, who in 1963 had led Milwaukee CORE's sit-ins. Civil rights activists differed on whether such appointments led to positions of power that could promote black advancement or were a co-optation that ultimately weakened the struggle.

The war in Vietnam, meanwhile, seized center stage, especially among Catholic activists, radicals on the left, and the counterculture youth movement in Milwaukee. The war came home most visibly on the night of Tuesday, September 24, 1968. Just after 6:00 P.M., fourteen antiwar protesters broke into the Selective Service office in downtown Milwaukee. They seized draft files, dragged them in burlap bags to the street, placed the bags at the foot of a nearby flagpole, doused the bags with "homemade napalm," and lit a match. As the files burned, the fourteen linked arms, sang hymns, read from the Gospel, and waited for police to arrive. They hugged and congratulated each other, remaining in high spirits as they were led into a police wagon.[7]

At the time, I was a senior at Holy Angels Academy, an all-girls Catholic high school in downtown Milwaukee. I was in a senior fog, biding my time until I could graduate. When I arrived at school that Wednesday, I hadn't heard about the draft files being burned. I expected it to be another uneventful day. Instead I saw some of the nuns wearing black armbands. I immediately knew something was up. Before long, one of the nuns replaced our schoolgirl rumors with facts. She explained they were wearing the armbands in solidarity with the burners of the draft files the night before, whom she referred to as the "Milwaukee Fourteen." I'm not sure exactly why, but I was profoundly affected. The war in Vietnam was no longer a faraway tragedy, and long-haired hippies weren't the only ones protesting. Nuns at my school were involved. That day seared into my young mind the awareness that there was a complicated yet compelling world beyond the parameters of my high school life. To this day, I look at the Milwaukee Fourteen as a reminder that commitment to one's beliefs has repercussions far beyond what one might imagine.

The Milwaukee Fourteen gained national notoriety along with the Catonsville Nine, who had burned draft files the previous May. In Milwaukee, the protest by the Milwaukee Fourteen was particularly shocking because six of those arrested were clergy, including Catholic priests. Father Groppi, meanwhile, co-chaired the Milwaukee Fourteen's defense committee. The cause had shifted, but the impassioned rhetoric and commitment remained. In a press statement the day they seized the draft files, the Milwaukee Fourteen said: "We who burn these records of our society's war machine are participants in a movement of resistance to slavery, a struggle that remains as unresolved in America as in most of the world. Our act concentrates on the selective service system because its relation to murder is immediate. Men are drafted—or 'volunteer' for fear of being drafted—as killers for the state. Their victims litter the planet."

The Milwaukee Fourteen represented a new era of activism. The events that followed their action were no less turbulent than those that had preceded it—when John F. Kennedy, Malcolm X, Martin Luther King Jr., and Robert F. Kennedy were assassinated; when police chased civil rights demonstrators with horses, tear gas, and dogs. But the scope of issues broadened. Inspired by the civil rights and black power movements, growing numbers of people took up emerging concerns such as women's liberation, the environment, and the rights of Native Americans and Latinos. The sense of urgency that propelled activists in the 1960s remained intact. But it broadened and increasingly shifted to developments thousands of miles away as the United States sent ever more troops to fight a war that it realized, only too late, it could not win.

The election of President Richard Nixon in 1968, meanwhile, signaled a shift in mainstream politics, with the federal government increasingly cool to civil rights concerns. The 1968 presidential race also highlighted the staying power of arch-segregationists, with Alabama governor George Wallace's third-party candidacy winning forty-six electoral votes and almost 15 percent of the popular vote.

The Milwaukee Public Schools ended the tumultuous 1960s much as it began: segregated, with a school board majority firmly committed to policies of intact busing and neighborhood schools. *Brown v. Board*, decided in 1954, had yet to make an impact.

Part II

Desegregation, Deindustrialization, and Backlash: 1970s and 1980s

8.

BROWN AND *MILLIKEN*: THE U.S. SUPREME COURT ADVANCES AND RETREATS

We conclude that in the field of public education the doctrine of "separate but equal" has no place. Separate educational facilities are inherently unequal.

—Unanimous U.S. Supreme Court decision, *Brown v. Board*, 1954

After 20 years of small, often difficult steps toward that great end [of equal educational opportunity], the Court today takes a giant step backwards.

—Justice Thurgood Marshall, dissenting opinion in *Milliken v. Bradley*, 1974

The desegregation era began with a momentous legal breakthrough and ended after a long, slow retreat. Two U.S. Supreme Court decisions stand out: *Brown* in 1954 and *Milliken* in 1974.

Nineteen fifty-four was a different time in more ways than one. At that time, most reporters covering the U.S. Supreme Court didn't bother to go to the Court to hear the justices deliver their opinions. It was much easier and faster to wait in the pressroom and write the story from there. Messages of an impending decision were sent from the Court via a pneumatic tube, and official copies of the rulings were handed out in the pressroom as a decision was read.[1]

On May 17, 1954, the justices began reading their decisions aloud around 12:30 P.M. The first dealt with monopoly and the Borden Company selling its milk in Chicago. The second dealt with indemnity and labor law. The third involved a union's right to picket retail stores. There was little to generate excitement. But then an unexpected message came via the pneumatic tube, and the court's press officer told the reporters: "Reading of the segregation decisions is about to begin in the courtroom." He then announced a change in protocol: the opinion would be handed out in the pressroom only after it was delivered from the bench. The reporters dashed upstairs. This was the decision everyone had been waiting for.

As Chief Justice Earl Warren began reading at 12:52 P.M., the Associated Press sent an alert to newsrooms across the country: "Chief Justice Warren today began reading the Supreme Court's decision in the public school segregation cases. The court's ruling could not be determined immediately." At 1:12 P.M., the AP sent its second bulletin, noting it was still unclear where the ruling was heading. It wasn't until 1:20 P.M. that the AP felt confident reporting that the U.S. Supreme Court said it was unconstitutional to segregate children by race in the public schools.

"We conclude that in the field of public education the doctrine of 'separate but equal' has no place," Chief Justice Warren intoned in reading the decision. "Separate educational facilities are inherently unequal."

Within an hour, Voice of America had translated the news into thirty-four languages and was sending reports across the world.[2]

More than half a century later, *Brown* has a troubled legacy. One of *Brown*'s many paradoxes is that it is primarily a ruling about public schools, yet it has been unable to deliver its promise of equal educational opportunity for all children.

At the time, however, *Brown* released a tidal wave of enthusiasm and hope not just about education but also about the Fourteenth Amendment's mandate of equal protection under the law for all people. Thus *Brown* is appropriately credited as a major catalyst of the civil rights struggles that soon engulfed the country and transformed racial relations. The late Derrick A. Bell, a professor of constitutional law at New York University School of Law and a thoughtful critic of *Brown*'s limitations, recalls that shortly after graduating from law school in 1957, he met with Judge William H. Hastie, the first black federal judge. Bell told Judge Hastie he hoped to become a civil rights lawyer. "Hastie nodded appreciatively," Bell writes. "He added, though, that while there might well be some mopping up to do, the *Brown* decision had redefined rights to which blacks were entitled under the

Constitution. 'Son,' he said, 'I am afraid that you were born 15 years too late to have a career in civil rights.'"[3]

Perhaps most important, *Brown* undermined the heart of *Plessy v. Ferguson*, the legal bulwark that upheld not only segregated schools but all of Jim Crow. (The term *Jim Crow* has a number of explanations. Some say it dates back to 1830, when a white minstrel man blackened his face, dressed as a bum, and danced, naming the minstrel skit "Jump Jim Crow" after a crippled slave.)[4] When white southerners retrenched and struck at the advances made by blacks during Reconstruction, they successfully replaced slavery with a system that segregated and disempowered blacks. Jim Crow laws, essential to that system, mandated segregation in just about every area of public life, from schools to hotels, restaurants, and water fountains. The U.S. Supreme Court upheld Jim Crow when, in 1896, it ruled in *Plessy* that separate but equal was constitutional.

There has long been an inherent bond between black education and liberation. Historian Peter Irons recounts the remembrances of Sarah Benjamin, a slave in Louisiana, and how slave owners responded when slaves secretly learned to read and write: "If yer learned to write dey would cut yer thumb er finger off."[5] In the antebellum South, meanwhile, a number of states outlawed the education of blacks, whether slave or free.

That fear of educated blacks did not dissipate after the Civil War. "The heart of the Jim Crow system, and the institution most central to its functioning, was the segregated school system," as Irons notes. "The combined power of racial prejudice and sexual phobia should not be underestimated as a motivating factor in the southern insistence on school segregation. But an equally important reason for maintaining separate schools was to make it simpler to provide a separate curriculum for black children, one that would provide the rudiments of literacy and training for manual labor and domestic service."[6]

Given the interrelationship of racism, education, and black liberation, schools in both the South and the North became the focus of resistance to desegregation. In the South, arch-segregationist governors received a reprieve after the U.S. Supreme Court, in what is known as *Brown 2*, called merely for desegregation "with all deliberate speed." Segregationists interpreted this to mean "as slowly as possible." During the 1955 school year, none of the southern states from Virginia through Louisiana had a single black student attending classes with white students.[7] In subsequent years, desegregation was essentially nonexistent as southern school boards interpreted *Brown* as a prohibition against state-sponsored segregation—but not as a mandate to approve plans that would actually desegregate schools. Once again the issue landed in the courts. It was not resolved until 1968, when the U.S. Supreme Court ruled in *Green v. New Kent County* and made clear that school boards must adopt realistic and immediate plans to integrate their schools. In 1970, the U.S. Supreme Court went a step further and approved busing of students to achieve desegregation. Segregationists, already upset by *Brown* and subsequent Court decisions, were incensed. "The word 'busing' soon became an epithet in the American political lexicon, hardly ever used without the adjective 'forced' to make the concept even more forbidding and frightening," Irons writes.[8]

Although northern whites were likely to support desegregation as public policy, in practice they often sought out segregated schools.[9] Housing segregation, not mandated by law but nonetheless an overarching reality in the North, made it easy to do so. Most whites, historian Thomas Sugrue notes, "had the flexibility to withdraw from public schools or to move across district lines."[10]

The U.S. Supreme Court, meanwhile, did not hear a northern school desegregation case until the early 1970s.[11] Of all the northern cases, none became more important than *Milliken v. Bradley*. Although the 1974 decision did not directly impact the Milwaukee desegregation case, which was limited to segregated schools within the City of Milwaukee, *Milliken* irrevocably shaped the legal parameters of urban desegregation in an era of increased suburbanization.

Vera Bradley, a leading plaintiff in the *Milliken v. Bradley* case that bears her name, fought for integrated schools because she wanted the best for her sons, Ronald and Richard. She didn't believe that sitting next to white children was a magic answer, or that her sons would suffer low self-esteem if kept in segregated schools. But she saw desegregation as the means to the goal of quality education. "We were upset because they [black schools] weren't getting as many materials as some other schools," Bradley said. "We figured if it was desegregated we would get the same."[12]

In 1970, the NAACP filed suit on behalf of Vera Bradley and other blacks in Detroit. The evidence was overwhelming that the school district had engendered and promoted segregated schools. But the issue became how best to desegregate in a city where whites were increasingly fleeing to the suburbs. In March 1972, Judge Stephen J. Roth rejected plans to desegregate merely within the district boundaries of Detroit. "School district lines," he said, "are simply matters of political convenience and may not be used to deny constitutional rights." That June, Judge Roth called for a desegregation plan that involved Detroit and fifty-three surrounding school districts.[13] The *Wall Street Journal* used one word to describe the reaction of suburban whites: "panic."

The country's political mood was far different in the mid-1970s than in 1954. Desegregation had been difficult, and both whites and blacks increasingly questioned *Brown*'s approach to educational opportunity. In addition, blacks all too often bore the brunt of the difficulties: long bus rides, disrupted communities, hostile white students and white teachers at integrated schools. Far more momentous was that President Richard Nixon had named four conservative justices to the Supreme Court. For two of them, Lewis Powell and William Rehnquist, opposition to federal judicial involvement in school cases had been a key factor in their nominations.[14] Rehnquist, for instance, had written a 1953 memo while a U.S. Supreme Court law clerk during the *Brown* case, saying, "I think *Plessy v. Ferguson* was right and should be reaffirmed."[15]

A sharply divided U.S. Supreme Court ruled 5–4 on *Milliken* on July 25, 1974—slightly more than two decades after *Brown*. In a decision with educational impact surpassed only by the *Brown* case, it struck down Judge Roth's desegregation mandate, which went beyond the Detroit city limits. After *Milliken*, the suburbs remained safe as an enclave for whites. By the end of the century, whites accounted for only 4 percent of the students in the Detroit schools. As Sugrue argues, "The *Milliken* decision spelled the end of the battle for educational integration."[16] In Detroit and throughout the North, he went on to note, racial segregation in housing and education became "the most persistent feature of life."[17]

Justice Thurgood Marshall, who had shepherded *Brown* through the courts, issued a dissent that was unequivocal, eloquent, and prescient: "In the short run, it may seem to be the easier course to allow our great metropolitan areas to be divided up each into two cities—one white, the other black—but it is a course, I predict, our people will ultimately regret."

9.

JANUARY 19, 1976: THE COURT RULES—MILWAUKEE'S SCHOOLS ARE SEGREGATED

I have concluded that segregation exists in the Milwaukee public schools and that this segregation was intentionally created and maintained by the defendants.

—Federal Judge John Reynolds Jr., January 19, 1976

On Thursday, June 17, 1965, attorney Lloyd Barbee walked up the granite steps of Milwaukee's federal courthouse, a majestic landmark built in 1892 and covering an entire downtown square block. On behalf of forty-one Milwaukee schoolchildren—thirty-two blacks and nine whites—Barbee filed a federal suit charging that the Milwaukee school board had deliberately implemented policies that led to segregated schools. It was the first suit in the nation in which parents of white children were plaintiffs, and one of twenty similar suits that the NAACP had filed in the North.[1]

Barbee asked for both "a speedy hearing" and a temporary injunction halting board policies that fostered segregated schools. Neither happened. It would be fourteen years, eight months, and two days before all appeals were decided. In contrast, the leading case in *Brown* was filed in 1951 and the U.S. Supreme Court issued its groundbreaking decision three years later.

The Milwaukee school board had long argued that housing patterns and not board policies had led to school segregation. The lawsuit, while noting segregated housing, argued that the school board had, over the years, fostered segregation and thus violated the U.S. Constitution's Fourteenth Amendment, guaranteeing equal protection. The suit alleged that the board had consistently redrawn school attendance boundaries "in such a manner as to produce greater segregation," promoted "intact busing," and designed transfer policies that allowed whites to leave black-majority schools easily while limiting choices for blacks. Finally, personnel policies kept black staff segregated in predominantly black schools.

The main facts were not in dispute. At the time of the lawsuit, thirteen elementary public schools in Milwaukee were more than 90 percent black, and eighty-six were more than 90 percent white. Statistics were similar in the middle and high schools.[2] A handful of schools in transition neighborhoods had a momentary balance, with whites often taking advantage of transfer policies to switch to white schools. Court documents also alleged that black schools were not only separate but also unequal, with blacks assigned to older buildings with less playground space, and black students more likely to be in substandard, overcrowded classrooms.[3]

The day after the suit was filed, a survey by the *Milwaukee Sentinel*, the city's morning newspaper, found that most Milwaukeeans "approved of the way the school board has handled racial imbalance in the school system."[4] Buoyed by such surveys, the school board remained intransigent and continued its segregationist policies.

In 1965, the lawsuit was still eclipsed by protests in the street. Indeed, on the day it was filed, Barbee was busy helping the five men and fifteen women arrested the day before at a demonstration against the intact busing of black students. (Neither the lawsuit nor the school protests were the day's top news. That was reserved for banner headlines reporting on a raid against the Vietcong by a fleet of twenty-seven B-52s flying in from Guam. It was the first time the B-52s were used in Vietnam.)

The lawsuit finally went to trial in September 1973, eight years after it was filed, and concluded the following spring. The federal courts offered little opportunity for public intervention. Thus by the time the suit went to trial, desegregation was in the shadows of the public spotlight. Far more electrifying events were unfolding, including the near-certain impeachment and subsequent resignation of a U.S. president following criminal activities that came to light after a burglary at a Washington, D.C., office complex known as Watergate.

But though the wheels of justice moved slowly, they did move. On January 19, 1976, two years after the trial ended, almost eleven years after the case was filed, with only five plaintiffs still enrolled in the Milwaukee schools, Judge John Reynolds Jr. made up his mind. In unequivocal language at the beginning of what would be a 141-page decision, Judge Reynolds wrote: "I have concluded that segregation exists in the Milwaukee public schools and that this segregation was intentionally created and maintained by the defendants."

Judge Reynolds had looked at board policies and actions from 1950 to 1974 and noted the many practices that promoted the growing racial imbalance in the city's schools. Dismissing the view that housing segregation was to blame, he said: "It is hard to believe that out of all the decisions made by school authorities under varying conditions over a twenty-year period, mere chance resulted in there being almost no decision that resulted in the furthering of integration."[5] At the time of the decision, 73 of the city's 158 schools were more than 90 percent white, while 30 were more than 90 percent African American.[6]

Within hours of the decision, battle lines were drawn. The school board immediately hinted it would appeal, and it did so by the end of the month. The appeal ultimately reached the U.S. Supreme Court and cost $2 million, making the desegregation case one of the most expensive of its day.[7] While the board did not prevail, it took years to emerge from the legal maneuvers. Equally important, the board's intransigence upset the momentum of desegregation and, because much of the debate was focused on legal issues, complicated the ability to organize parents and community members.

Despite the board's resistance, most people realized that the court order was likely to stand. The bus, not segregation or equal educational opportunity, became the hot-button issue. "Desegregation Order May Require Busing," the front-page headline blared in the *Milwaukee Sentinel* the day after the federal court ruling. Anti-integrationists quickly took up the demand of "no forced busing." Others bemoaned the loss of "neighborhood schools." Both slogans became code for opposing desegregation without having to openly embrace racism or defy a federal court order.

Within the white community, most public reaction was cool or openly negative. Milwaukee-area congressman Clement Zablocki said he was so upset by Judge Reynolds's opinion that "it makes my blood boil every time [Reynolds's] name is mentioned."[8] State senator F. James Sensenbrenner, representing a suburban district at the edge of Milwaukee, complained that the decision "spells the end of the neighborhood school system in Milwaukee." Other political leaders ran for cover—from the state's two U.S. senators to Mayor Henry Maier and Governor Patrick Lucey. All had "no comment." Mayor Maier later clarified his stance, saying of Judge Reynolds's decision: "I would obey, but I would resent it."[9]

The retired head of Northwestern Mutual Life Insurance, a corporate mainstay, set the tone for the business community's response when he said busing "doesn't seem to be the answer." An unidentified bank vice president was more blunt: "I don't care who's bused into my kids' school, but I don't want them bused into the inner core. . . . You also owe your kids physical safety."[10]

Father John Hanley, superintendent of the Milwaukee archdiocesan Catholic schools, said it would be "un-Christian" for parents to transfer children to parochial schools to avoid integration. But it was already well known that Catholic schools had become a safe harbor for anti-integrationists, especially on the city's South Side. Father James Groppi, then heading the VISTA program in the city of Racine, about thirty miles south of Milwaukee, said, "The Milwaukee Catholic school system should have taken the lead a long time ago and integrated its own system. I'm also afraid that the Catholic school system is going to become a haven for white segregationists."[11] (A 1967 report by the Catholic Interracial Council noted that de facto segregation existed throughout the Catholic parochial schools, with black pupils concentrated in just four of roughly a hundred parish schools in Milwaukee County. Most of the schools had no blacks.)[12]

Although politics had shifted in the black community since the suit's filing in 1965, the response was generally positive. Mildred Harpole, a well-known black educator and activist, said the decision was "long overdue." Former councilwoman Vel Phillips "applauded" the decision. Doss Bender, president of the local NAACP, hoped for "complete integration." A poll by the *Milwaukee Journal* in March 1976 found that 73 percent of black respondents said racial integration was a desirable goal. Barbee said that ten of the eleven elected black officials at the local and state levels approved Judge Reynolds's decision. The main critic was state senator Monroe Swan, who had long supported black community schools as an alternative to desegregation: "[School integration] hasn't really worked anyplace outside the South. . . . If quality education is the purpose, [community schools] is the most effective route to take."[13]

The *Milwaukee Sentinel*, summarizing reactions from notable women as part of its "World of Women" column in its women's pages, addressed the concern that was on most everyone's mind. The column quoted an un-identified woman who worked for the schools and who said, " 'Oh my god. I hope it will not be another Boston.' "[14]

By the 1970s, public schools in the North were more segregated than in the South. Just as Little Rock symbolized southern resistance, two decades later Boston became the symbol of northern resistance. In the South, resistance centered on a defense of Jim Crow. In the North, the bus became the enemy.

President Richard Nixon had emboldened northern opposition to desegregation by calling busing a "classic case of the remedy for one evil creating another evil."[15] President Gerald Ford went a step further and distanced himself from the federal court order to desegregate Boston's schools. "I have consistently opposed forced busing to achieve racial balance as a solution to quality education," Ford said in a press conference. "And, therefore, I respectfully disagree with the judge's order."[16] The message was clear: the federal government would not help Boston police keep order.

The stage was set for Boston's first day of desegregated schooling on September 12, 1974. At the time of the court order, roughly one-third of Boston's students were already being bused or took public transport to school—but to segregated schools.[17] "Forced busing" became the anti-desegregation rallying cry.

Opposition was strongest in South Boston, a working-class Irish neighborhood with a fierce reputation for protecting its turf. Federal judge W. Arthur Garrity had called for almost eighty blacks to be bused into South Boston High and an equal number of whites from "Southie" to be bused to Roxbury, in the heart of the city's black community.[18] To resist, the militantly anti-busing white group ROAR—Restore Our Alienated Rights—called for whites to boycott school. In addition to angry parents, truant students were thus on hand to cause trouble for the roughly twenty blacks from Roxbury entering South Boston High that first day of school.

The initial yellow bus bringing the black students, No. 218, pulled up to South Boston High School just before 8:00 A.M. The first of many rocks thrown that day bounced off No. 218's side. The white crowd on the sidewalk cheered. "Go home, nigger," some yelled. Others shouted, "Turn the bus over."[19]

The crowd's hostility was crystallized by one man who told the *New York Times*, "Any white kid that goes to school out of his neighborhood should be shot, and any black kid that comes out of his neighborhood to school here should be shot."

Boston police finally cleared the streets, and the black students entered South Boston High. But the school was almost empty, as white students had followed ROAR's call for a boycott.

As the months wore on, the boycott continued and violence spread throughout the city. The civil rights days of nonviolent resistance had long since passed, and angry black students responded in kind. When the schools opened again in September 1975, the situation was still explosive. The following spring, on April 5, 1976, an already awful situation got worse.

White students from Charlestown and South Boston had marched on city hall to read an anti-busing statement to the press. They then headed to the federal courthouse to picket Judge Garrity. They came across a black lawyer, Theodore Landsmark, on his way to city hall. A group of the white students tried to impale Landsmark with the sharp end of a flagpole, then knocked him down with the flagpole and clubbed and beat him. The next day, newspapers across the country carried a picture of the students charging Landsmark with the flagpole, "exposing Boston's ugly racial wounds to the nation."[20]

One night two weeks later, white auto mechanic Richard Poleet was stopped at a red light in Roxbury. He was spotted by a group of black youth, who shouted, "There goes whitey." Poleet was dragged from the car and severely beaten. Louise Day Hicks, the leader of ROAR and a South Boston mother whose anti-busing stance had won her elections to the city council and Congress, blamed Poleet's beating on "forced busing, which has made this city fertile ground for such brutality."

Both Landsmark and Poleet survived their attacks. Boston's image did not. "The long series of explosions over busing in Boston did not end for several years, and the reverberations still echo through the city until the present," notes historian Peter Irons.[21] As Milwaukee prepared for desegregation in the spring and summer of 1976, Boston's experience was an ever-present cautionary tale.

Memories of Milwaukee's 1967 riots and racial disturbances were still strong, and anti-integration sentiments remained high in many white neighborhoods. When George Wallace spoke to hundreds of whites at Milwaukee's Serb Hall in the spring of 1976, in a reprise of his presidential ambitions, he was greeted by chants of "Wallace yes, busing no." Wallace called for freedom of choice in education and derided the "social experimentation" of forced busing.[22]

Faced with the federal court order and fearful of violent confrontations, the city's power brokers united around one overriding goal: Milwaukee would not be a Boston.

Shortly after Judge Reynolds issued his decision, Milwaukee superintendent Lee McMurrin went to see Mayor Henry Maier. It was McMurrin's first year in the job and the two did not know each other well. Maier made clear that civil unrest would not be tolerated in Milwaukee. "He said he had already called the Department of Justice and the governor, and that he could have the National Guard keep order if necessary," McMurrin recalls.[23]

Such options were not preferred, of course. So Maier asked McMurrin, who was white, about his plans. "Mayor, we are not going to have that situation," McMurrin responded.

"How are you going to avoid that?" the mayor asked.

"We have a plan to desegregate the schools based on volunteers and educational incentives. And we will recruit parents and community workers to join us in this effort." McMurrin, the affable, unflappable salesman, was at his best.

The outgoing superintendent, Richard Gousha, was a respected educational leader but lacked the gregarious one-of-us personality that Milwaukeeans prefer in their public leaders. When the board hired McMurrin away from Toledo, Ohio, they knew they needed someone who could smile, shake hands, slap backs, and sell board policies. McMurrin was their man. The bitterly divided fifteen-person board, with anti-integrationists in the majority, unanimously chose him from a field of a hundred candidates.[24]

Described alternately as "everyone's Dutch uncle" and "relentlessly optimistic," McMurrin even sported an "Everything Is Beautiful" button.[25] Schoolchildren who visited his office often drew portraits of McMurrin, many of them resembling the "Have a Nice Day" stickers popular at the time.[26] Rick Janka, the education reporter from the *Milwaukee Sentinel*, wrote in an article about McMurrin's first day: "It's not a hard job to describe

McMurrin. If the comic strip character Charlie Brown ever grows up, he'll probably look like Lee McMurrin."[27]

That optimism came in handy. McMurrin got a taste of the city's tense politics at his first official meeting with the school board in July 1975. Nazis showed up in full uniform with black boots and swastikas and filled the front row of seats; their girlfriends, in brown uniforms, were in the second row, and parents and other supporters filled in behind. At the second meeting, members of the ultra-right-wing John Birch Society (whose national headquarters were in Wisconsin) showed up and called McMurrin a communist.[28]

As he did with many of the charges leveled against him, McMurrin shrugged it off. His smile and happy-go-lucky persona masked his political perception and understanding of who did and didn't have power in Milwaukee. While many were unsure of the way forward, McMurrin unequivocally believed he had a plan that was educationally and politically superior to all others.

Throughout the fall, knowing that the federal courts would likely order desegregation, McMurrin had worked on that plan. Its driving vision was integrated citywide "specialty schools" that would attract whites who would choose to voluntarily bus their children to the schools. The specialty schools, often referred to as "magnet" schools nationally, would receive extra resources and would offer innovative programs, from Montessori to "open education," "individually guided education," language immersion schools, and arts schools. They would be open to students throughout the city, with admission based on a lottery. "By concentrating public attention on the specialty school concept and the broadening of educational opportunities, leaders assumed that some of the negative imagery of desegregation could be ameliorated," David Bennett, a deputy superintendent who was the behind-the-scenes implementer of Milwaukee's desegregation, later wrote.[29]

To avoid a Boston, Superintendent McMurrin used the carrot of voluntary choice and specialty schools to win over whites and beat back the anti-desegregation mantra of "forced busing." While a questionable move in terms of equitable treatment of blacks and whites, the move was politically shrewd. The rhetoric of choice, combined with innovation and extra resources, was seductive. "I remember thinking at the time that choice was a brilliant way to defuse potentially violent opposition," recalls William Lynch, an attorney long involved in education and civil rights issues in Milwaukee. "In Boston, the South Boston High School neighbors all knew what was happening to their kids, so they could get together and organize resistance. But the system of allowing preferences, and allowing people to go to school anywhere and everywhere, that made it made it very hard for opposition to organize."

In his decision, Judge Reynolds ordered desegregation to begin the following September, to be phased in over three years. But he had no intention of following the path of Judge Garrity in Boston, who became intimately involved in specifics and, in essence, seized control of the school system. Judge Reynolds left it to school officials to propose a plan. Understandably lacking trust in a school board he had just found responsible for unconstitutional segregation, Judge Reynolds appointed a special master to help guide the process, who would be paid by and report to the court. Judge Reynolds named John Gronouski, a man he knew and trusted. Like Superintendent McMurrin, Gronouski had a flair for appealing to the common person. More important, he had a long political career that included serving as U.S. postmaster general and as U.S. ambassador to Poland—a plus given Milwaukee's strong Polish community. But it also meant that yet another white man would play an essential role in implementing the desegregation of the Milwaukee Public Schools.

Milwaukee's winters are long, cold, and gray. When the winter sun goes down, Milwaukeeans survive by going into a state of near-hibernation. On a snowy evening in February 1976, however, scores of parents and community people left their homes and gathered in the gym at Pierce School in Milwaukee's Riverwest community. A working-class area also known as a haven for artists and political activists, Riverwest was one of the few Milwaukee neighborhoods that could be considered even remotely integrated. It was also home to some of the Latinos immigrating to Milwaukee, especially Puerto Ricans.

Aurora Weir, a Panamanian who had gained prominence for her ability to organize across ethnic and racial divides, addressed the crowd at Pierce School in Spanish, then English, and finally Italian. "For our information," she told the crowd as she switched back to English, "I am going to conduct the meeting trilingually this evening because we have some families that recently arrived from Italy."

Schools across the city were holding similar meetings, albeit not in three languages. As part of the desegregation planning process, representatives from the schools and community groups were being elected for the citywide Committee of 100. The committee was the official advisory group to the Milwaukee school board, the administration, and the court's special master, with a mandate to ensure community input into desegregation plans.

In the months following Judge Reynolds's desegregation order, the school board was seen as the main obstacle to successful desegregation. With the court order to back them up, civil rights supporters in both the black and white communities prepared for the new era, their energy strong and their hopes high. Milwaukee's segregated, unequal schools had been declared illegal. It was time to move forward and make desegregation work.

After the federal court order mandating desegregation, three major forces were in motion. First was the school board majority, representing the attitudes of many white voters and opposed to desegregation. Second was an alliance of power brokers, led by Superintendent McMurrin and including key media and business players. They knew the power of Judge Reynolds's decision and that desegregation was coming, but they wanted to avoid both civil unrest and mandatory busing of whites into black neighborhoods. Third were the community groups, led by the Committee of 100. With the involvement of both white and black activists, the community groups focused on a vision of equitable integration that did not cater to white privilege and preferences. (Nationalists within the black community who didn't support integration kept a low profile that spring and summer, realizing "that current community sentiment and the law supported desegregation.")[30]

The Committee of 100 was the most important and broad-based of the community groups organizing to promote desegregation, and the only one to hold official advisory status. It was co-chaired by Cecil Brown Jr., a longtime activist in the black community, and Grant Waldo, a white activist. Blacks were represented proportionately on the Committee of 100 (about one-third, in line with a black enrollment of 34 percent in Milwaukee's public schools in 1976). The Coalition for Peaceful Schools was also formed, representing community and religious organizations, with voting members ranging from the League of Women Voters of Greater Milwaukee to the Milwaukee Urban League, the Episcopal Diocese, and the Milwaukee City Council of PTAs. That summer a third group formed, People United for Integration and Quality Education, comprising community and radical activists and with an explicit focus on fighting racism.

From the beginning, the community groups' vision went far beyond Superintendent McMurrin's approach. They focused on desegregation plans that grouped schools and called for equitable busing of black and white students. A core component of Superintendent McMurrin's plan, although neither the administration nor media liked to acknowledge this reality, was that desegregation would be accomplished via the voluntarily integrated specialty schools and by mandatory busing of blacks into formerly predominantly white schools. Whites, meanwhile, would generally be allowed to remain in their neighborhood schools if they wanted.

After the court order in January, the clock was ticking on developing specifics of how desegregation would unfold the next fall. The community groups were organizing, but Superintendent McMurrin's plan had the momentum. Gronouski, the court-appointed special master who had Judge Reynolds's trust, came to accept reluctantly the voluntary-for-whites plan. He believed it had to be given a chance since so many powerful forces were behind it and McMurrin himself was so enthusiastic. "Nor could I ignore the fact," Gronouski wrote in a June 9, 1976, statement to Judge Reynolds, "that were I to endorse a mandatory integration plan before the people of Milwaukee had an opportunity to try a voluntary plan, I would have been unresponsive to the people of Milwaukee."

While heaping praise on everyone from the Milwaukee PTA to the Milwaukee business community and media, Gronouski had nothing but scorn for the school board majority: "My deepest concern, and Milwaukee's most serious dilemma, is the wholly negative attitude of the bare majority presently in control of the School Board. It has adamantly refused to countenance any significant positive movement toward development of a meaningful integration plan."[31]

The community groups were not content with plans for the first year of desegregation but realized that time was running short before school was to begin. They reluctantly accepted that blacks would be disproportionately bused in year one, believing they had the influence to shape years two

and three of desegregation. There were a number of reasons for disproportionate busing of blacks that first year. One was that older, inner-city
schools were crowded to begin with, because over the years the administration had failed to build enough new schools in black neighborhoods.
Second, several black schools were in such dilapidated condition that they
were closed. Third, a number of black neighborhood schools were being
reopened as specialty schools reserved for black and white volunteers from
across the city.

After weeks of back-and-forth, on July 9, 1976, Judge Reynolds signed
off on a school desegregation plan for the first year, giving the go-ahead to
McMurrin's approach. The agreement called for one-third of the schools to
be desegregated by September, beginning with elementary schools. Another
one-third of the schools were to be desegregated by September 1977, and
the rest by September 1978. A school would be defined as desegregated and
racially balanced if it had a 24–45 percent black student population. The
door was left open for mandatory busing of whites in years two and three
of desegregation, which the community-based groups argued was un-
avoidable if blacks and whites were to be treated equally.

Even before the court decision the previous January, McMurrin had
been the man with the plan. For the immediate future, accepting his approach seemed the best way to sidestep the school board's intransigence
and move forward. As the *Milwaukee Courier*, a black community newspaper, argued: "After all, why do we seek desegregation? Because inner city
schools are inferior to outlying white schools. . . . We want our children
out of bad schools."[32]

There were only fifty-nine days before the start of school, with more
than fifty of the schools to be transformed from segregated to racially balanced. *Chaos* would be too strong a word to describe those final weeks. *Near
chaos* would be more apt.

10.

SEPTEMBER 7, 1976: THE BUSES ROLL
AND DESEGREGATION BEGINS

People need to remember the reasons we had a court order in the first
place. The reasons were valid; the remedy was flawed.
 —Joyce Mallory, desegregation activist and school board member

In July 1976, just weeks before Milwaukee was to begin its first year of desegregation, Joel McNally and his wife, Kit, were relaxing on their couch
watching the local television news. That day, the school district had released a report on how many people had volunteered to help integrate the
new specialty schools that were being developed in the central city to promote integration.

"I still remember that night," recalls McNally, the father of three young
children at the time. "They put up the number for Lloyd Street School,
which we and some friends had chosen for our kids, and it was such a small
number. What's more, we personally knew every single person on that list.
The MPS [Milwaukee Public Schools] administration hadn't done a thing
to recruit people."[1]

McNally, a white reporter at the *Milwaukee Journal* helping to cover the
desegregation controversy, knew that the board and administration "weren't
gung-ho on integration," as he puts it. But he was both appalled and a bit
frightened by that evening's news. "I thought desegregation wasn't going to
happen," he recalls. Given that the school board had already appealed the
desegregation order in hopes that Judge Reynolds's decision would be overturned, it wasn't a cavalier concern.

The McNallys came of age during the political movements of the 1960s
and were committed to issues of social justice. They had been working with
a group of progressive whites, primarily on the city's liberal East Side but

also from other neighborhoods, including the South Side. They strongly opposed segregation and wanted integration to work. They immediately doubled their efforts to recruit people to Lloyd and its program of "individually guided education." "We realized we had to put a push on integration ourselves, citywide, because the administration was so lackadaisical," McNally says.

The group organized an open house at Lloyd, taking advantage of the warm weather to set up tables on the playground. They contacted people and organizations throughout the city, inviting parents to come to the potluck, tour the school, and meet others interested in sending their children to Lloyd. Turnout exceeded expectations, and the playground was jammed. "The assistant principal, probably one of those totally dispirited administrators stuck at Lloyd for whatever his past sins might have been, he could not believe what was happening," McNally recalls. "White, black, and Latino parents were descending on his school."

McNally believes the potluck turned recruitment around. More parents, black and white, started choosing Lloyd. The involvement of a number of white parents went beyond merely choosing an integrated school. "We did this voluntarily, yes, but that doesn't begin to describe it," McNally notes. "We didn't just passively volunteer. We organized and actively recruited other white parents through house meetings and phone banks."[2]

Another shock was awaiting the white parents at Lloyd, however. The library, indicative of overall conditions at the school, was all but nonexistent— a small classroom with outdated books, complete with tattered pages and covers torn off. "It was pathetic to even call it a library," McNally says. "We raised hell immediately and a library was created. I don't believe for a minute that black parents weren't upset about that library before integration. But until white parents started yelling and screaming, the administration didn't care. I've always believed that the very fact that it was a racist system is why white parents needed to be in those schools."

Grassroots organizing to promote integration was not unusual during the summer of 1976. Dating back to the civil rights movement, a significant number of whites and blacks had worked in organizations that crossed the city's racial divides. That legacy was still strong, helping to build a level of white support for equitable integration that politicians and school officials underestimated and, ultimately, dismissed.

* * *

Milwaukee began its much-anticipated desegregation of schools on Tuesday, September 7, 1976. The biggest news was the non-news. There were no jeering white crowds, no rocks thrown, no mass protests. Nor were there fistfights or major racial conflicts at the schools. The biggest problem was late buses, as newly hired drivers scrambled to figure out their routes. Parents across the city, even newspaper reporters and school board members, took children to school in their own cars when the buses didn't arrive—a reflection of the good-neighbor, pitch-in-and-help mentality that is part of Milwaukee's blue-collar identity.

Even the *Milwaukee Sentinel*, the more conservative of the city's two daily newspapers, admitted that the only "hitch" in the opening week of desegregation "has been widespread confusion over transportation . . . The important thing is that a foundation is being laid for the implementation of future stages of voluntary desegregation."[3]

In those first weeks, Milwaukee was enjoying a honeymoon phase with desegregation. After the relief that there was no violent backlash from whites, however, other realities came into focus. It was quickly apparent that the burden of busing was falling primarily on blacks. In that first year of desegregation, African American children accounted for about 90 percent of those bused.[4]

Community groups were raising the alarm, but the city's power elite remained committed to the voluntary busing of whites. For its part, the press remained mute about the facts of disproportionate busing for blacks. As *Milwaukee Sentinel* reporter Rick Janka later admitted, "I saw but never wrote about what was a very heavy burden on blacks. I really think blacks got the raw end of the deal. But I didn't want to be the one to get the community up in arms. I wanted to see integration work. And I think all the other TV and news reporters felt the same way."[5]

Although Milwaukee did not become a Boston, and although many whites worked hard to make the administration's desegregation plan work, anti-integration sentiment in Milwaukee's white community remained formidable. In school board elections the year after Judge Reynolds's decision, the top three vote getters were school board members opposed to desegregation.

The pro-integration community groups, spearheaded by the Committee of 100, increased their organizing. They knew that Judge Reynolds was to sign off on proposals for years two and three of the desegregation timetable. The community groups all favored equitable busing of blacks and whites, and all of them promoted a plan called "pairing and clustering" of schools.

The pairing and clustering proposal called for linking together predominantly black and predominantly white schools within a particular geographic area. The schools would then work, as a group, to reach the court's desegregation goals. The emphasis was on collaboration within groups of schools rather than, as in McMurrin's plan, on individualized choice and busing. As explained in a newsletter in September 1976 by the Coalition for Peaceful Schools:

> These techniques [pairing and clustering] have several advantages:
>
> 1. All [elementary] students involved attend their neighborhood school for several years and also attend one school outside their neighborhood.
> 2. Students in each grade are kept together throughout their elementary years. They attend classes in two school buildings—one in their neighborhood and one in the neighborhood of the other race.
> 3. The burden of busing is fairly equitable for both races.

The community groups also called on the district to modify policies so that the elementary schools involved in pairing and clustering would, as a group, feed into the same secondary school. The specific focus was on a court deadline in January 1977 for the school administration to submit its plan for year two of desegregation. Community groups put in tens of thousands of volunteer hours, held community meetings, and developed detailed proposals. They demanded equitable busing, quality education for all, and pairing and clustering. They were suspicious of the administration's claim that it was open to modifying its approach in years two and three of desegregation.

That November, the administration desegregation architect, deputy superintendent David Bennett, assured the *Milwaukee Journal*, "It's absolutely untrue that the administration is walking around with a plan in its pocket."[6] However, Bennett also admitted in a 1984 academic article, "We were never into pairing and clustering." Bennett further acknowledged that the administration never saw the Committee of 100 as an equal partner. Instead, it was viewed as a politically useful counterbalance to the board majority's anti-desegregation intransigence. One of the administration's main goals in desegregation, he wrote in his 1984 academic article, "was to maintain control of the school system in the hands of the board and the administration."[7]

Bennett, it appears, has a long-standing habit of speaking out of both sides of his mouth. In the 1984 academic article he defended the massive busing of blacks by saying, "The fact that nine times as many blacks are transported as whites reflects the difference in their choice patterns, not a difference in burden or responsibility." Yet at a Milwaukee forum in 1999, he reportedly admitted that the entire desegregation plan was designed to benefit and placate whites.

Bennett was "unavailable" when the *Milwaukee Journal Sentinel* asked him to confirm his remarks, which had created a buzz of gossip throughout the city. But Anthony Busalacchi, a school board member at the time and board president in 1978–79, spoke up. "I think it was an unspoken issue with the School Board at the time," Busalacchi told the *Journal Sentinel*. "It was an issue of how do we least disrupt the white community."[8]

By the spring of 1977, with Milwaukee's desegregation effort not even a year old, the media was forced to admit problems. "Integration Gets a D," the *Milwaukee Journal* noted in a Sunday feature that April.[9] The headline was journalistic hyperbole, but it got people's attention. What's more, there was no denying that desegregation, as structured by the administration and school board, was leading to separations between the specialty schools and traditional schools. Staff and parents at traditional schools were often bitter at the two-tier system developing not so much along lines of race but along those of class.

"There's nothing special about Parkview," a *Milwaukee Journal* feature noted. "Staff members and parents say that's the problem."

Before desegregation, Parkview was nearly all white. It was one of nineteen formerly segregated elementary schools that were to become integrated that first year—but not by a specialty program that attracted both white and black volunteers. "On the contrary," the paper noted, "the schools were integrated because black parents of children in crowded Inner City schools were persuaded, cajoled—in some cases, just told—to volunteer their children to be bused to places like Parkview."

Before desegregation, only 14 of Parkview's roughly 425 students were nonwhite. In the fall of 1976, about 140 African Americans were bused in. There were minor changes in staffing, but no training to help the teachers through what everyone knew would be a difficult transition. Cultural differences too often were viewed as disciplinary infractions, and disciplinary problems often escalated into racial animosity. The *Milwaukee Journal* told the story of ten-year-old Eric Carter to demonstrate the problem.

> Like nearly all black pupils at Parkview, Eric had attended the crowded, all-black Auer Avenue School last year. His mother claims that Eric never got into trouble at Auer, so she was surprised to discover what happened after he got in a fight [at Parkview].
>
> "As punishment, the teacher put his desk in a corner for two weeks," said Marlene Carter. "What kind of incentive is that, having a child staring at the wall? He cried every day about it when he came home. He felt self-conscious. Punishment should last one day. Every day's a new day."
>
> As a result of the incident, Mrs. Carter transferred Eric to Garfield Avenue School, which specializes in open education.

The division between specialty and traditional schools would grow in coming years. To its credit, the school district implemented a lottery system for both blacks and whites for admission to the specialty schools. But the specialty schools tended to have more resources. The parents who chose the specialty schools tended to be more middle-class and more involved in their child's education. In addition, staff at the new specialty schools tended to be united both in their support of integration and in their commitment to their school's specialty, whether it was open education or the arts. Traditional schools had a disproportionate number of staff who needed, but did not receive, human relations training to counterbalance racial stereotypes and assumptions.

At Parkview during the first year of desegregation, the average was twenty-eight students for every teacher, including reading and music specialists. Overall, there were twenty students for every adult in the building. At Lloyd Street, a specialty school, there were about fifteen students for every teacher and fewer than ten students for every adult.

Desegregation proponents felt the disparities were yet another indication that leading administrators didn't have their hearts in successful integration. The *Milwaukee Journal*, for once, seemed to agree. "There is considerable evidence," the *Journal* reported, "that Milwaukee's educational decision makers doomed Parkview desegregation to failure initially by unrealistic staffing policies and inadequate human relations training."

At a number of newly desegregated schools, teacher-student relations were tense, with the predominantly white teaching staff too often falling back on racial misconceptions as they taught increasing numbers of black students. Nor did it help matters when the teachers union went on strike in April 1977. Teachers had been without a contract since January. Key issues involved money, class size, and flexibility in staffing. But, as with everything, issues of race were involved.

Bob Peterson, a twenty-three-year-old activist involved in desegregation, was working at the docks that spring. He also had been a leader in the community/labor/antiwar group the Wisconsin Alliance. His natural sympathies were with both workers on strike and communities of color demanding justice.

Shortly after the teachers union went on strike, he called up his friend Virgil. The two walked three blocks through the Riverwest neighborhood to Pierce Elementary School and joined a picket line of about fifteen teachers. Grabbing a protest sign was second nature to him, and soon he was marching with a placard that read, "Fair Contract Now."

"It seemed pretty clear to me that the school board, which was stonewalling on desegregation, was doing no better in negotiating with the teachers," he later reflected. "But, as always, things were more complicated than one first imagined."[10]

Later that day, Peterson got a phone call from a close friend, Clara White, an African American woman whose involvement in civil rights dated back to the 1963 March on Washington. Both Peterson and White were leaders in the community group People United for Integration and Quality Education.

White did not share Peterson's enthusiasm for joining the teachers on the picket line. "Bob, we got a problem," she told him. "The strike."

Peterson agreed that the walkout was taking attention away from the desegregation effort, and he also agreed that it was never a preferred option for children to miss school. But he saw the recalcitrant school board as the problem, not the strike.

"See any black people on the picket line?" White asked Peterson.

"Just Virgil and Frank from People United," he replied.

"No black teachers?"

"Not that I recall," Peterson admitted.

"That's my point," White said.

Peterson came to understand that one of the strike's flash points, contract language on staff transfers, was grounded in the union's insistence that the transfers be based strictly on seniority.

Clarence Nichols, a public school teacher and member of the NAACP, had organized a black caucus within the union a few months earlier to protect the rights of black teachers. Black teachers tended to have less seniority, and the caucus demanded separate seniority lists for whites and blacks. Nichols estimates that as many as 50 percent of the district's 866 black teachers refused to honor the strike and crossed the picket lines.[11]

The strike was settled seventeen school days after it began. Seniority remained mostly unchanged, but the district won flexibility in assigning staff to the specialty schools.[12] A more lasting effect was that the strike damaged already fragile relations between the union and both black teachers and the black community. In a pattern that held for years to come, the union believed its power lay in electing school board members who would agree with the union, not in building bridges to the community. The *Milwaukee Courier*, a black community newspaper, called the union "racist"—not for the last time.[13]

On Labor Day 1977, the day before the second year of desegregation was to begin, a multiracial crowd gathered at Washington Park in Milwaukee to show their support for integration. It had been a rocky first year as the Milwaukee school district took its initial steps to overcome decades of segregationist policies. Community groups felt it important to publicly reaffirm their commitment.

"Do not lose hope, and do not lose heart," Cecil Brown, co-chairman of the Committee of 100, told the crowd of several hundred people.

While Brown was urging desegregation supporters to keep the faith, many parents were more focused on the checklist of concerns that accompany the beginning of school. Would the buses arrive on time? Would their child like school? Would the teacher like their child?

Kathy Williams, who a generation earlier had taken part in the Freedom School boycott of Milwaukee's segregated schools, shared those concerns. The mother of two young children, with the youngest less than six months old, she didn't have time to follow all the ins and outs of desegregation policy. She just knew she wanted the best school possible for her daughter, four-year-old Manika.[14]

In the spring, in what became an institutionalized and complicated ritual in Milwaukee, Williams had filled out various forms listing her first, second, and third choices of school for her daughter—and crossed her fingers. When a school did not have enough slots for all those who chose the school, assignment was by lottery. If Williams's daughter did not make it through the lottery and get one of her three choices, the district would assign her daughter to a school. (Similarly, those who did not take part in the choice process were generally assigned a school.)

Educational quality was certainly a key issue when Williams listed her top three choices, none of which were schools in her neighborhood. But there were other reasons. "The schools in the neighborhood didn't have a four-year-old kindergarten program. That was the main reason," Williams recalls. Although the media put so much attention on busing, Williams felt that putting her young daughter on a bus was the least of her concerns. "I had been working in the school system as a paraprofessional for a number of years," she explains. "While there wasn't busing for desegregation, kids were bused on field trips. I had the normal concerns at the beginning—would my daughter get off at the right stop? Would there be appropriate supervision at the school when she got there? But I wasn't overly concerned about the bus."

Williams had listed MacDowell Montessori, one of the new specialty schools, as her first choice, and her daughter was admitted. She made a point of visiting the school early in the year, introducing herself and letting the teacher know she would be a concerned, active parent. "I wanted it to be clear that I was available for my child in the event of any need or questions," Williams explains. "I wanted the teacher to know there were adults available who cared about that child."

"To say there was no racism at the school would be a silly thing to say, because racism is so institutionalized and permeates schooling and society to this day," Williams adds. "But I don't recall any overt incidents or problems. It was a smooth schooling experience for my daughter."

Other black families were not so lucky. For many, busing was the result not of a choice but an assignment system that seemed the work of a mentally unbalanced bureaucrat. Black students forced to leave their segregated neighborhood schools were assigned in a scattershot blast going in all directions. When the *Milwaukee Journal* ran a story in October 1977 headlined "Busing Nightmare: 3,194 Ways to Go to School," the story rang true for too many parents.

> Take a city map. For every elementary school pupil, draw a line from the school in his neighborhood to the school he attends.
>
> From Auer Avenue School in the Inner city, you have lines going to 95 locations.
>
> From Berger School, you have lines extending in 67 directions. From Clark School, 70, and from Franklin, 76 . . .
>
> When you're finished, you have a maze of 3,194 lines, each representing a different combination of sending and receiving schools. You have a picture of the interplay among the neighborhoods that school desegregation has created. . . .
>
> Because of the school choice system, virtually every public school has become a citywide facility. On the average, pupils in the neighborhood of each elementary school attend 20 schools outside the neighborhood.

The pro-integration community groups continued their call for "pairing and clustering" and a more rational and equitable plan for desegregation. None of the power brokers, however—neither the media, the administration, nor the school board—had the political will to support plans that mandated white children attend schools in predominantly black neighborhoods.[15] "The various community groups were way ahead of the elected officials," noted Mary Bills, a white activist later elected to the school board. "They were prepared to desegregate and to do it fairly. The administration and the board majority were not."[16]

The intransigent, anti-integration school board majority won an important victory in June of 1977, leading to what can only be described as legal ping-pong. The U.S. Supreme Court, taking up the school board's appeal of

Judge Reynolds's desegregation order, vacated Judge Reynolds's decision and threw the matter back to the appeals court. Just days before school was to begin in September for year two of desegregation, the appeals court told Judge Reynolds to hold additional hearings on evidence of the school board's segregatory policies. The appeals court refused to reverse Judge Reynolds, but many people were understandably confused. They thought the appeals court had put a stop to desegregation in Milwaukee.

The hearings were held in the winter, and in June 1978 Judge Reynolds confirmed his original decision. But there was a cost. The momentum of desegregation had slowed, anti-integrationists felt vindicated, and whites increasingly had fled to either the suburbs or private schools within the city. What's more, the appeals court had eliminated the job of John Gronouski, the special master that Judge Reynolds had appointed to act as an arbiter and liaison to the court. This deprived desegregation supporters of a powerful ally who, despite his vacillation and readiness to compromise, supported equitable busing. "I have a hunch that the movement of blacks would have been a little more equal had I not been fired," Gronouski reflected almost a decade later.[17]

At the same time, after the first year of desegregation began, a group of black activists, influenced by a nationalist perspective, launched a campaign known as "two-way or no-way." They demanded an end to desegregation unless whites and blacks were equally bused. While the campaign did not gain widespread traction within the black community, it underscored the growing concern that Milwaukee's desegregation plan privileged whites and forced blacks to bear the burden of fixing a problem they had not caused.

After affirming his original decision, Judge Reynolds once again ordered the desegregation of the Milwaukee Public Schools. There was no special master this time, however. With little trust in the school board, Judge Reynolds ordered both the plaintiffs and the defendants to submit plans by February 23, 1979. The desegregation attorneys and the school board entered into negotiations to reach a mutually agreeable settlement. In May 1979, more than three years after his original decision, Judge Reynolds approved the settlement, which continued Superintendent McMurrin's approach of choice, specialty schools, and inequitable busing of blacks.

The settlement was to remain in effect for five years, during which there could not be any further legal action against the board. It required that only about 75 percent of students attend desegregated schools in the third year of desegregation, as opposed to the original goal of 100 percent. As a result, an estimated twenty-four schools would remain almost all-black. The definition of a desegregated school was also loosened, to 20–60 percent black at the high schools and 25–60 percent at middle and elementary schools. The settlement did not require any mandatory busing of whites. In addition, resegregation would be legally permissible if the total enrollment of blacks exceeded the number of non-blacks—a phenomenon that, given white flight and demographic trends, was only a few years away. The rationale was that with a decreasing number of whites, it would be impossible to maintain desegregated schools. The court-brokered settlement also took up the complicated issue of staffing. Judge Reynolds okayed guidelines for a minimum number of black teachers at every school—which also meant a reduced percentage of black teachers at schools that would remain all-black.

Civil rights activists uniformly condemned the settlement, calling it everything from a "capitulation to racism" to "a travesty of justice."[18] James Koneazny, a board member supporting integration, said of the settlement, "To leave all-black schools in this day is a travesty and a tragedy, and to vote for it, I think, is sinful."[19]

The U.S. Supreme Court had signaled its retreat from desegregation, however, and a disheartened Lloyd Barbee saw the legal writing on the wall. Believing half a loaf was better than none, Barbee accepted the settlement. But he had no illusions. "Integration didn't fail," he said years later, responding to the view that desegregation didn't work in Milwaukee. "It was never tried. It was sabotaged."[20]

The NAACP, upset at the less-than-complete blueprint for desegregation, appealed the settlement. Various community groups submitted briefs agreeing with the NAACP. On February 19, 1980, however, the appeals court rejected the NAACP appeal. The Milwaukee Public Schools embraced "three systems," as civil rights attorney William Lynch noted: "an integrated specialty school system, an integrated non-specialty school system, and an all black system."[21]

The long and tortuous legal battle for desegregation was over. Segregated schooling was no longer Milwaukee school board policy. But true desegregation remained a distant dream. Before long, it became popular for the media to declare desegregation a failure—a judgment it had never made about segregated schooling in Milwaukee. "People need to remember the reasons we had a court order in the first place," Joyce Mallory, a black parent activist at Lloyd who later served on the school board, reminded people. "The reasons were valid; the remedy was flawed."[22]

Or, as Vel Phillips might say, desegregation in Milwaukee became a classic example of the NAACP waltz: two steps forward, a side step, and one step backward.

As the school buses rolled, other factors were in play that significantly affected not only the public schools but all of Milwaukee.

In an acceleration of a trend that had begun in the 1960s, whites moved to the suburbs, especially families with young children. Roughly one-third of nonblack children four years old or younger in 1975 had left the city by 1985.[23] In that same decade, the percentage of white elementary students attending private schools doubled, particularly on the South Side. Most of those attended Catholic schools. In 1976, the archdiocese publicly had stated it opposed white flight to its schools. But an archdiocesan official involved in integration admitted that white flight to its schools after the court desegregation order was "more than we care to admit."[24] By 1985, one-half of white elementary students in Milwaukee went to private schools. In comparison, 94 percent of nonwhite elementary students attended the public schools.[25]

Educational disparities were not the only problem. In 1977, just as desegregation was unfolding, the city's manufacturing industries began their historic decline as Milwaukee and the heartland became synonymous with the term "rust belt." The black community was thrown backward as it bore the brunt of both racist employment patterns and the tradition of last hired, first fired. "For blacks, Milwaukee is the toughest place to find a job," the *New York Times* wrote in a December 31, 1977, feature. Official black unemployment was 19.8 percent, the highest in the nation. The rate for Milwaukee white adults was 5.3 percent, one of the lowest in the country.

Anger and frustration erupted throughout the black community, this time sparked by police brutality.

11.

1981: POLICE BRUTALITY MOVES TO CENTER STAGE

There comes a point where you don't take any more. The Lacy case was the straw that broke the camel's back.

—Milwaukee NAACP President Chris Belnavis

On Thursday, July 9, 1981, Ernest Lacy was helping his cousin paint an apartment near Twenty-fourth Street and Wisconsin Avenue, on the western edge of downtown. Just before eleven o'clock on that warm summer evening, the twenty-two-year-old Lacy took a break.

Lacy, an African American, walked to a nearby Open Pantry Food Mart for a snack. Near the store, he was stopped by three members of Milwaukee's all-white elite Tactical Squad. The squad was looking for a rape suspect.

Certain details will never be known. But four eyewitnesses—three white students from nearby Marquette University and a black church elder—later testified at the inquest that they saw Lacy facedown on the ground, his feet near the curb and his head almost in the lane for oncoming traffic. He was handcuffed with his wrists behind his back, his arms jerked high into the air. An officer was kneeling on him. The only disagreement among the eyewitnesses was where the officer had put his knee—the neck, the base of the neck, perhaps the upper back—and whether Lacy's arms were at a right angle to the street or "nearly" a right angle.[1]

Lacy was thrown into a police wagon. The police drove a few blocks to arrest another man, Tyrone Brown, on old parking warrants. What happened during that ride is unclear. But as Brown got into the van, he stepped over Lacy, who was still handcuffed and on the van floor. It became apparent that Lacy was not breathing, and an officer administered smelling salts. There were no other attempts at resuscitation. By the time paramedics arrived, Lacy's heart had stopped. Lacy was taken to a nearby hospital, where just before midnight he was pronounced dead on arrival. His body was badly bruised.[2] In the meantime, another man had been arrested for the rape.

Lacy was thin and slightly built. He had a history of emotional problems. His family said he was easily intimidated, with a particular fear of police and being in enclosed places. This led to the headline in the *Milwaukee Sentinel*'s first major story on the killing: "Fright May Have Caused Man's Death After His Arrest."[3] Friends doubted police accounts that Lacy aggressively fought back when arrested. Jurors at a subsequent inquest, after a month of testimony from one hundred people, unanimously found that Lacy died due to an interruption of oxygen to his brain because of the pressure applied to his chest and neck.

For almost two years, sparked by Lacy's death, race relations in Milwaukee were dominated by the long-standing issue of police brutality. Education, jobs, and housing were still important concerns, but they took a backseat to what was so starkly a matter of life and death.

As was common throughout urban America, there had long been tensions between the police and Milwaukee's black community. The tensions were often the flash point for anger over broader issues of entrenched, institutional racism. Milwaukee was slow to do anything about police-community relations, which only bolstered the perspective that the police's function in the black community was primarily one of control. By the early 1980s, despite a 1975 court order calling for more blacks to be hired, the force was still overwhelmingly white. Although 25 percent of the city's population was black, there were only 129 black police officers on a force of 2,000. None was above the rank of sergeant.[4]

Harold Breier, appointed as police chief for life, had been running the department almost two decades. He had cemented a reputation as a no-nonsense, law-and-order cop with a disdain for black people. A 1967 report to the U.S. Commission on Civil Rights noted that "in [Milwaukee's] inner core, no man is hated more than police chief 'two-gun' Breier," the name often used for the police chief in the black media.[5] Critics in the white community dubbed him "Milwaukee's Fuhrer."[6] Supporters credited him with keeping crime low. Mayor Henry Maier, known for doing little to address concerns in the black community beyond establishing commissions and issuing reports, refused to publicly challenge the seventy-year-old Breier.

It didn't ease the community's anger when, about a week after Lacy's killing, a jury exonerated the police in the death of a young black man shot during the 1967 riots. A policeman had shot eighteen-year-old Clifford McKissick while he was running away from the scene of a firebombing. The family had filed a civil suit, which took fourteen years to work its way through the courts.

A few months later, in December 1981, the Lacy case again overlapped with past allegations of police brutality. This time the black community was vindicated. A federal civil jury awarded $1.8 million to the estate of Daniel Bell, a twenty-two-year-old black man killed in 1958 after being stopped for driving a car with a broken taillight. One of the officers, Louis Krause, admitted more than two decades later that fellow officer Thomas Grady shot Bell in the back, the gun's muzzle only six inches away. Officer Grady then drew a knife, put it in Daniel Bell's hand, and pressed Bell's dead hand around the knife.[7] The burgeoning civil rights community had launched protests against Bell's killing at the time. But in 1958 it did not yet have the strength to successfully challenge the police version of events. An all-white inquest found that Officer Grady "had justifiably shot and killed" Bell in self-defense.

Organizing around Lacy rekindled the grassroots fervor that had been a hallmark of the 1960s. Some of those involved personally remembered not only the Bell and McKissick killings but also the Tactical Squad's attempts to intimidate open housing activists. A Coalition for Justice for Ernest Lacy was formed, at its height including more than 125 groups not only from the black and white communities but also from the city's growing Latino population. The coalition was led by Howard Fuller and Michael McGee, two men who, in their own ways and with widely diverging tactics, would go on to become recognized leaders in the black community.

Lacy's death lit a spark. "There comes a point where you don't take any more," the president of the Milwaukee NAACP explained to the *Chicago Tribune*. "The Lacy case was the straw that broke the camel's back. He is the 23rd victim in the last 10 years who has lost his life at the hands of our police."[8]

Thousands of people marched throughout the summer, demanding justice. "Fire Breier," they would chant, referring to the police chief. Breier, in turn, would show up at the demonstrations, all but taunting the crowd.

Jurors at the inquest that fall recommended that three of the police officers be charged with reckless homicide, the first time an inquest into the death of a black recommended criminal sanctions against the police.[9] Charges were eventually dropped, with the district attorney citing difficulties in getting a conviction. The Coalition for Justice for Ernest Lacy continued organizing, however, and forced the Fire and Police Commission to take disciplinary action. One officer was fired and four others suspended. More satisfying, the Lacy family received a $500,000 settlement the day before its civil suit was to go to trial in federal court.

The most lasting effect involved changes in state law. One bill, dubbed the "Lacy Bill," made it a crime to abuse or neglect a suspect in police custody.[10] The other bill, a 1984 measure known as the "Breier Bill," ended the life term for Milwaukee police chiefs and transferred authority over the police to the city's Police and Fire Commission, the mayor, and the Common Council. Breier retired shortly afterward, citing age and declining health. The day he announced his retirement, a reporter asked Breier if he would have done anything differently. "I wouldn't change a damn thing," Breier replied. "I say to hell with my detractors."[11]

The Lacy case earned a place of honor in Milwaukee history as the most-sustained, best-organized community campaign ever against police misconduct. But it was not the last example of outrage.

A decade after Lacy's killing, in 1991, Milwaukee suffered through its most heart-wrenching murders ever. Serial killer Jeffrey Dahmer murdered seventeen men and boys, with Dahmer's gruesome crimes including torture, dismemberment, necrophilia, and cannibalism. A number of the victims were young African Americans and Asians. Concerns were soon raised that police racism and homophobia helped Dahmer remain beyond scrutiny as he killed so many for so long. By the time he was caught, Dahmer was killing one person a week.

One incident was particularly disturbing. Two months before Dahmer was arrested, an African American woman called 911 and reported a naked Asian boy bleeding and staggering on the street. Police arrived to find Dahmer running after the boy. Dahmer, a seemingly well-mannered white man, convinced the police the boy was a friend who had had too much to drink. The officer reported the resolution of the incident to the 911 dispatcher, saying that "an intoxicated Asian, naked male, was returned to his sober boyfriend." That report is followed by laughter.[12]

Throughout Milwaukee, people of all ages, races, and sexual orientations were deeply disturbed when tapes of the dispatch reports were made public. "If that boy had been white, he'd be alive today," community advocate Reverend LeHavre Buck said, reflecting a common view.[13]

In 1994, an African American inmate at a state prison attacked and killed Dahmer and white inmate Jesse Anderson. Anderson had gained notoriety for blaming two black youths for viciously stabbing his wife to death in the parking lot of a mall frequented by blacks. Police later detailed how Anderson had meticulously planned the attack, thinking his story of a robbery-by-black-youth-gone-wrong would not be seriously questioned.

"The distance between civilization and barbarity, and the time needed to pass from one state to the other, is depressingly short. Police officers in Milwaukee proved this the morning of October 24, 2004."

So begins a federal appeals court decision involving the police beating of Frank Jude Jr., who describes himself as biracial. The incident—almost half a century after Bell, thirty-six years after McKissick, twenty-three years after Lacy, and thirteen years after Dahmer's arrest—was noteworthy for its raw racism, prolonged brutality, and widespread police involvement.

Jude, along with a black male friend and two white women, showed up at a party on the city's South Side. Most of the guests were off-duty police officers. Jude and his friends immediately felt uncomfortable and left. Cops stormed out of the house after them, with one of the cops alleging the group had taken his police badge. As the cops threatened the group, Jude's friend tried to wake up the neighbors. "Nigger, shut up, it's our world," the cops warned. They then proceeded to beat the two men. The women called 911, but when two policemen arrived, one of them joined the assault. At one point, Jude was kicked so hard in the crotch that "his body left the ground," according to the federal appeals court ruling. Pens were stuck into Jude's ear canals, and his fingers were broken "by bending them back until they snapped." One of the police thrust a gun to Jude's head and said, "I'm the fucking police. I can do whatever I want to do. I could kill you."[14]

In 2006, an all-white jury acquitted the three police officers charged in the beating, the prosecution hampered by perjury and the police department's "code of silence."[15] Thousands marched through the streets in indignation, demanding a federal investigation. They were led by Michael McGee Jr., an alderman who was the son of the co-leader of the Lacy coalition.

For reasons that have never been adequately analyzed, the protests were muted. One factor is that the most disturbing details took years to emerge, coming out only during a subsequent federal trial. Second, Jude himself was not the most upstanding of citizens. On the night of his beating, he was on parole for felony convictions for selling marijuana and bribing a police officer, and he had earlier performed as a stripper at a bachelorette party.[16] Third, there was no well-respected leader or coalition to organize the public's disgust. Howard Fuller had moved on to an exclusive focus on school vouchers. The elder McGee had used his recognition from the Lacy campaign to become an alderman, but he then increasingly developed a penchant for hotheaded, inflammatory rhetoric. Although designed to scare whites into action, the rhetoric instead scared everyone. After two terms he was defeated by a black police sergeant. The younger McGee was also fond of off-the-cuff, bombastic statements, some of them homophobic and misogynistic. This hamstrung his ability to organize. (The younger McGee ended his aldermanic term in a prison cell, convicted of nine felony counts including bribery and extortion.)

After the police were acquitted in state court of the Jude beating, even the district attorney called the outcome "a cover-up."[17] Federal officials then investigated. Ultimately, four officers pled guilty to lesser charges including perjury, one officer was acquitted, and three were convicted of assaulting Jude and violating his civil rights.

On January 6, 2011, the *Milwaukee Journal Sentinel* published a front-page story about a group of rogue police officers known as "the Punishers." Members of the group, named after a vigilante comic-book character, reportedly wore black gloves and caps with skull emblems while on duty. Some had skull tattoos. Jude himself had referred to one of the police officers who beat him as "Mr. Punisher," referring to the policeman's skull tattoo, which looked exactly like the logo of the comic-book vigilante.

The Punishers first came to the attention of a police commander after the Jude beating. "This is a group of rogue officers within our agency who I would characterize as brutal and abusive," the commander wrote in a 2007 report. "At least some of the officers involved in the Jude case were associated with this group, although there is reason to believe the membership extended beyond those who were convicted in the case."

The department briefly investigated the group, but little was done.[18] Police chief Edward Flynn declined to be interviewed for the 2011 *Journal Sentinel* story. Instead, he issued a statement calling the existence of the Punishers a "rumor." There was no follow-up story, no public statement of concern from any official, no editorial calling for further investigation. The story died after one day.

12.

MILWAUKEE'S GREAT MIGRATION #2: WHITES MOVE TO THE SUBURBS

Until the black ghetto is dismantled as a basic institution of American urban life, progress ameliorating racial inequality in other arenas will be slow, fitful, and incomplete.

—Douglas S. Massey and Nancy A. Denton, *American Apartheid*[1]

On a cold winter morning when he was five years old, Kurt Chandler's life was turned upside down. Happily running around his central-city neighborhood one day, the next he woke up in a former cornfield surrounded by half-acre lots filled with snow. "I was a city kid," he remembers. "And suddenly, it was like I was transported to Mars. I was a suburban kid."

Unknowingly, Chandler was making history. He was part of the great migration of white families leaving the city for the suburbs. Like the great migration of blacks from the South to the North, this migration forever changed Milwaukee's urban landscape.

Chandler has fond memories of his early years in Milwaukee. He'd run around with other kids, hiding under porches, playing catch, and rushing home when, three doors down, he could hear his mom calling, "Come home for dinner!" There was a neighborhood bakery, a neighborhood meat market, and, most important to a young child, a neighborhood candy store complete with candy cigarettes, candy teeth, and Tootsie Rolls—"all that great stuff," Chandler says.[2]

The neighborhood was a community, filled with wonderful characters—the milkman, the rag man who doubled as scissors sharpener, the carny who, for a few bucks, would dress kids up in cowboy clothes and set them on top of a pony. Some fifty years later, Chandler still has a photograph of himself on that pony, complete with a black cowboy hat, a cowboy vest, and spats over his shoes.

Chandler lived near Twenty-second and Wright, in what was a German and Jewish stronghold. But the neighborhood was changing. Blacks were moving in. To Chandler's five-year-old mind, a kid was a kid, with the ability to catch a baseball far more important than skin color. But his parents saw it differently.

When Chandler was older, his parents talked of why they moved to New Berlin in 1959. Like many young families, Chandler's parents wanted to live the American dream. They were tired of renting, and land was cheap out in those cornfields. His father, a carpenter, had long thought of helping to build his own home, and suddenly it seemed possible. The suburb they chose, New Berlin, captured in both name and spirit the desire for a fresh start. Even their subdivision's street names evoked a mood of adventurous optimism, named after New World explorers such as Magellan, Balboa, and Cortés.

But race, the often unspoken but ever-present factor in Milwaukee's history, was undeniably an issue. Census Tract 51, a few blocks to the east of the Chandlers' Milwaukee home, changed from less than 1 percent black in 1950 to 67 percent black in 1960.[3] As the line of transformation spread to the west and north, the Chandlers' neighborhood was just a few years behind in moving from predominantly white to predominantly black.

"My parents wanted out of the inner city," Chandler says. "There was this idea that integration was a bad thing. My parents' attitude, particularly my father's, was very negative toward people of color. He was prejudiced. He wanted out."

The migration of Milwaukee's white families to the suburbs was under way by the late 1950s. The number of whites in the city dropped from 668,351 in 1960 to 411,287 in 1985. By the 2000 Census, the city's 298,379 white residents were officially a minority.

Once again, Milwaukee mirrored national patterns. "The suburbanization of America proceeded at a rapid pace and the white middle class deserted inner cities in massive numbers," write sociologists Douglas S. Massey and Nancy A. Denton in *American Apartheid*. "Only one-third of U.S.

metropolitan residents were suburban residents in 1940, but by 1970 suburbanites constituted a majority within metropolitan America."

Unlike some urban areas, Milwaukee also became known for a suburban migration that, by and large, left behind not only the poor but also working- and middle-class blacks. It is one of Milwaukee's many contradictions that even as blacks entered professional and higher-paying jobs, life in the suburbs was less than welcoming.

As suburbanization accelerated, sociologists coined a new term to describe the entrenched and severe segregation in urban areas, especially in the North and East—*hypersegregation*. The term stuck to Milwaukee, becoming as much a part of its identity as beer and brats. In a 1989 study, Milwaukee's concentration of segregation was the worst among thirty metropolitan areas with significant black populations. Some years it slipped to number two, three, or four, trading places with other rust belt cities such as Gary, Indiana, Buffalo, New York, and Detroit, Michigan. By the 2000 Census, not much had changed in Milwaukee. People of color dominated the city, with African Americans the highest percentage followed by a growing Latino population. Yet in the three counties surrounding Milwaukee County, whites accounted for 95 percent of the residents.

Millions of individual decisions were behind the suburban migration. For whites, these individual decisions were bolstered by institutional and governmental policies—real estate practices, mortgage and home insurance policies, and the development of the interstate highway system. Whites eager to move to the suburbs, for instance, "demanded and got massive federal investments in highway construction that permitted rapid movement to and from central cities by car," Massey and Denton note.

In 1956, President Dwight Eisenhower signed legislation popularly known as the National Interstate and Defense Highways Act, becoming the largest public works project in U.S. history at the time. The Milwaukee region, not to be left behind, poured money into its interstate. When work began on the Marquette interchange in downtown Milwaukee in 1964, it was the largest single construction project ever in Wisconsin.[4] To build the interstate, huge swaths of homes were torn down in Milwaukee. The African American community was particularly affected, as its neighborhoods were literally cut in half. As the suburbs sprawled, housing became even more overcrowded in the central city. Cars were essential to the suburban lifestyle—but in Milwaukee in 1980, almost 40 percent of African American households did not have a car available.[5]

Federal housing policies played a role in the growing divide between city and suburb. Even when the U.S. Supreme Court outlawed restrictive housing covenants in 1948, the Federal Housing Authority (FHA) held on to racially shaped policies for determining the suitability of neighborhoods when granting loans. The tenor of those policies is reflected in an FHA underwriters' manual stating that new subdivisions should protect against "adverse influences" such as "infiltration of inharmonious racial or nationality groups."[6]

"As a result of these policies, the vast majority of FHA and VA mortgages went to white middle-class suburbs, and very few were awarded to black neighborhoods in central cities," according to Massey and Denton.[7]

In the 1970s, following federal, state, and local policies on open housing, hopes for housing integration remained high. But enforcement of housing discrimination laws was weak. More important, discriminatory policies were replaced by "discrimination with a smile."[8] Real estate people quietly steered whites and blacks in different directions. Suburbs used zoning laws such as minimum lot sizes and prohibitions on multifamily housing to restrict low- and moderate-income families. Home insurance and mortgage lending policies favored whites. The suburban "white noose" tightened.

In 1988, Milwaukee gained another distinction, this time for having the highest rate of black mortgage loan denials in any urban area. Blacks were almost four times as likely as whites to be rejected for mortgage loans.[9] In more recent years, African Americans in the Milwaukee area were far more likely than whites to obtain home mortgages through subprime lenders charging higher interest rates. When the subprime housing bubble burst in 2008, African Americans in Milwaukee were particularly affected by the foreclosure crisis. (Rejections were common in bank loans in general. A 1995 study found that loan denials in Milwaukee affected middle-class blacks the most, with lending disparity between whites and nonwhites growing in higher-income brackets. As a *Milwaukee Journal* article noted, the study "is troubling, because it raises the possibility that many blacks do not encounter less racism as they move up the economic ladder; they encounter more.")[10]

Redlining in home insurance practices exacerbated the home-buying difficulties for people of color. In 1995, American Family Insurance Company agreed to a $14.5 million settlement in a federal lawsuit against its discriminatory lending practices in Milwaukee. Among the discriminatory practices: telling agents not to sell to black people, offering higher prices to black customers, and charging lower rates in white neighborhoods. "Together, these practices set the pattern for and re-enforced neighborhood segregation and created a vicious circle in which the region's reputation for segregation drives continued segregation," noted a 2002 report on housing in southeastern Wisconsin by the nonpartisan Public Policy Forum.[11]

Problems went beyond racial segregation, however. In Milwaukee, as throughout the country, suburbanization also meant economic flight as businesses increasingly settled outside the city. The city's tax base declined. "Thus, at the same time that urban schools had larger numbers of disadvantaged children to teach," one historical analysis noted, "city school systems had to look far afield to get the resources needed to teach them."[12]

After graduating from New Berlin High School in 1971, Chandler went to college on and off, traveled, and lived for a number of years in Boulder, Colorado, and Minneapolis. He settled back in Milwaukee in 1995, a move set in motion by his father's death and a sense of responsibility to help out his mother.

Chandler had never liked the suburban lifestyle, but he had two children and schools were important. Both he and his wife, Cathy, had reservations about the quality of Milwaukee's public schools. They decided to live in Wauwatosa, an inner-ring suburb that is only a twelve-minute car ride from his downtown job as a senior editor at *Milwaukee Magazine*. They can walk to grocery stores and restaurants, and there's an urban feel without drawbacks such as too much noise and grime. But, Chandler admits, "Wauwatosa is not as diverse as we would like it to be. It's getting there but slowly, slowly, slowly."

In 2010, in line with the hypersegregation that is a hallmark of the Milwaukee metropolitan region, Wauwatosa was 90 percent white.[13] The poverty rate was roughly 5 percent.[14] Just a few blocks away, in the City of

Milwaukee, the 2009 poverty rate was 27 percent and the number of children in poverty approached 40 percent.[15]

In New Berlin, controversy exploded in the summer of 2010 over an apartment complex that included "workforce housing" priced for people earning $35,000 a year or less.

New Berlin, with a population of about 39,000, is 95 percent white.[16] Opponents feared that the housing would attract undesirable elements from Milwaukee. Mayor Jack Chiovatero, who supported the complex, received threatening phone calls; a sign that read "Nigger Lover" was put in his yard, "Bigot" was spray-painted on his driveway, and "Leave or ____" was written on his fence. A frustrated Chiovatero sent out an email saying, in part, "Our City is filled with prejudiced and bigoted people who with very few facts are making this project into something evil and degrading." The email became public, Chiovatero became the target of a recall, he apologized, and he withdrew his support of the development. The New Berlin Plan Commission formally rejected the proposal.

In June 2010, the U.S. Justice Department filed suit against New Berlin on the grounds that the city had violated the Fair Housing Act. A month later, New Berlin agreed to an out-of-court settlement allowing the affordable housing project.

13.

THE 1980S: THE RUST BELT AND REAGANOMICS

No city collapsed during the 1980s more than Milwaukee.

—Myron Orfield, urban planning expert[1]

The legal challenges to the desegregation of Milwaukee's schools were not settled until 1980. Just as the legal hurdles were cleared, however, the city was hit with an unexpected and devastating reality: deindustrialization.

Descending slowly at first, deindustrialization soon enveloped every institution, from families to schools to neighborhoods. At the very time the schools were attempting their most difficult transformation ever, Milwaukee's economy fell apart.

On Monday, January 17, 1983, that new reality could no longer be ignored.

Milwaukee's A.O. Smith Corporation was holding a job fair for welders and press operators. The company expected a large turnout, so the event was at the state fair complex nestled on the city's southwest side. Job seekers started lining up the afternoon before. Hundreds waited all night, huddled in sleeping bags and blankets to ward off bone-chilling temperatures that hovered in the teens. Some people started fires in nearby trashcans, evoking images of the Depression. Police estimated that fifteen thousand people showed up for the job fair. There were 150 to 200 openings.

The job fair was a sign of the times, as the 1982 recession hit Milwaukee hard. It was also a sign of the future. Before long, major Milwaukee factories would be gone and thousands of family-sustaining jobs would vanish. Milwaukee, the "machine shop of the world," settled into its status as a creaking cog in the rust belt.

Once-mighty cities of the Midwest, from Gary to Detroit to Milwaukee, painfully declined as they adjusted to deindustrialization and globalization.

Milwaukee's black community, younger and less established than in other rust belt cities, was especially affected. Poverty grew. Segregation intensified. Homelessness expanded. Crime increased. New problems emerged—in particular AIDS and crack cocaine—and came to symbolize all that was wrong with the nation's cities. Amid all this, conservatives started dismantling the social safety net and redistributing wealth toward the wealthy, calling on the poor to rely on their bootstraps and take advantage of trickle-down economics.

All in all, the 1980s wreaked havoc on Milwaukee. No problem, however, was more wrenching than the loss of jobs. Manufacturers that were household names in Milwaukee—Kearney & Trecker, Allen-Bradley, Harnischfeger, Briggs and Stratton, A.O. Smith, American Motors—began shipping jobs to low-wage factories down South or, increasingly, overseas. Even Schlitz, "the beer that made Milwaukee famous," left the city, bought by an out-of-state brewer.

Allis-Chalmers, once Milwaukee's largest employer and known worldwide for its farm implements and tractors, symbolized the shift from a manufacturing-based economy to a service- and consumer-based economy. The Allis-Chalmers complex in the Milwaukee area employed eleven thousand people in 1965; there were only five hundred employees by the mid-1980s, and in 1987 the company declared bankruptcy.[2] Over the years, as deindustrialization escalated, significant chunks of Allis-Chalmers's multi-acre complex were razed to make way for a shopping mall.

Pick almost any major manufacturer and the story was similar. In 1967, there were 118,600 manufacturing jobs in the city of Milwaukee. By 2002, there were only 34,957—a loss of 83,643 jobs.[3]

The loss devastated Milwaukee's black community. As a 2004 article in the *Milwaukee Journal Sentinel* noted, "In little more than a generation, Milwaukee has morphed from an El Dorado of unrivaled opportunity for African-Americans—and a beacon for their middle-class aspirations—to a locus of downward mobility without equal among other big U.S. cities. The result: A depression in the region's urban core far more severe than the Great Depression of the 1930s."[4]

A few select statistics tell the story. In 1970, when Milwaukee was at the height of its industrial power, the city's black family median income was 19 percent higher than the national black family median. By the year 2000, Milwaukee's median black family income was 23 percent lower than the national figure.[5]

Milwaukee black poverty rates showed a similar flip. In 1970, Milwaukee's black rate was 22 percent lower than the U.S. black figure. By 2000, Milwaukee's black poverty rate of 34 percent was the highest for blacks in the country's twenty largest cities.

When the 2008 recession swept across the country, a bad situation got worse. In 2009, 53.3 percent of working-age black males in metropolitan Milwaukee were either unemployed or not in the labor force—a rate that had tripled in a generation. The rate was 31 percentage points higher than for white men, leading to the highest black/white jobless disparity in any major metropolitan area.[6]

Milwaukee found little solace in the fact that it routinely traded worst-in-the-country status with other rust belt cities such as Detroit, Chicago, Buffalo, and Cleveland. Some years Detroit had the worst unemployment; some years Buffalo was the most segregated. But the overall trends were depressingly static.

One might think that deindustrialization cast an unprecedented pall over the entire Milwaukee metropolitan region. But it didn't. New jobs surfaced, but in suburban areas beyond the reach of most central city residents. In the 1980s, when Milwaukee lost 28,000 jobs, jobs in the suburbs increased by 33,000.[7] Not surprisingly, poverty has consistently been lower in the suburbs, especially those farther from the city. Waukesha County, just west of Milwaukee County, had the third-lowest poverty rate (3.5 percent) of the nation's largest counties in 2005. Waukesha County was 93 percent white.

Generations earlier, the "Promised Land" of the North helped spur the great migration of southern blacks to the North. Deindustrialization and globalization transformed these manufacturing powerhouses in the North into the home of the "truly disadvantaged."[8] Concentrated joblessness, segregation, and poverty reinforced each other and presented seemingly insurmountable barriers that affected families, neighborhoods, and schools alike. As sociologist William Julius Wilson notes in his book *When Work Disappears*, northern industrial cities became synonymous with urban dysfunction not because of the personal shortcomings of their increasingly poor and nonwhite residents but because deindustrialization ripped out the cities' economic heart. As Wilson writes, "Most of today's problems in the inner-city ghetto neighborhoods—crime, family dissolution, welfare, low levels of social organization, and so on—are fundamentally a consequence of the disappearance of work."[9]

Father James Groppi, the Catholic priest who had led Milwaukee's open housing marches in the 1960s, was one of many who grappled with the new reality. And not always in ways he would have predicted.

Groppi left the priesthood in 1976 to marry Margaret Rozga, who had been active in Milwaukee's civil rights movement. They had three children together. Groppi remained politically active, in particular around welfare, the Vietnam War, and the rights of Native Americans. But he increasingly found himself confronting a problem he had not experienced in the priesthood: he needed to get a job and help provide for his family. In 1979, he became a bus driver for the Milwaukee County transit system, involving himself in the union and ultimately rising to president of the bus drivers union.

On Monday, January 17, 1983, the *Milwaukee Journal* carried a feature on Groppi—just below the story on the job fair for A.O. Smith. Groppi's bus route traversed blighted neighborhoods, and the experience sapped not just his energy but his soul. In the article, Groppi worries about the growth in gangs. "You can't look at these kids as kind of an oppressed minority because they have become the worst kind of oppressors," he says. "They are terrorizing blacks and whites. They are really a negative force in that community." He explains how he would love to work with the youths, but the church's prohibitions against marriage meant he had to find his living elsewhere. In sorrow more than anger, Groppi relates a recent incident as a bus driver when seven or eight youths, one with a baseball bat, jumped on the bus, refused to pay, and demanded transfers. Two passengers—a black and a white—help Groppi defend himself.

Groppi explains how in the 1960s, the youth channeled their energy into demanding civil rights. But that sense of purpose was gone with the jobs. "Right now," Groppi says of the new generation, "the way they're headed, they're either going to be dead in the street or in jail."

Groppi never got the time to figure out how to confront the new realities. He died of brain cancer in 1985.

*   *   *

Behind every jobless statistic in Milwaukee is a working person, someone such as Ken Thompson.[10] The growth and demise of Milwaukee's manufacturing frames the story of his life.

Thompson, an African American man now in his fifties, went to work at A.O. Smith in 1976 out of high school. He made good money as a welder and punch press operator. Today he does handyman work for friends and family.

He still has his dreams, however. He hopes to open a business—"Kennie's Home Improvement, or something like that," he says. But, he adds with a shrug, life is unpredictable. "I used to think I could look ten years down the road and get a good idea of where things are going to be. But now, I don't know."

Thompson lives with his wife and younger children in the upstairs unit of a Milwaukee duplex, near the Thirtieth Street Industrial Corridor. The corridor, built along a rail line that allowed industries to easily transport raw materials and finished products, connected some of the city's most well-known foundries, tanneries, breweries, and manufacturers. During the corridor's heyday, the companies employed nearly 40 percent of neighborhood residents. Today, most of the factories are hollowed-out buildings, their future uncertain as contamination remains a major issue. The neighborhood is not doing much better.[11]

It wasn't always like that. When Thompson graduated from Riverside University High School, he did what his father and grandfather had done before him. He went to work at A.O. Smith, a sprawling complex churning out truck and auto frames and at its height employing almost ten thousand people.[12]

Thompson thought he had it made for life. But then the 1982 recession hit and he was laid off. He was called back about a year later, but laid off again in 1985. Thompson wasn't worried at first—layoffs and recalls seemed as natural as the change in seasons. But this time the layoff lasted for five years. While laid off, Thompson got into an electrician class, going to school at night while working at various temp agencies during the day. He and his wife started raising a family, and before long there were two young children. Between the temp agency and school, he was rarely home. Tensions increased, and Thompson started drinking more and taking part in the drug culture that had started booming in the city. His life began to fall apart. He dropped out of night school. His drug use increased. He and his wife separated.

After A.O. Smith called him back to work in 1990, Thompson put in another six years before he lost his job again. He decided to seriously address his drug use and got into treatment programs. He went back to the temp agencies, usually working as a machinist or welder. The pay was okay, but there were no benefits. And every time Thompson reached the ninety-day limit when a company was to formally hire a temp worker, he was transferred to a new job.

"I lost a lot of hope back in the nineties," Thompson says. "Even when I had those temp jobs, I couldn't see a future. I felt worthless."

A.O. Smith continually cut back on its manufacturing in Milwaukee, eventually selling its car and truck operations to Tower Automotive in the late 1990s. Jobs dwindled and before long were shipped completely to Mexico.

Thompson's father, who retired from A.O. Smith before the jobs collapsed, had bought various rental properties over the years. Thompson, who remarried and says he's been free of substance abuse for four years, started doing maintenance and repair for his father. Word got around, and Thompson picked up handyman jobs throughout the neighborhood. "I do it all," Thompson says. "Plumbing, electricity, drywall."

Older and wiser, he tries to remain hopeful. "The work situation is still gloomy, but now I don't have the drugs to get in the way. I have a greater sense of making it, and I am my own boss. I feel good about that."

His biggest regret in life? That he went to work at A.O. Smith immediately after high school and didn't go to college. "I had friends, they went on to get their college degrees and a lot of them are teachers and principals now," he says.

While deindustrialization and globalization transformed Milwaukee's economy, the 1980s also ushered in an equally far-reaching political phenomenon: the Reagan era.

A smiling actor who perfected an aw-shucks populist image, President Ronald Reagan was stunningly effective in promoting a conservative ideology that transformed politics and the role of government for decades to come. Public schools became a significant battleground as conservatives promoted tax dollars for private schools, embraced curriculum initiatives such as creationism, and dismissed the importance of school desegregation.

Former president Richard Nixon had taught the GOP the value of coded rhetoric, "persuading working-class voters to vote their prejudices rather than their economic interests."[13] But Reagan became the master.

In his first campaign stop as the GOP presidential candidate, Reagan chose the Neshoba County Fair in Philadelphia, Mississippi. He told an enthusiastic white crowd of ten thousand fairgoers, "I believe in states' rights." If elected, he promised he would "restore to states and local governments the power that properly belongs to them."[14]

To those who knew their not-too-distant history, Reagan's message was clear. Just sixteen years earlier, Philadelphia, Mississippi, had been the scene of one of the most notorious political murders in U.S. history. White segregationists had murdered three young civil rights activists who had come to Mississippi in 1964 as part of Freedom Summer to help win voting rights for African Americans. What's more, "states' rights" had long been the rallying cry of segregationists opposed to federal civil rights legislation.

"Everybody watching the 1980 campaign knew what Reagan was signaling at the fair," *New York Times* columnist Bob Herbert writes. "Whites and blacks, Democrats and Republicans—they all knew. The news media knew. The race haters and the people appalled by racial hatred knew. And Reagan knew.

"He was tapping out the code. It was understood that when politicians started chirping about 'states' rights' to white people in places like Neshoba County, they were saying that when it comes down to you and blacks, we're with you."[15]

Reagan also perfected the art of policy by anecdote, using his storytelling skills to take advantage of racialized stereotypes and promote the conservatives' agenda. One of Reagan's favorite stories involved the Chicago "welfare queen," a tale he repeated "to congressional and foreign leaders alike, inflated with each telling." Nor did the media seem to mind when Reagan told his story of a "strapping young buck" who used food stamps to buy a T-bone steak, booze, and cigarettes; in the South, it was well known that *buck* was a slave-auction term for black males.[16] (Three decades later, presidential hopeful Newt Gingrich wooed voters by tapping out a similar code, accusing President Barack Obama of being a "food-stamp president.")

Reagan used his stories not only to win over white voters but also to further shift the national debate. The War on Poverty morphed into a war on the poor and their personal failures. Demands for civil rights and racial equality segued into critiques of affirmative action and charges of "reverse discrimination." Adding policy bite to his rhetoric, Reagan cut federal student aid, and the fraction of black high school graduates going to college dropped from 35 percent to 26 percent in Reagan's first term.[17]

While Reagan saw affirmative action as a problem, he did not feel the same about school and housing segregation. In Reagan's first two years as president, his administration filed only two cases under the Fair Housing Act of 1968, compared to about sixty-four cases every two years under previous administrations. As for schools, Reagan's assistant attorney general in charge of civil rights said, "We are not going to compel children who don't choose to have an integrated education to have one."[18]

For major metropolitan areas, no policy was more devastating than Reagan's New Federalism. When Reagan took office in 1980, the federal government provided aid that amounted to 18 percent of city budgets. The money was used for a wide swath of programs, from mass transit to job training to social services. By 1990, the federal share had dropped to 6.4 percent.[19]

Reagan's political genius, meanwhile, lay in his ability to harness seemingly disparate forces—white workers susceptible to rhetoric about the "special privileges" given to blacks and the poor, corporations promoting an anti-tax and anti-regulation agenda, neoconservative intellectuals providing an ideological framework, and evangelical Christians focused on issues such as abortion and school prayer. A powerful conservative coalition emerged, its contradictions smoothed over by the ever-affable Reagan.

In Milwaukee, the uncertainty of the nation's shifting political climate was complicated by continued white flight to the suburbs and the crumbling of the city's manufacturing economy. Historian Marc Levine notes that one of the distinguishing features of Milwaukee's economy before the 1980s is that "a disproportionate percentage of blacks were employed in manufacturing, which is what made deindustrialization so particularly devastating here."[20]

At the same time, education reform was clearly more important than ever, as education became essential to a family-supporting job in the postindustrial, knowledge-based economy. But how best to move education reform forward?

Throughout the 1980s, reformers in Milwaukee came up with different answers. Desegregation activists realized the Milwaukee schools would find it difficult to completely desegregate because so many whites were fleeing the city, and so they advocated metropolitan-area-wide initiatives. A small but increasingly influential group of nationalists in the black community was comfortable with segregated schools, both in the city and the suburbs, and championed black community schools. Conservatives centered in the Republican Party, meanwhile, shifted their focus away from public education and pushed for taxpayer funding of private schools, reaching out to the black nationalists for support.

The clarity of the 1960s civil rights agenda—oppose segregated schools and demand open housing—was gone.

14.

DESEGREGATION:
FORWARD AND BACKWARD IN THE 1980S

I went to an all-black school, so I am not enamored with
integration per se. But I look at the economics of schooling,
and I've never seen green follow black.

> —Joyce Mallory, former Milwaukee school
> board member and plaintiff in a lawsuit seeking
> metropolitan-area-wide desegregation

Demond Means was a young child when the federal court ordered Milwaukee to desegregate its public schools. He lived in a diverse yet transitional neighborhood and attended nearby Thirty-eighth Street School, an integrated specialty school that highlighted project-based learning. He then went to Daniel Webster, an integrated middle school, taking the bus about six miles each way. In 1990, he graduated from Riverside University High School, one of the most diverse and high-achieving high schools in Milwaukee.

In 2008, Means became superintendent of the Mequon-Thiensville school district, just north of Milwaukee. His rise to superintendent in an affluent white suburb is a noticeable accomplishment for an African American man in Milwaukee. It is the same suburban area where, half a century earlier, Hank Aaron's sister Alfredia endured such harassment at school that she moved back to Memphis.

As a young man, Means worked part-time at his grandfather's bar near the Thirtieth Street Industrial Corridor and saw firsthand how the black community faltered when the factories collapsed. Education was Means's ticket forward. He went on to college after high school and ultimately earned a doctorate in education. He lives in Milwaukee, along with his wife, who is a principal in the Milwaukee Public Schools.

Means is befuddled by criticisms that became popular in the 1980s and that continue to this day—that the push for desegregation undermined a focus on quality education for African Americans, and that there is little good happening in the city's public schools. "I had teachers that were committed to diversity," he says of his experience in integrated Milwaukee schools. "I had white teachers, I had black teachers. And they were forcing us to elevate our performance." Having worked in a variety of suburban districts, Means also believes the Milwaukee schools get a bad rap: "There are Milwaukee public schools that are outperforming schools in the suburbs, if you look at the criteria of what people are dealing with in terms of facilities, foundations, socioeconomics, you name it."[1]

The Mequon-Thiensville district takes part in Chapter 220, a voluntary integration program with Milwaukee named after its authorizing legislation. Means is perplexed by those who dismiss the benefits of metropolitan-area-wide desegregation efforts, attributing the criticisms to Milwaukee's parochialism. "We have a metro area that hasn't really dealt with race," he argues. "So young people leave the city and never come back and we wonder why. For God's sake, why should they come back? We're still arguing about Chapter 220 and desegregation. How progressive is that?"

Jeannie Ullrich, an African American a few years older than Means, took a different educational path. As a young child, she experienced the best and worst of Milwaukee's public schools. As a high school student, she attended a suburban district during the initial years of Chapter 220.[2]

During the first year of court-ordered desegregation in Milwaukee, Ullrich started at Elm School of the Arts, one of the most popular specialty schools. She loved Elm and stayed there until sixth grade, when she graduated. "It was a wonderful school, with wonderful teachers," she says. "It was everything I think a school ought to be."[3] But Ullrich also experienced the flip side of the city's public schools. After Elm, she went to Fritsche, a middle school specializing in the arts. "It was horrible," she says, without a trace of equivocation in her voice. Academic expectations were low, homework was nonexistent, students were disrespectful of teachers, and the school seemed on the verge of being out of control. Two incidents stick in her mind.

The first happened shortly after she started at Fritsche as a seventh grader. A clique of five girls started picking on her. It wasn't a racial thing—Ullrich is African American, as were the five girls. But Ullrich became a target. "The girls said, 'You think you're cute, we're beating you up,'" she remembers.

One day, as the bus approached school, Ullrich saw the girls waiting for her. She froze.

"You getting off?" the driver asked.

"No," Ullrich replied. "I'm going to stay on the bus and go back home."

It was the first and only time she ever skipped school.

The next incident happened at school. A group of girls had gotten a pass to go to the library. "Suddenly these other girls started asking me if I had had sex yet," she says. "I was only twelve years old!"

From that moment, Ullrich knew that Fritsche was not a good place for her. She transferred the next year to a parochial school close to home. When it came time to choose a high school, she applied to Rufus King, a Milwaukee public specialty high school with an International Baccalaureate program. Admission was by lottery, and Ullrich didn't get in. She's not sure how, but she had heard of the Chapter 220 program. Ullrich applied to Nicolet High School, a suburban school on the northern edge of Milwaukee, one that is often considered the best-funded and academically most comprehensive high school in the region. "My fourteen-year-old mind didn't know that Chapter 220 was controversial," she says. "I just knew I wanted to be somewhere where I had peers who would support me academically."

As a freshman, every morning at 6:15 A.M. Ullrich would leave her home in the Sherman Park neighborhood of Milwaukee, walk a few blocks, and catch a yellow school bus. The bus would drive throughout the city, picking up another thirty-five to forty students, mostly black but some Latinos. They would arrive at Nicolet High School around 7:15 A.M., just before the school day was about to begin.

Ullrich is quick to caution that her experience cannot convey the totality of Chapter 220. For one, her background is not the norm. The youngest of five siblings, she was adopted as a baby into a white family. Her mother worked at a battery factory and her father was a firefighter. Her siblings attended Milwaukee public high schools and did well, but when she was a sophomore her family moved into the Nicolet school district.

Ullrich notes that complicated family situations that cross racial lines are increasingly common in twenty-first-century America, and multiculturalism is a fact of life across the globe. Nicolet High School helped prepare Ullrich for that world. Partly it was the academics, partly it was the chance to mix with both black and white students, and partly it was because the school's large Jewish population exposed her to yet another cultural and religious reality. With a bachelor's degree from the University of Wisconsin–Madison and a master's in education from Harvard University, Ullrich today works in the field of philanthropy and facilitates education grants in Milwaukee.

"It's funny, but I talk to my other friends and ask, 'Do you remember any racial incidents at Nicolet?' And we're like, 'No,'" she says. "That's not to say there weren't problems, but we just weren't aware of them. Besides, there were black kids on the basketball team, and they were cool. This was the beginning of that time when suburban white kids started thinking black kids were cool."

Class, not race, seemed to be the dividing issue at Nicolet. "We were mostly middle-class blacks," Ullrich says. "The kids that were considered different, they were called the burnouts. They wore black shoes, army clothes, they smoked. They were 'the other,' not the 220 kids."

About the same time Ullrich was attending Nicolet High School in the Milwaukee suburbs, some activists in the black community intensified their criticisms of desegregation, saying it detracted from a necessary focus on the problem of low academic achievement of African Americans. A number also blamed desegregation for the increasingly fragile sense of community in black neighborhoods. A significant core of both black and white activists, meanwhile, remained committed to school desegregation as the best way to promote educational opportunities within a context of intense residential segregation. As they saw whites continue their flight to the suburbs, they advocated metropolitan-area-wide solutions, in particular redistricting that combined city and suburban schools into the same school district.

Dennis Conta, a white legislator from the Milwaukee area, was one of the first to shake this hornet's nest of a controversy. It was early on, in 1975,

when the federal district courts had not yet ruled on the Milwaukee desegregation suit, and no one really knew if the court might embrace a regional
solution.

Conta proposed a modest redistricting that would have merged a few
Milwaukee schools with two nearby suburban districts, Shorewood and
Whitefish Bay, in order to promote racial integration. A public meeting to
discuss the proposal attracted a thousand people, most of them whites and
most of them strongly opposed. Representative F. James Sensenbrenner, a
Republican representing the suburban areas, attacked the plan for "using
children as pawns for some social technician's wild-eyed scheme." He received thunderous applause.[4]

Interestingly, Conta's plan came surprisingly close to passing the state
assembly, in part because some legislators felt it might stave off more drastic
plans for metropolitan desegregation. Conta needed fifty votes, but he could
only muster forty-six. "I just couldn't get those final four votes," Conta
recalls, more than a tinge of sadness in his voice.[5]

Despite the defeat of Conta's redistricting plan, desegregation proponents remained hopeful. In the next ten years they put forth various proposals to redistrict area schools. The Metropolitan Integration Research
Center, a multiracial group formed by desegregation activists in the late
1970s, spearheaded many of the efforts.

The center refused to view school districts as fixed entities, and knew that
boundaries were merely lines drawn on a map to serve a political and/or educational purpose. When purposes changed, or when districts were too small
to provide a range of opportunities for their students, it was common for
boundaries to be reconfigured. In fact, massive redistricting had taken place
throughout Wisconsin's history. In the mid-1930s, for instance, Wisconsin
had 7,777 school districts. By changing boundaries, the number of districts
had dropped to only 498 districts in 1967. As the state superintendent of public instruction noted in 1983, school district boundaries and organization
"had never been permanent or static nor was it ever intended to be. Changes
in school district organization are a normal, on-going process necessary to
keep pace with changing needs, expectations, and conditions."[6]

In the early 1980s, many of the suburban districts surrounding Milwaukee were small, with the average size about 3,000 students, compared
to the roughly 88,000 Milwaukee public school students in 1984. The baby

boom generation after World War II had initially swelled suburban school enrollment, but those boomers were getting older and leaving school. Even white flight from Milwaukee could not compensate. Suburban districts faced the possibility that if enrollments continued to decline, they would have to cut academic and extracurricular opportunities or, in some cases, consider merging. Desegregation activists saw not only a need but also an opportunity: Milwaukee needed the suburban schools in order to truly desegregate, and the suburban schools needed to maintain enrollment. Redistricting seemed a mutually beneficial solution. Except for one complication: redistricting was tied up with race.

In the spring of 1984, the Metropolitan Integration Research Center developed a specific proposal: take Milwaukee and the surrounding twenty-four suburban districts and reorganize into six districts. The new districts would be roughly equal in size and property value and would provide increased possibilities for racial and socioeconomic integration. In addition, administrative costs would be reduced, busing would be restricted, educational disparities would be significantly lessened, and proposals for site-based management would safeguard parent input into decision-making. The proposal also called for efforts to counteract housing segregation.

The research center developed its restricting plan in collaboration with the Milwaukee school board, emphasizing the organizational, academic, and financial benefits to the suburban districts. There was also a stick—the threat of state legislation or a federal lawsuit that might lead to solutions the suburbs would not like.

Given racial stereotypes, however, redistricting was the suburbs' worst fear. Politically astute, suburban leaders did not attack desegregation itself. They emphasized "local control," with local being defined narrowly in order to separate the suburbs from Milwaukee. They also called for "voluntary" plans that could leave key decisions in suburban hands. (In testimony to the Milwaukee school board in March 1984, a representative of the Metropolitan Milwaukee Fair Housing Council warned against "voluntary" plans: "Our definition of the term voluntary as it is frequently used in the fair housing field is 'to delay, forestall the inevitable or produce cosmetic changes without substance or merit.' All too often, voluntary ends up being the furthest distance between two points.")[7]

In May 1984, the Milwaukee Public Schools asked the state to change school district boundaries throughout the Milwaukee metropolitan area. The suburbs unrelentingly opposed the plan, and it had no political future. The Milwaukee school board took up the only weapon left in its hands. On June 28, 1984, it sued the state and twenty-four suburban school boards, saying that they had conspired over the years to keep blacks confined to city schools and neighborhoods.

"We have here in the metropolitan area an established housing apartheid sanctioned by government for many years," the Milwaukee Public Schools' attorney, Irvin Charne, argued when the case came to trial three years later.[8] At the time, 97.52 percent of all blacks living in the four-county metropolitan area lived within the Milwaukee city limits.[9] The lawsuit asked the court to "declare the public schools in the Milwaukee metropolitan area to be unconstitutionally segregated," and to mandate a desegregation plan.

Almost nineteen years to the day after Lloyd Barbee sued the Milwaukee Public Schools, the federal courts once again became the arena of last recourse against segregated schools. The region's business community took what was then an unusual step and publicly entered the fray. While giving a nod to good education as "the door to individual opportunity and community advancement," it rejected any solution that went beyond voluntary measures. "Only through voluntary action can we create the public will to make integration really work," argued the Greater Milwaukee Committee, the city's most powerful business group.[10]

The business community and the suburbs were not the only ones derailing regional desegregation. An increasingly vocal network of African Americans, in line with nationalist and black power perspectives that had gained strength throughout the country, rebuffed desegregation and instead called for improving black neighborhood schools. "One of the great fallacies of our day is the notion that a discussion about desegregation and integration are automatically prerequisites or are somehow inherently dealing with the question of an effective education," Howard Fuller, a prominent leader in the black community, told a school board hearing in 1984. "This is an illusion that this society can no longer afford to accept."[11] Fuller demanded a moratorium on metropolitan desegregation discussions until academic achievement in the Milwaukee Public Schools could be studied. The move was widely seen as a tactic to stall and undermine support for metropolitan desegregation.

Politically sophisticated suburbanites realized the value of black activists promoting what in essence was a "separate but equal" perspective (the same perspective declared unconstitutional in *Brown*). The alliance between black nationalists and whites dismissive of desegregation did not become publicly apparent until years later, when voucher proposals surfaced as a way of providing public tax dollars for private schools. But as early as 1984, when metropolitan-area-wide desegregation was the top educational issue, the suburbs' lobbyist in the state legislature outlined the value of courting blacks who denigrated desegregation.

Referring specifically to Fuller and to state representative Polly Williams, lobbyist Gary Goyke called on his suburban clients to voice public support for the general idea of voluntary metropolitan-area-wide desegregation, in order to head off the possibility of stricter measures ordered by the courts or the state legislature. In a December 19, 1984, letter to suburban school districts, Goyke wrote that appearing cooperative would buy time "for the 'Fuller' group to gain strength in Milwaukee. Fuller, Representative Polly Williams and other black leaders favor local neighborhood schools. They will be able to help us if they become strong enough. However, this group is still weak. . . . We need this Milwaukee ally in our effort to defeat reorganization, but they won't be ready to help effectively for several years."[12]

Joyce Mallory does not like to be pigeonholed into an ideological box. She was a prominent desegregation activist in the 1970s and 1980s, active with the NAACP. From 1983 to 1993 she was a member of the Milwaukee school board, and for several years the only African American. On a policy level Mallory is best remembered for two issues: first, her role as a plaintiff in the metropolitan desegregation lawsuit, and second, her advocacy years later of African American immersion schools within the Milwaukee Public Schools. The approaches might seem diametrically opposed. To Mallory, both stemmed from the same core belief: do what's best at the time, in ways possible at the time, to promote better educational opportunities, especially for African Americans.

Today, Mallory heads an early childhood education center in Milwaukee's central city. In early 2011, while the children at Mallory's center were napping and a modicum of silence had descended, she talked about her involvement in education. She reminisced about the personalities that shaped policy debates, her comments often punctuated by laughs of disbelief at the cast of characters. She rolls her eyes when the subject of the teachers union comes up, angry that contracts seemed to always outrank the needs of children. She is proud that during her time on the board, women played a leading role and helped the board sidestep landmines of crass political partisanship. She bemoans the stubborn backwardness that permeates Milwaukee and explains why she tells her grown-up son not to move back to the city.

But if you want to hear Mallory's true passions emerge, listen to her talk about educating Milwaukee's African American children. She is a no-nonsense, no-excuses educator. "Whether kids are learning has to do with a good teacher and a good leader, and whether they have the resources necessary to teach kids who are poor," she says. But she knows that such basics are often missing. She doesn't romanticize poor people, and she is the first to demand that parents teach their children the value of self-control and discipline. But the broader society also has to step up to the plate and concretely help struggling families, communities, and schools.

"It takes more damn resources to get poor kids where they need to be," she says. "And if you aren't going to equalize resources, it isn't going to happen. Policy makers can tiptoe around the margins if they want to. But at some point they have to deal with the fundamental issue of resources."

Access to schools with better resources was a driving force for Mallory when, in 1984, she was a plaintiff in the Milwaukee Public Schools' lawsuit against the suburbs. Having learned from mistakes in previous desegregation plans in Milwaukee, she advocated for a metropolitan plan that included the transfer and busing of both blacks and whites, an emphasis on a multicultural curriculum and integrated staffs, and a housing component that would promote residential desegregation.

Like most lawsuits, the metropolitan desegregation effort did not work its way through the courts either smoothly or quickly. Voluntary out-of-court settlements were proposed, with terms favorable to the suburbs.

The Milwaukee school board was split over accepting the settlements, with some members holding out for more favorable terms for the district and its students. The NAACP sided with the holdouts. Some in the black community believed the entire effort was a waste of time. Nationally, the Reagan administration had signaled it was comfortable with school segregation, reflecting a changed political climate.

By early 1987, Judge Thomas J. Curran of the federal district court was pressing for a settlement. The suburbs and most of the Milwaukee school board agreed on key points. But Mallory wanted a better deal. "I reviewed the settlement and said, 'I don't agree with this. It is not in the best interests of black children.'" Pressure increased on Mallory to agree—with the board even suing her in federal court to force her to acquiesce. That summer, it became clear that no better deal would be forthcoming. The Milwaukee school board approved the main parts of the settlement by a vote of 6–2. Mallory abstained. In October 1987, the federal district court approved the negotiated settlement.

The heart of the settlement called for a voluntary program under which nonwhite students in Milwaukee could enroll in twenty-three suburban districts, and seats would be saved in Milwaukee's highly popular specialty schools for white suburban students. The overwhelming majority of the transfers were of Milwaukee students to the suburbs. Housing integration programs that were part of the settlement, meanwhile, had been stripped of meaningful impact. The state sweetened the deal for the suburbs by providing significant dollars to the districts for every student who took part in the program. The suburbs also wrote into the original agreement that they did not have to accept students with special educational needs, nor those who did not speak English as their primary language. If the suburbs failed to meet hoped-for goals of accepting more public school students from Milwaukee, there were no penalties.

"The settlement was just horrible," recalls school board member Mary Bills, a white advocate of metropolitan redistricting who refused to vote in favor of the settlement. "Everyone with power—the lawyers, the judges, the media, businesses, and union leaders—all lived in the suburbs, and Milwaukee's children didn't stand a chance. The settlement showed, once again, how racism is the ring around Milwaukee's wonderful blue collar."[13]

At the same time, Bills and others cite the benefits of opening up suburban schools to African Americans and other minority students. Also a plus, the state paid for yellow school buses to transport the Chapter 220 students. An estimated 40 percent of black households did not own a car (1980 figures), and there was no public bus system extending beyond Milwaukee County and into many of the suburban districts.[14] The state-funded busing made the program accessible to blacks throughout Milwaukee.

While policy makers debated the merits of metropolitan desegregation, black parents took advantage of the program. Within a year, more than four thousand Milwaukee public school students were transferring to suburban schools, with the number rising to almost six thousand students by the mid-1990s.[15] In 1998, there were three times more applicants from Milwaukee than suburban seats available.[16]

Mallory, who held out as long as possible for a better settlement, understands the program's strengths and shortcomings. She has no regrets. "The lawsuit was the means to achieve an end, and that end was increased access to suburban seats for black children in Milwaukee," she says. "I went to an all-black school, so I am not enamored with integration per se. But I look at the economics of schooling, and I've never seen green follow black."

"The sad part is," she continues, "is there was never a definitive study done of 220 to see if kids did better."

The stated purpose of Chapter 220 was to promote cultural and racial integration, not to promote achievement. Several reports showed generally positive academic results for students taking part in Chapter 220, which voluntarily continues on a small level even though the court-brokered settlement has lapsed. A 1994 report by Wisconsin's nonpartisan Legislative Audit Bureau found that Milwaukee public school students transferring to the suburbs scored better than Milwaukee students who applied for but did not get into the program. The report, based on eighth- and tenth-grade achievement tests, also found, however, that the Milwaukee public school students scored below their suburban classmates.[17]

While the Milwaukee school board was pushing for metropolitan-area-wide desegregation, others within the black community were questioning the time and money put into integration. Suburban lobbyist Goyke had proved prescient in his 1984 prediction that in "several years" Fuller and Williams would have enough support to become effective allies.

In the summer of 1987, at the very time the Milwaukee school board was trying to reach a desegregation deal with the suburbs after years of litigation, Fuller promoted a substitute education reform: carving out a separate school district in the black central city. The proposal dominated the news for months, gaining a level of support unthinkable a few years earlier.

There was also a national context. By 1987, desegregation had been coming under increased scrutiny as the promise of *Brown* was tarnished by realities that fell so short of the dreams. In Milwaukee, there was the added factor of desegregation coinciding with deindustrialization. "Had desegregation been implemented while Milwaukee's black community was participating in an expanding citywide economic boom, then the outcomes might have been different," notes a 1992 report by the Wisconsin Advisory Committee to the U.S. Commission on Civil Rights.[18]

The economy aside, Milwaukee's desegregation efforts had a mixed record after ten years. On one hand, the integrated specialty schools proved highly popular with both blacks and whites. They also tended to have higher academic achievement, and showed the educational value of well-funded integrated schools organized around a coherent curricular theme. At the same time, it was impossible to deny that Milwaukee's desegregation relied on voluntary choice for whites and mandatory busing for blacks. There were only haphazard attempts to provide diversity training for teachers and staff, and suspensions for blacks were some of the highest in the country.

The Milwaukee administration stressed only the positives, calling the desegregation framework an "immense success" that was a national model. The Milwaukee school board, meanwhile, was focused on metropolitan desegregation. As a result, calls for a separate black district resonated with a range of people who, regardless of ideology, wanted a renewed commitment to educational achievement. As Peter Murrell Jr., an African American educator at Marquette University, wrote: "Dr. Fuller, Representatives Williams and Coggs, and other proponents of the New North Division School District represent a community struggling to improve the quality of education for its children. [Milwaukee Public Schools acting superintendent] Dr. Faison represents a bureaucracy."[19]

* * *

When Fuller and his allies proposed a separate black district in the central city, controversy exploded. Support for integrated schools remained high in the black community, especially among professionals and the middle class. Fuller and his allies focused on desegregation's shortcomings, dismissing metropolitan-area-wide plans as "body shuffling."[20]

The public airing of differences within the black community spilled into the daily newspapers—an unusual move in a city where African Americans rarely voiced their disagreements in the white-controlled media. The proposal was also the first public glimpse at an emerging alliance between whites and blacks opposed to desegregation. That alliance would come to shape not only the future of desegregation in Milwaukee but also the entire structure of public and private education.

Fuller argued that a separate district controlled by the black community could do a better job educating blacks than the Milwaukee Public Schools, and he pointed to bureaucracy and the teachers union as key impediments to reform. He also put forth an argument he would effectively resurrect in future controversies: "there is no way that things could be worse" than the current situation.[21]

Some supporters of the separate school district, such as Williams, fit comfortably within a black nationalist framework that was deeply suspicious of whites and focused on power for the black community. Larry Harwell, an influential aide to Williams, succinctly summarized this view when he called integration "a way for white people to take us over."[22] Fuller was more complicated. Moving from grassroots activist to well-connected insider, he had used his prominence in the Ernest Lacy police brutality campaign in 1982 to secure an appointment as secretary of the Wisconsin Department of Employment Relations. At the time of the proposal for a separate black district, Fuller was dean of the School of Liberal Arts and Sciences at the Milwaukee Area Technical College (MATC). More than one person wondered about his ultimate intentions—or, as *Milwaukee Magazine* asked in a cover-story profile in 1988, "Who is Howard Fuller and what does he want?" In that profile, one black leader argued that the idea for a separate black district gained traction in part because Fuller was telling white people what they wanted to hear: "White people have seen Howard as a useful tool for keeping blacks out of the suburbs, for making black people a problem for black people—which takes a large burden off whites."

A tally of those for and against a separate black school district defied easy predictions. Two state representatives from the black community, Williams and G. Spencer Coggs, were in support. So were three black aldermen on the city's Common Council. The city's two African American newspapers were split on the issue.

State senator Gary George, the most powerful elected official from the black community, opposed the plan, as did Representative Marcia Coggs. Walter Farrell, a well-known black educator at the University of Wisconsin–Milwaukee and president of the Milwaukee Afro-American Council, said he was "real saddened" by the Fuller-Williams proposal. Black school board members Joyce Mallory and Jeanette Mitchell were opposed, with Mallory noting that schools in the proposed district had been largely black for decades, giving the black community plenty of time to provide support. "What will be different now that hasn't happened in the last 15 to 20 years?" Mallory asked.[23]

The NAACP condemned the plan, labeling it "urban apartheid."[24] Clergy from the city's two most prominent black congregations were also opposed. Lloyd Barbee, by then only peripherally involved in Milwaukee issues, said it was an attempt to commit the legislature to racial segregation.

White advocates of metropolitan-area-wide desegregation opposed the plan. More surprising was the positive response from influential people such as Governor Tommy Thompson, a Republican. Thompson announced on a radio call-in show that "Howard Fuller and myself are friends—don't look so shocked. He is a very astute and articulate individual, and I have a great deal of respect for him."[25] (Thompson later backed away from his support.) George Mitchell, an influential business community consultant, also supported the separate district, as did representatives from the Reagan administration.[26] Business and professional leaders in the suburbs, meanwhile, began "to look favorably on Fuller and Williams as respected and popular leaders who offered non-integration strategies for dealing with Milwaukee Public Schools problems," Milwaukee historian Bill Dahlk writes.[27]

State legislation to create the black district was drafted in early 1988. Located in the central city, the district would include one high school, two middle schools, and seven elementary schools. Roughly 6,400 students would be affected, 97 percent of whom were black.[28]

On March 18, 1988, during what the media described as "an emotional and angry session that lasted until nearly 5 A.M.," the state assembly passed the proposal for a separate black district by a decisive 61–36 margin.[29] An impassioned Williams helped win the day with her plea to "give us a chance to educate our own." The plan faced an uphill battle in the state senate, especially given Gary George's opposition, and did not survive. But even in defeat, the proposal forever changed education politics in Milwaukee. The desegregation era was over.

In 1997, Jonathan Coleman published *Long Way to Go: Black and White in America*, using Milwaukee as a case study. Education plays a prominent role in the book, including the call for a separate black district. Citing conversations with Fuller in the mid-1990s, Coleman writes that Fuller "now realized that if they had been successful in that strategy [for a black district], they would actually have made things worse; they would have wound up with a district 'so damned impoverished' that nothing of substance could have been achieved anyway."[30]

15.

LATINO STUDENTS: MOVING BEYOND BLACK AND WHITE

People wanted to transform communities, to have more community
control, to change the curriculum. They viewed bilingualism as part of
that larger vision.

—Latino activist Tony Baez

While metropolitan desegregation and a separate black school district
dominated education headlines in the late 1980s, other, less noticeable developments had a lasting impact. The slow but steady increase in Latino
students is a prime example.

Milwaukee's response to the Latino community's growth mirrored its
reaction to black immigration after World War II. The growth was recognized but basically ignored until a threshold was crossed and it became
clear that the city's racial demographics had irrevocably changed. Throughout the 1950s and 1960s, segregation in Milwaukee was a black/white issue.
By the 1980s, that was no longer possible. The city's Latino population was
growing too large to be an afterthought.

Puerto Ricans were particularly active in school issues. Many came from
middle-class backgrounds, with educational credentials such as a college
degree. In addition, Puerto Ricans are U.S. citizens due to the island's com-
monwealth status; activists did not have to worry about their legal status,
which allowed them to play a public role.

More often than not, Luis "Tony" Baez was near the epicenter of any
given controversy. In 1969, Baez was a student at the University of Puerto
Rico, a hotbed of the movement to free Puerto Rico from the U.S. control
imposed after the Spanish-American War. He was involved in student
protests demanding the island's independence. He also became a potential

target, as police arrested student leaders on often-spurious charges. Baez's mother was worried about her son's safety. She sent him to live with relatives in Chicago.

But times were no less turbulent in Chicago. Baez's relatives were active in the Young Lords, a militant group defending the rights of Puerto Ricans in neighborhoods plagued by police brutality, gentrification, turf battles, and anti-Latino harassment. "Within days of arriving in Chicago, I became involved with the Young Lords," Baez recalls. "I went from one fire to another."

Baez learned to improve his English in Chicago by negotiating between the Young Lords and the Black Panthers. Navigating those complicated politics served him well when, a year later, he moved to Milwaukee to work with Latino students organizing at the University of Wisconsin–Milwaukee. Before long, he was immersed in broader issues involving the Latino community and the city's public schools. In the early 1970s, Baez was a founding member of the City-Wide Bilingual Bicultural Advisory Committee for the Milwaukee Public Schools, and in 1975 the school district hired him as its first bilingual parent co-coordinator. He went on to work in higher education, often at the center of bilingual, desegregation, and gender equity struggles; in the 1990s, he was a vice president and dean at Hostos Community College in New York City. Today, Baez is head of the Council for the Spanish Speaking, Milwaukee's oldest Latino community-based organization. Mention a well-known Latino activist anywhere in the United States and Baez will likely be one or two degrees of separation away from knowing the person on a first-name basis, if not personally acquainted himself.

Milwaukee offered its first bilingual program in 1969, at the Vieau Elementary School on the near South Side. The school is proof that while Milwaukee is slow to change, it is not immune to the forces of history.

Built in 1894 and expanded in 1928, Vieau Elementary encompasses an entire city block, its three stories rising high above nearby homes. It is one of a surprising number of Milwaukee schools that date to the late nineteenth century. (Brown Street School, originally built in 1882, is the oldest.) The longevity of the schools is due not just to Milwaukee's frugality but also to the pride in craftsmanship and education that the Germans brought with them to Milwaukee. While the schools built in the 1950s are known

for their cinder blocks and bomb-shelter ambiance, the older buildings relied on marble, lannon stone, terrazzo, and other quality materials expected
to last hundreds of years. Pleasing architectural flourishes—such as the sky-
lights in the boiler house and over the gymnasium roof at Vieau Elementary—
were a given rather than an extravagance. The schools were designed as
neighborhood institutions building the future, not as mere warehouses.

Vieau Elementary is named after the French Canadian fur trader Jacques
Vieau, the first white settler in what later became Milwaukee. In one of the
earliest examples of the city's multicultural/multiracial heritage, he married
Angelique Roy, a woman of French and Menominee ancestry. Jacques Vieau's
place in Milwaukee's history was permanently fixed when, in the early
1800s, he brought to Milwaukee the man who would later become the city's
first mayor.

For much of the twentieth century, Vieau Elementary taught the German and Polish immigrants who settled on the South Side and worked at
the area's factories and foundries. In the 1960s, the neighborhood evolved.
It was once again home to immigrants, but this time from south of the U.S.
border rather than Europe. By 2009, 97 percent of Vieau's seven hundred
students were Latino, with 40 percent classified as English-language learners. Some 90 percent were eligible for free or reduced-price lunch.

When Spanish became part of the classroom at Vieau Elementary, it
was a continuation of past practice. As far back as 1870, a school board
recommendation to the superintendent noted that three-fifths of public
school students in Milwaukee were of German descent. "As nearly all German parents want their children to learn German in connection with English, it becomes a matter of duty on the part of the Board to have the
German language properly taught in the public schools," the board noted.[1]
An 1897 outline of the school schedule allotted two hundred minutes per
week of instruction in German after the second grade—more time than was
given for science, writing, U.S. history, or geography.[2] Until World War I,
when anti-German hysteria descended, German was an integral part of the
school day throughout Milwaukee.

It wasn't until the 1960s, in an era of increased immigration and growing sensitivity to the rights of racial minorities, that language issues forcefully reemerged. Immigrant communities called upon schools to meet the

educational needs of students with limited English skills. Advocates of bilingualism took the demand a step further and called upon schools to help students maintain their home language while learning English. The Bilingual Education Act of 1968 provided federal funding to address such language issues, and also allowed school districts to provide bilingual education without running afoul of desegregation mandates.

Not surprisingly, the issue of language rights landed before the U.S. Supreme Court. The case involved Kinney Lau, a Chinese student in the San Francisco schools. As was common at the time, all instruction was in English. Lau, who spoke Chinese, couldn't understand the teacher. He started failing his classes. What's more, his predicament was not unusual—some 1,789 Chinese-speaking students had a similar problem. In 1970, attorney Edward Steinman filed suit on behalf of the students, using the logic of *Brown* to argue that because they could not understand instruction given only in English, they were being denied education "on equal terms."

The San Francisco school district argued that it wasn't its fault that the Chinese children had a "language deficiency." Therefore, the district said, it was under no obligation to provide any special support for the students. The U.S. Supreme Court unanimously disagreed. In a 1974 decision in *Lau v. Nichols*, Justice William O. Douglas wrote, "There is no equality of treatment merely by providing students with the same facilities, textbooks, teachers and curriculum; for students who do not understand English are effectively foreclosed from any meaningful education." Citing the Civil Rights Act's prohibitions against discrimination on the grounds of race, color, or national origin, the Court ruled that a failure to provide English language instruction to the Chinese-speaking students denied them educational opportunity. The decision did not specifically call for bilingual education as a remedy, nor did it advocate any specific curricular reform. Advocates of bilingual education nonetheless considered the decision a significant victory.[3]

Unlike the *Brown* ruling, *Lau* received little publicity at the time—only a one-sentence summary in the *New York Times*. To this day, however, *Lau* provides the legal framework for the special help due students who fall under the category of English-language learners.

In Milwaukee, Latino activists had been organizing ever since passage of the Bilingual Education Act in 1968. Reflecting the demographics and politics of the times, they encompassed a range of identities, from Puerto Ricans to Mexican nationals to Chicanos from southern Texas. Their priorities sometimes differed, but they were united by their pride in Spanish, their determination to fight discrimination, and their rejection of the idea that speaking Spanish reflected a "language deficiency." Milwaukee's activists defended bilingualism and invariably linked it with biculturalism—an orientation reflected in Wisconsin's Bilingual Bicultural Legislation Act of 1975. The emphasis was far broader than merely helping students learn English, which was the framework established by *Lau*. "The theme for us was equity and access," Baez says, "with a strong emphasis on multiculturalism and community control. These were grassroots movements advocating that bilingualism was a human right."

Rolling his eyes and shaking his head in dismay at today's marketplace model of reform, Baez struggles to articulate that earlier era's vision. "People wanted to transform communities, to have more community control, to change the curriculum," he says. "They viewed bilingualism as part of that larger vision.

"But now it is all assimilation," he continues. "Schools have become a way to say, 'Oh, you are the newcomers and as soon as you learn English, you're out, no more bilingual education.'"

The Latino activists differentiated between programs designed to "transition" students into English-only classrooms as quickly as possible and bilingual programs that sought to "maintain" one's native language and culture. In Milwaukee, advocates of a maintenance approach won. They also fought for, and won, district support to involve parents in the bilingual programs.

Despite vacillating attitudes in recent years toward immigrants, those originating visions remain strong. Bilingual education in the Milwaukee Public Schools has emphasized maintaining and improving one's first language—both to build a foundation for learning English and also to acknowledge the importance of being truly bilingual in today's global world. Throughout the country, the Milwaukee Public Schools are known for their strong bilingual programs, for their two-way bilingual schools, and for their language immersion schools in French, Spanish, German, and Italian.

Starting with just one bilingual classroom at Vieau Elementary in 1969, the bilingual program in the Milwaukee Public Schools blossomed. By 1977, there were nineteen schools providing bilingual services to 2,560 students.

The district's bilingual staff encompassed seventy-four teachers, forty-five aides, thirty-one paraprofessionals, six administrators, and four counselors.[4]

At the height of the grassroots desegregation movement in the 1960s, the Latino community was small, focused on adjusting to life in a new country. "At the level of community, people didn't really follow the desegregation issue," Baez recalls. "In 1976, when the court case came down, the understanding was almost zero."

Because the Latino community was not involved in the desegregation movement, Latinos were invisible in the court case. When federal judge John Reynolds Jr. issued his decision in 1976, Latinos were defined as "non-black." The future of the bilingual schools was in doubt, because they were viewed as "white" schools that had to be integrated. The fear was that Latinos would be sent to schools in the black community that did not have any bilingual programs, and blacks who did not speak Spanish would be sent to the bilingual schools.

"We had a meeting with Lloyd Barbee," Baez recalls, "and we said, 'Lloyd, we have a concern with defining this as black and white. What about Latinos?'" Baez says Barbee was sympathetic but did not want to change the parameters of the legal debate and argue that, for purposes of desegregation, Latinos should be treated as a separate racial minority with specific language needs. "Lloyd said, 'Tony, I understand, but I fought like crazy for this case and there is no way I am going to open it up again,'" Baez recounts.

Because the court case was subjected to so many legal appeals, this bought time for the Latino community. While Latinos were unsuccessful in their attempt to formally intervene in the court case, the final settlement made it possible for the bilingual programs to continue and expand. The school board signaled its support when it approved a statement in 1976 noting, "Bilingual Bicultural education and integration are compatible and feasible. Both efforts are attempts at providing equality of educational opportunity for pupils."[5]

The Latino community, meanwhile, learned an important lesson: it could not remain aloof from the city's broader educational debates. When the issue of metropolitan desegregation came to the fore, the Latino community was prepared. The Chapter 220 metropolitan settlement, finalized in 1987, defined Latinos as a "minority" and thus eligible to transfer to suburban schools. Latinos were only 8 percent of Milwaukee's public school students at the time, but it was clear that their needs could not be neatly folded into a black/white framework.[6]

In September 1988, I held the hand of my four-year-old daughter Caitlin and we walked up the stairs of La Escuela Fratney/Fratney Street School. We were both scared, although I was better at hiding my feelings.

After I graduated from high school in 1969, I left Milwaukee as soon as I could. Two decades later, when I was pregnant with my second child in a one-bedroom apartment in Brooklyn, Milwaukee's family-friendly nature beckoned. Along with my husband, also a Milwaukee native, we returned to the city of our youth, the veritable prodigal children. Shortly after we moved back to Milwaukee, however, my husband was diagnosed with AIDS. When he died in the spring of 1987, I became the harried single mother of two young children. The Milwaukee Public Schools selection process was one of the last things on my mind, and I wasn't tuned in to the middle-class grapevine that let parents know the preferred schools.

When it came time to choose a school for my daughter, I felt there were two good schools close by, one of them just down the block. To this day I'm not exactly sure why I chose Fratney. It was a little farther away, six blocks, but I liked what it offered. What's more, a yellow school bus would pick up and drop off my daughter at day care, making my working life oh so much easier.

Fratney was a beautiful school built in 1903, with a spacious playground. But its two-way bilingual program was new, with absolutely no track record. Students would spend half their time learning in English and the other half in Spanish, with an equal split between English-dominant and Spanish-dominant children. The bilingualism was part of a broader vision of a multicultural education. The program appealed to me. I wanted my children to learn to live in the world, not to escape into a privileged enclave.

Fratney's two main founders, Bob Peterson and Rita Tenorio, had been active in community and school organizing, and I felt a kinship with their progressive politics. There were definitely details to be worked out in the school's program. But I had grown up in a family of six children and had lived in New York City for nine years, so I was comfortable with creative chaos. Peterson was Norwegian Lutheran and Tenorio was a German Mexican who had started her teaching career in Catholic schools; I felt reassured that things would never get completely out of control.[7]

I enrolled Caitlin in Fratney. For the next fifteen years I was a Milwaukee Public Schools parent.

16.

MONEY: THE ROOT OF ALL SOLUTIONS

The best things in life are free
But you can keep them for the birds and bees
Now give me money
That's what I want
That's what I want, yeah
That's what I want

—The Beatles

School funding is one of the most complicated issues in education, perhaps outdone only by special education. Entire forests have been cut down to print the many books written about school finance. With few exceptions—most notably Jonathan Kozol's eloquent and persuasive *Savage Inequalities*—the books are as complicated (and boring) as income tax manuals.

A few things are clear, however. First, across the country there is a gulf between the funding of most urban schools and their suburban neighbors. Second, the U.S. Supreme Court, in a 5–4 decision in *San Antonio v. Rodriguez* in 1973, washed its hands of the problem. It ruled that public education was not a fundamental right protected by the U.S. Constitution, and that unequal funding did not violate the Fourteenth Amendment's mandate of equal protection. In essence, the Supreme Court gave its stamp of approval to separate and unequal school funding.

In metropolitan Milwaukee, as in many urban areas across the country, school funding is both separate and unequal. A 2001 report by the education publication *Rethinking Schools* noted, "As the percentage of students of color has risen in the Milwaukee Public Schools, funding per pupil has plummeted compared to funding in overwhelmingly white suburban districts."

A few figures tell the story. In 1981, when the white and African American populations in Milwaukee were roughly equal, Milwaukee's "shared costs per pupil" were only $127 below the suburban average.[1] As the percentage of white students dropped in the Milwaukee Public Schools, the spending gap widened. By the 1998–99 school year, when whites were only 20 percent of the district's enrollment, the Milwaukee Public Schools had $1,254 per student less than the suburban average, based on "shared costs."

The *Rethinking Schools* report noted parallels with the 1976 federal court decision that found Milwaukee's segregated school system unconstitutional. "Instead of isolating only majority African-American schools and providing those schools with fewer educational resources," the report said, "the current system isolates an entire school district and provides the whole district with fewer resources."[2]

School finance reformers in Wisconsin challenged the funding system in state court, arguing that it violated the state constitution's mandate for uniform educational opportunity. In 2000, a 4–3 majority on the Wisconsin Supreme Court rejected the lawsuit, saying the finance system was as equal as "practical."

State aid has never fully compensated for the insufficient property tax base in poverty-stricken Milwaukee. In recent years, moreover, the state share of school funding has decreased. The Milwaukee Public Schools have faced ever-decreasing resources.[3]

In the spring of 2003 I walked up well-worn granite steps at Riverside University High School, as part of a reporting assignment on school budget cuts. I chose to focus on Riverside in part because my daughter Caitlin had graduated from the school the year before. I wouldn't have to rely on other people's claims that, despite the budget cuts, the school was academically strong and had a lot going for it.

Riverside is the prototypical comprehensive urban high school, from sports teams to school plays and car washes to support extracurricular activities. The student body of some sixteen hundred is distinctly multiracial—mostly African American, but with a significant percentage of Latino, Hmong, and white students. Located near the University of Wisconsin–Milwaukee, the school bridges the city's affluent East Side and nearby working-class neighborhoods. Academically, the school has a strong college prep curriculum and a solid bilingual program. Its students are among the most politically active in the city, whether on issues of homelessness, the rights of non-heterosexual students, or immigrant rights. The four-story brick building, complete with tower, dates from 1912 and was built to last. It has the iconic look and feel of an urban high school.

On this particular day, I was headed for the office of school principal Rosana Benishek. She had been told to cut $317,000 from the school's budget for the 2003–4 school year. In talking about the budget cuts, Benishek faced a daunting problem. How could she convince people that despite the budget cuts, despite the incessant media message that urban public schools were failing, and despite the unspoken yet prevalent bias that low-income minority kids were less academically talented, Riverside was a good school?

A similar dilemma faced teachers and administrators across the Milwaukee Public Schools. They knew the effects of yet another round of cuts on top of cuts the year before and the year before, going back to 1993, when the state legislature imposed spending limits on public schools. But if they painted too dire a picture, would even more families opt for the private voucher, charter, and open enrollment options outside of the Milwaukee Public Schools?

"It's a fine line," Benishek said. "We want to show people that there is a budget crisis in our schools. But I don't want people to get the notion that we are not still functioning at the highest levels."

Statistics backed up Benishek's claim that Riverside—as was true of a number of the district's schools—was able to complete successfully with suburban schools. Riverside was particularly noted for its Advanced Placement courses providing high schoolers with college credit. Riverside has been especially proud of the number of low-income and minority students who take AP classes. Of the top thirteen AP schools in Wisconsin in 2002, the year before I interviewed Benishek, Riverside had 44 percent of test takers who were minority, compared to the next highest at 15 percent.[4]

"It's a terrible irony," noted Riverside's Jean Fleet, who at the time taught AP World History and Comparative Government. "The kids are great and are better than ever. But the resources aren't there."

By 2011, the budget crunch in the Milwaukee Public Schools had gotten worse. Take the case of Elm Creative Arts School, an elementary school (kindergarten through fifth grade) specializing in arts education.

It's mid-June, two days before the 2010–11 school year is to end. Vicki Samolyk, the lone art teacher at Elm, is packing up her art room, alternating between cleaning out shelves and making sure children get their work before they leave for the summer. Tanika, a third grader, enters the room.[5] "Ms. Samolyk, I need my mask," she says. Samolyk starts rummaging through boxes and cluttered desktops. "Is this it?" she asks, holding up a black and white mask. "No," Tanika says. But then Tanika sees a ceramic fish she had painted. She gives a squeal of delight, is satisfied, and goes back to her regular classroom. "Bye, Ms. Samolyk," she says as she cheerfully bounces out of the room.

Elm started in the 1970s as a part of the desegregation plan. The school used its arts offerings to attract an integrated student body, and it quickly became an example of how an adequately funded, integrated school can be both popular and successful. Before long, it was one of the most sought-after public schools in Milwaukee. Admission followed race-based guidelines and was by lottery.

In its early years, Elm was roughly balanced, with equal numbers of white students and black students. The school had six full-time art teachers providing instruction in music, dance, drama, and visual arts. Classroom teachers were required to have a background in the arts so that the arts could be incorporated throughout the curriculum (that requirement remains, even today). In 1991, Elm moved into a new building with an art gallery, a performance space, and a cluster of art rooms. It's a wonderful building for arts education. But then came years of budget cuts. The librarian position was cut, with the job taken over by an educational assistant. The jobs of various art teachers were eliminated, including the dance teacher, who doubled as the phys ed teacher. By 2010–11, the school could only afford Samolyk's part-time position. (It also had a six-week music teacher and a six-week physical education teacher, as part of a district program helping schools who did not have music or phys ed teachers on staff.) Samolyk worked three days at Elm and two days at a school on the South Side. She taught almost a thousand children. In the 2011–12 school year, Elm's art position was slated to be half-time, which meant Samolyk would have needed a third school to maintain a full-time job. Except at Elm, which has dedicated art rooms, she would have taught with art supplies crammed onto a cart that would be wheeled into the classroom and wheeled out after thirty minutes. The prospect made Samolyk's head spin. She decided to retire.

Samolyk has taught at Elm for twenty-eight years. Her spirits are bittersweet this day in June as she sits at a paint-stained art table to talk about Elm. She has enjoyed teaching, is proud of all that Elm has done over the years, and understands the essential role of the arts in encouraging creativity and in making learning fun. On this particular day, however, she feels an overwhelming sense of sadness. "When I began, we had full-time art, full-time dance, drama, and music," she reminisces. "We had a huge string program, with Suzuki violin, regular violins, violas, cellos. And a brass brand with wind and percussion." Her voice trails off as the enormous size of the cuts sinks in. Samolyk's hope is that the classroom teachers will find time in their already crammed schedules to infuse art into the traditional curriculum.

There's no one factor in the art program's demise at Elm. It happened gradually, a little one year, a little the next. In the 1990s, it really got bad. Some cuts affected all schools. Some cuts targeted specialty schools, which had tended to receive a higher per-pupil budget in order to finance the specialties. Some cuts happened when the specialty schools fell out of favor (although not with the parents) and the administration pushed other reforms, such as small schools, neighborhood schools, and K–8 schools. "It was death by a thousand cuts, a small but steady bleed," she says.

Samolyk does see one overarching factor in the cuts: the school's changing demographics. As budgets declined and as whites fled the city, Elm's student body became less and less integrated. By 2010, the school was 13.2 percent white, with 19 percent of all students requiring special education services and 65.7 percent eligible for free or reduced-price lunch.[6] Samolyk can't prove that changing demographics are the reason underlying the problems facing Elm and other Milwaukee public schools, but she feels it in her bones. "What's sad is that now, more than ever, the kids need the arts," she says. "When else might these kids have a chance to go to the symphony, to the art museum, if not through school?"

Michelle Nate, who for ten years had the unenviable task of overseeing finances within the Milwaukee Public Schools, has seen the effect of changing demographics on the district as a whole. "It's very hard to convince people in Madison [in the state legislature] to give Milwaukee more money," she notes. "And what distinguishes Milwaukee from the rest of the state? It's not our tall buildings. It's our black and brown kids. But they don't say that, of course."[7]

Slavery flourished for about 250 years in the United States before it was ended by a bloody civil war, which was followed by short-lived transformations during Reconstruction and then by almost a century of Jim Crow.

The federal court approved a final settlement for Milwaukee's school desegregation in 1979. Less than ten years later, desegregation was no longer a priority. Within another decade, neighborhood schools would once again became official policy in the Milwaukee Public Schools. Judged by historical standards, it was a brief attempt to redress injustice.

As support for desegregation waned, a disturbing number of policy makers and power brokers preferred reforms that increased private and semiprivate school options in Milwaukee. Most significantly, in 1990 the state legislature established a nominally experimental voucher program in Milwaukee under which public tax dollars would pay for private school tuition. Milwaukee quickly became known nationally for this program, the country's oldest and largest. An era of resegregation and abandonment was under way.

But history is never simple. When Governor Scott Walker unleashed his agenda in 2011—from expanding the private school voucher program to cutting public education and prohibiting collective bargaining by most public sector workers—he inadvertently unleashed an upsurge of popular protest unprecedented in Wisconsin's history. The era of resegregation and abandonment had spawned a new era of protest.

Part III

Resegregation, Abandonment, and a New Era of Protest: 1990s and 2000s

17.

1990: VOUCHERS PASS, ABANDONMENT BEGINS

Privatizing public education is the centerpiece, the grand prize, of
the right wing's overall agenda to dismantle social entitlements and
government responsibility for social needs.
                          —Ann Bastian, senior program officer at the New
                                                     World Foundation[1]

The long, painful, and conscious abandonment of Milwaukee's public schools
began in September 1990. Publicly funded vouchers for private schools
evolved from conservative dream to on-the-ground reality.

Given the plethora of educational options in the twenty-first century,
the public is often confused about vouchers. Are they just a variation on
charter schools?

The answer, unequivocally, is no.

Charter schools, although they tend to operate as semiprivate institutions, remain public schools. By definition, voucher schools are private—
even when every single student may be receiving a publicly funded voucher
to attend the private school.

Because they are defined as private schools, voucher schools differ inherently from public schools, whether charter or traditional. Voucher schools,
for instance, need not respect constitutional rights of due process and free
speech. They are not subject to the same standards of public oversight or
transparency as public schools. They also tend to be religion-based schools,
able to use public tax dollars to incorporate religion into the curriculum and
to circumvent a host of nondiscrimination requirements.

As a journalist, parent, and concerned citizen, I have followed Milwaukee's voucher program for over two decades. People often ask me to summa-
rize my perspective, expecting an analysis of test scores, parent satisfaction,

and similar issues. While important, these concerns sidestep the essential problem: vouchers have nothing to do with improving public education and everything to do with funneling public tax dollars into private, often religious, institutions. They are, at their core, an abandonment not only of public education but also of this country's commitment to democracy and educating all children.

The repercussions of vouchers go far beyond education. As a 2008 analysis in *Washington Monthly* noted, conservative activists "seized on vouchers as a particularly potent example, in part because they struck at the heart of the nation's most deeply established governmental activity—public schooling. If conservatives could show that private schools worked better than public ones, and that the introduction of competition improved entire school systems, that would advance their arguments for welfare rollbacks, Social Security privatization, and other initiatives to replace government programs with the free market."[2]

For more than twenty years, vouchers have dominated and distorted educational reform in Milwaukee. From the program's limited beginning in 1990, vouchers have repeatedly expanded as conservatives kept their eyes on their prize—replacing public education with a system of universal vouchers. By 2010, voucher schools in Milwaukee enrolled more than twenty thousand students, approaching the size of Wisconsin's second-largest public school district. In line with the resurgence of conservative political power after the national 2010 elections, voucher proposals were also gaining momentum throughout the country.

Milwaukee is ground zero in the nationwide voucher movement. It is home to the country's oldest and largest voucher program, and has been a model for similar initiatives in Cleveland, Washington, D.C., and New Orleans. For public school systems across the country, Milwaukee provides a unique chance to look into the future.

Like most people, I didn't give vouchers much thought when the Wisconsin legislature passed the voucher program in 1990. I remember vouchers being billed as "choice" for poor people, an experimental effort under which public dollars would pay the tuition at a handful of private, nonreligious community schools serving a couple of hundred poor children. It seemed worthwhile and noncontroversial, akin to throwing a few dollars in the missionary collection basket at Sunday church.

My first actual encounter with vouchers, on November 14, 1990, was unexpected but enlightening. It started as just another day as I dropped my two daughters off at day care, changed my focus from harried single parent to no-nonsense journalist, and walked into my job at the *Milwaukee Journal* metro desk. As a general assignment reporter, I was never quite sure what would come my way—perhaps a weather story, perhaps an overnight shooting, perhaps a human interest feature.

I ate the peanut butter and jelly sandwich that passed for breakfast, downed some coffee, and got ready for my day's assignment. The city editor, a gray-haired Irishman who filled every stereotype of the gruff, disheveled newshound, called me over. I was to go to Bruce Guadalupe School, one of the community schools receiving vouchers, and give an on-the-scene report on daily life at a voucher school.

I headed off to Bruce Guadalupe, located in an old parish school on the South Side, its brick exterior walls bearing testament to years of smoke from nearby factories. About 44 of the school's 130 predominantly Latino students received publicly funded vouchers to pay tuition. (At the time, voucher schools were required to have 51 percent of students privately paying tuition, in order to ensure that a school did not rely on public tax dollars and was a functioning private entity. Over the years, that requirement was gradually eliminated.) I talked to various teachers at Bruce Guadalupe, trying to get a handle on what the story might be. I decided to sit in on a seventh-grade reading class, where students were studying vocabulary.

Constancies Morales, thirteen, groaned as she tried to use the words *reticent* and *benignly* in the same sentence. She was stumped. Her teacher tried to come to her rescue. Did she know what the words meant? "One word sort of means 'shy.' The other means 'kindly,'" the teacher prompted. It didn't help. Connie was allowed to move on and try again later. Relieved, Connie began matching definitions with words, pairing "a community of dolphins" with possible answers such as "cetaceans," "oral tradition," and "pod."

The class brought back memories, and I was quickly transported back to my own education decades earlier. As I reported at the time, "It was a typical reading class for Connie. In some ways it could have been a typical class for thousands of other children across Milwaukee."

There were only thirteen students in Connie's class, one reason she liked the school. "Indeed," I wrote, "the key features of her school are not radically different from reforms mentioned for public schools: small class sizes, parental involvement, high expectations and a positive school spirit."

As I found out, however, not all staff shared the "positive school spirit." In between classes, several teachers approached me with vague stories of turmoil and tension. They couldn't say more, they said, because they feared for their jobs. The principal was equally upset and vague. The teachers advised that I attend the parent meeting scheduled for the following evening.

I wrote my story, without the unsubstantiated claims of turmoil, and my editor agreed that I should attend the parent meeting to find out what was going on. The night of the meeting, I walked up the school steps, reporter's notebook in hand, ready to get the story. I immediately found my way blocked by a somewhat beefy lawyer physically barring me from the meeting's door. He told me that Bruce Guadalupe was a private school, this was a private meeting for parents, and I would not be allowed to attend.

I huffed and I puffed, citing the power of the press and arguing that Bruce Guadalupe was receiving public dollars and thus was subject to Wisconsin's open meetings and records legislation. No, the lawyer explained, Bruce Guadalupe was a private school and I could not enter the meeting. He made it clear that he was prepared to call the police.

I returned to the newsroom and vented to my editor about what had happened. He subsequently got in touch with the *Milwaukee Journal*'s lawyers. Before long, the opinion from the paper's lawyers filtered down. The voucher legislation did indeed define the schools as private. The Bruce Guadalupe lawyer was right. The public and the media had no right to attend the school's parent meetings.

I never did find out what happened at that parent meeting. But within two weeks, the nonprofit agency overseeing the school announced that the teaching staff would be slashed by a third, classes would be combined, and the bilingual program would be cut in half. The much-beloved small classes I had written about were financially unsustainable. Within another two weeks, the principal was gone.[3]

It was the first but certainly not the last time I ran up against voucher schools refusing to provide basic information available from public schools. The next time, in 1999, my opponent was not a beefy lawyer but a church with two thousand years of experience in handling dissent and controversy.

By this time I had left my job at the *Milwaukee Journal* and was managing editor at *Rethinking Schools*, a teacher-led publication that tried to walk the minefield of demanding reform of public schools but also protecting the institution of public education. *Rethinking Schools* was based in Milwaukee and, more often than I would have liked, I found myself reporting on vouchers for both local and national audiences.

In 1990, the voucher program began with seven private schools serving roughly 340 children. By 1998, religious schools were allowed to receive vouchers and the program served almost six thousand students at eighty-three schools, most of them religious. My experience at Bruce Guadalupe had made me wary of getting reliable information from the voucher schools. But my request to the Archdiocese of Milwaukee seemed innocuous: could I have the racial breakdown of students at the various Catholic voucher schools? Segregation and resegregation were important issues within Milwaukee, and I was curious what was going on at the Catholic voucher schools.

I made the request in writing to Maureen Gallagher, director of Catholic education for the archdiocese. No response. I called Gallagher on the phone. She initially gave me the runaround, such as complaints of not enough time to go through reports. When I told Gallagher that *Rethinking Schools* had the time to compile the data from her records, she was blunt. "Are you kidding?" she told me. "We don't open our files to anybody."

It was the end of the discussion, but not the end of our back-and-forth. A short time later, I heard through a well-placed source that the archdiocese itself was worried because test scores at some of the voucher schools were extremely low. In some cases, this person reported, the students were doing worse than their public school counterparts.

I sent another letter to Gallagher, asking for the test scores at archdiocesan voucher schools. Gallagher was again blunt, although more formal. She wrote a letter explaining that the archdiocese "cannot provide you with the additional information you requested." The Catholic schools, she wrote, were accountable to the Church, to the parents, and, as far as voucher funds went, to the reporting requirements of the Department of Public Instruction. As she knew, the department was prohibited at that time from requiring voucher schools to report data on academic achievement and test scores.[4] Private schools, like private roads and private country clubs, don't have to answer to the public.

Federal judge Terence Evans puts the matter more eloquently in a case that laid out a fundamental difference between public and private schools, both those that take part in a voucher program and those that don't. In 1995, Evans ruled on a case involving Tenasha Taylor, an African American who since third grade had been a student at the private and prestigious University School of Milwaukee, located in a nearby suburb.[5] Taylor had given a speech on black separatism in her junior-year English class, in which she quoted the view that "all white people are devils." School officials also said she criticized the school as racist. Suspended and not allowed to return to the school for her senior year, Taylor sued on grounds of free speech. She lost.

"It is an elementary principle of constitutional law," Evans wrote, "that the protections afforded by the Bill of Rights do not apply to private actors such as the University School. Generally, restrictions on constitutional rights that would be protected at a public high school . . . need not be honored at a private high school."[6]

For more than twenty years, policy makers in Milwaukee and Wisconsin have privileged this private system.

An unusual alliance helped spawn Milwaukee's voucher program— conservatives, libertarians, black nationalists, business leaders, and religious-school advocates in both the Republican and Democratic parties. Over time, especially as the Milwaukee program abandoned its focus on community-based schools serving poor children, various people have joined or left the voucher movement. But one force has consistently been a mainstay both ideologically and financially: Milwaukee's Lynde and Harry Bradley Foundation. For more than two decades, the foundation has used its local and national clout and its bankroll to nurture, protect, and expand Milwaukee's voucher program. From 1986 to 2003, it made an estimated $41 million in grants for school voucher initiatives.[7] Subsequent grants have maintained a similar pace; in recent years, the foundation has increasingly funded corpo-ratized charter school franchises.

Michael Joyce, the president of the Bradley Foundation from 1985 to 2001, helped shape both the foundation's ideological direction and the ori-entation of Milwaukee's voucher program. To this day, the voucher move-ment remains dominated by foundations, organizations, and philanthropists who share Joyce's free-market worldview and who, in the name of reform-ing education, seek to replace public education with a universal voucher system that includes private and religious schools.

Joyce's physical appearance obscured his power and influence. When I interviewed him several times in the mid-1990s for a profile in *Rethinking Schools*, he seemed to delight in the "man in the gray suit" persona he shared with so many Milwaukee executives. He could easily have been mistaken for a professor or a middle-aged Clark Kent: thick glasses in oversized frames, hair thinning at the top, a waistline growing but not out of control, a well-tailored but bland suit and tie. Nothing compelled one to take a second look. Beneath that Clark Kent façade, however, was a man fond of wielding power. And the Bradley Foundation ensured he had lots of power to wield. "Michael Joyce plays for keeps," then Milwaukee mayor John Norquist said in 1993. "He is interested in advancing his agenda. He's very much into the rough and tumble of politics and influencing policy."[8]

Raised in a blue-collar, Irish Catholic Democratic household in Cleve-land, the young Joyce supported the civil rights demands of Martin Luther King Jr. But like many neoconservatives, he became alarmed by the more radical demands of the black power movement, the women's movement, and opponents of the Vietnam War. By 1972, he had shed his liberal lean-ings and voted for Richard Nixon. Over the years he slowly worked his way up the political and ideological hierarchy of the Republican Party. In 1979, he was asked by William Simon, secretary of the treasury for Presidents Nixon and Ford, to head the Olin Foundation—one of several that at the time dominated conservative funding. While there, Joyce gained a national reputation for using foundation grants to nurture a free-market conserva-tive political agenda and to fund conservative think tanks such as the Heritage Foundation, the American Enterprise Institute, and the Manhat-tan Institute.

In 1985, the Bradley Foundation was flush with money after the Allen-Bradley Company's sale to Rockwell International Corp. Andrew "Tiny" Rader, chairman of the foundation's board, wanted an aggressive leader who could take the foundation in new, more politically focused directions. He went to the Olin Foundation and talked to Joyce. "We've got money, and we want to do what you did at Olin," Rader told Joyce. "We want to become Olin West."[9] Joyce accepted the job as president of the Bradley Foundation, remaining until 2001, when he left to help lead President George W. Bush's "faith-based" initiative funding religiously oriented social services.[10]

To those familiar with the history of the Allen-Bradley Company, it was no surprise that Joyce took the foundation far beyond the usual role of a local philanthropy subsidizing a city's symphony, art museum, or ballet. The founders and leaders of Allen-Bradley, Harry Bradley and Fred Loock, were passionately interested in politics and "gravitated to the far reaches of the right wing," according to a history of the company. Both were active supporters of the far-right John Birch Society, which rejected unions, the minimum wage, and Social Security and whose founder, Robert Welch, accused President Eisenhower of being "a dedicated, conscious agent of the Communist conspiracy." Welch regularly spoke at Allen-Bradley sales meetings.[11]

The foundation carried on that ideological torch, albeit with a modern twist. In alignment with the evolution of conservatism, Joyce eschewed the overt nativism and racism of the John Birch Society. He embraced neoconservative politics that emphasized "traditional" cultural values, promoted free-market economics, criticized government social safety net programs as promoting dependence on the "nanny state," and advocated a strong military and intervention in global affairs. At the same time, Joyce's neoconservative orientation sidestepped contentious issues popular with activists on the religious right, such as abortion rights and school prayer. It was modern conservatism for modern times, with an emphasis on free-market economics and a disdain of government social programs.

Although the Bradley Foundation's size never has matched that of leading liberal-oriented foundations, Joyce targeted his grants for maximum political effect. By 1990, under Joyce's leadership, 60 percent of the Bradley

Foundation's grants were related to public policy and the world of ideas. Milwaukee, in turn, became "a showcase for public policy reforms [the foundation] sought nationwide."[12]

Joyce's grant-making helped build a modern-day intellectual framework for reshaping the role of government while giving priority to the role of the market. Joyce was named in an *Atlantic Monthly* article as one of the three people most responsible for the successes of the conservative intellectual movement. The conservative magazine *National Review* once called Joyce the "Chief Operating Officer of the conservative movement." John J. Miller, best known as a national political reporter for *National Review*, argued in a 2003 report that the Olin and Bradley foundations "reshaped America" with "extraordinary and conspicuous success," and should be studied by conservative philanthropists eager to advance the cause of limited government and individual freedom.[13] Over the years, the Bradley Foundation has remained a key funder of conservative causes. Although not as well known as the Koch and Scaife family philanthropies, Bradley is arguably more powerful. As the *Milwaukee Journal Sentinel* has noted, "From 2001 to 2009, it doled out nearly as much money as the seven Koch and Scaife foundations combined."[14]

In the late 1980s, the Bradley Foundation's foray into educational policy advocacy was uncharted territory. By the twenty-first century, with the rise of Bill Gates and other hands-on billionaire reformers, foundation-driven reform was the norm rather than the exception.

In education, Joyce had a single-issue agenda: school vouchers. Unfailingly critical of public schools, Joyce considered them examples of socialism that promoted "everything from environmental extremism, to virulent feminism, to racial separatism, to a radical skepticism about moral and spiritual truths."[15] Within Milwaukee, the discussion of vouchers invariably focused on their potential value for low-income students of color. When speaking to media beyond Wisconsin, Joyce was more frank about his true beliefs. As he told the *Baltimore Sun*, if a voucher system "is good public policy for the poor, why isn't it good public policy for middle or high-income wage earners?"[16]

Joyce argued that vouchers were the only worthwhile reform because "it is about changing power relationships." He dismissed all other reforms— smaller class sizes, improved teacher training, curriculum reform—as palliatives. "They are incremental at best," Joyce said. "They palliate and disguise."[17] It was classic Joyce: take a complicated issue, present a simplistic solution that furthered a conservative agenda, and wrap it in intellectual-sounding rhetoric.

Bradley-funded research rarely stirred controversy, with a few notable exceptions. The first was in 1992 for a book on Anita Hill, who had shocked the nation with her allegations of sexual harassment against U.S. Supreme Court nominee Clarence Thomas. The book was a follow-up to an article in which author David Brock called Hill, among other things, "a bit nutty and a bit slutty." Joyce defended Brock's book as a "very thorough and meticulous piece of research."[18] (In subsequent years, Brock recanted his conservative views and reporting and also apologized to Anita Hill.)[19]

In 1993, another Bradley grantee was accused of smear tactics. This time the incident involved Clint Bolick, who torpedoed President Clinton's nomination of Lani Guinier to head the Justice Department's Civil Rights Division. In an opinion piece in the *Wall Street Journal*, Bolick branded Guinier as one of "Clinton's Quota Queens."[20] The name stuck and her nomination was withdrawn. (Bolick, meanwhile, went on to become nationally prominent in defending voucher programs, including the Milwaukee initiative.)

Joyce enjoyed such controversies. In announcing his retirement from Bradley he said: "My style was the style of the toddler and the adolescent: fight, fight, fight, rest, get up, fight, fight, fight. No one ever accused me of being pleasant."[21]

Nothing, however, compared to the controversy that followed the Bradley Foundation's funding of *The Bell Curve*. Skyrocketing onto the bestseller lists in late 1994, the book argues, in essence, that blacks are inherently and genetically not as smart as white people. It posits that intelligence overwhelmingly determines social class, that this intelligence is unchangeable and largely determined by genetics, that IQ tests accurately measure this intelligence, and that African Americans are disproportionately poor because as a group they score lower on IQ tests than whites and therefore are irremediably less intelligent.

The Bradley Foundation paid Charles Murray nearly $1 million over eight years to research and co-author *The Bell Curve*. It did so with eyes wide open. When Murray was asked to leave the Manhattan Institute in 1989 because of the controversy surrounding the project, the Bradley Foundation specifically decided to continue Murray's funding when he moved to the American Enterprise Institute. By 1994, the year *The Bell Curve* was published, the foundation liked Murray's work so much that it raised his annual stipend. Joyce reiterated throughout the controversy that he was proud to sponsor Murray's work. He called Murray "one of the foremost thinkers of our time" and applauded him for tackling a "taboo subject."[22] Murray and co-author Richard Herrnstein, meanwhile, cite Joyce in the book's acknowledgments as one of those who "offered advice, or at least raised their eyebrows usefully."

Interestingly, Murray and Herrnstein list a few select policy recommendations at the end of *The Bell Curve*. Their key education reform is school choice, including publicly funded vouchers for private and religious schools. Among other things, they argue that parental choice will lead to "orderly classrooms and well-enforced codes of behavior."

The book also calls for a shift in focus, from "disadvantaged" students toward "gifted" students. Policy makers, the authors warn, "need to be more realistic about what can be done to improve the education of students in a heterogeneous, nontotalitarian country. Specifically, critics of American education must come to terms with the reality that *in a universal education system, many students will not reach the level of education that most people view as basic.*"[23]

Joyce, in an interview shortly before publication of *The Bell Curve*, made a similar comment. "To expect perhaps that someone of somewhat limited intellectual ability manage a rigorous curriculum in foreign language, or for that matter in any language, could explain some of the frustrations which young people exhibit," he told me. "It might explain, for example, fairly high dropout rates."[24]

Publication of *The Bell Curve* coincided with a resurgence of conservative Republican power during the presidency of Bill Clinton, not unlike the growth of the Tea Party during the Obama administration. Somewhat surprisingly, *The Bell Curve* received extensive and balanced treatment from a variety of mainstream media, from the *New York Times Book Review* to the *New Republic* to the *Wall Street Journal*. It was left to social scientists and academics to refute the book's scientific pretensions. Stephen Jay Gould, perhaps the most renowned science historian and evolutionary biologist at the time, was one of several who traced the book's popularity to the conservative political climate. "Should anyone be surprised that publication of *The Bell Curve* coincided exactly with the election of Newt Gingrich's Congress and with a new age of social meanness unprecedented in my lifetime?" he asked.

Murray later boasted that *The Bell Curve* played an important role in shaping policy, especially in countering calls for affirmative action and in torpedoing a federal initiative by President Clinton to help everyone attend at least two years of college. *The Bell Curve*, Murray said in 1998, "is the stealth public-policy book of the 1990s. It has created a subtext on a range of issues. Everybody knows what the subtext is. Nobody says it out loud."[25]

On a theoretical level, the modern-day voucher movement is traced to the work of economist Milton Friedman of the University of Chicago.

Deeply suspicious of publicly controlled institutions, Friedman argued in 1955 that funding of public schools should be replaced with vouchers for any approved school, public or private, secular or religious. The vouchers would be "subsidies," providing a minimal level of education, with better-off parents adding to the voucher to pay tuition at more expensive private schools. Regulation of schools would be minimal, on par with health inspections of restaurants.[26] Friedman's free-market approach to education mirrored his dislike of government social programs in general, including what he considered "socialist" initiatives such as Social Security and Medicare.

Friedman never abandoned his dislike of public schools, which he referred to as "government schools." In a 2005 interview a year before he died, the ninety-three-year-old Friedman told the libertarian magazine *Reason*, "There are many kinds of possible vouchers, but there are two basic varieties, which I label charity vouchers and educational vouchers. Charity vouchers are unfortunately what we've gotten mostly so far. They are intended for low-income people who are unquestionably the worst victims of our deficient school system. . . . I want vouchers to be universal, to be available to everyone. They should contain few or no restrictions on how they can be used."

Bolick, the opponent of affirmative action who went on to defend the legality of voucher programs, notes that the idea of vouchers might have died if not for a decline in urban education. He blames this decline in part on the *Brown* decision and desegregation's "stern remedies, especially forced busing."[27] Ironically, however, the first use of vouchers was not by poor black parents but by whites hoping to escape desegregation. For five years, until federal courts intervened, officials closed the public schools in Prince Edward County, Virginia, rather than comply with orders to desegregate. White parents took advantage of vouchers to attend a private, whites-only academy.

Such an association between vouchers and white supremacy was not useful to voucher advocates in the 1980s. It took the publication of the book *Politics, Markets and America's Schools*, by John Chubb and Terry Moe, to modernize the case for vouchers and portray vouchers as a way to counter bureaucracy, promote consumer choice, and stimulate education reform. As education historian Robert Lowe wrote shortly after the book's publication, the book was an attempt "to theoretically justify the abandonment of all public education on the grounds that choice will produce educational excellence."[28]

The Chubb and Moe book was the Bradley Foundation's first direct involvement in the school choice movement, beginning with a $75,000 grant in 1986 and a follow-up grant of $300,000 in 1990.[29] The book was highly influential in policy circles across the country, with the *Chicago Tribune* noting that it "rocked the education world." The book also played an essential role in building support for vouchers in Milwaukee.

There are competing creation myths about Milwaukee's voucher program. Then governor Tommy Thompson, in his memoir *Power to the People*, takes credit. He writes that he stumbled onto the idea of vouchers "by using my common sense," and then promoted the idea among African American activists such as Representative Polly Williams and Howard Fuller.[30] Williams, a Democratic legislator from Milwaukee who championed the successful 1990 voucher legislation, says Thompson is rewriting history and she played the essential role.

Regardless of whether one believes Williams or Thompson, Joyce played an important behind-the-scenes role. As Bolick notes in his book *Voucher Wars*, outlining the legal battle in support of vouchers, "The three-way marriage of [the] Bradley [Foundation], Thompson and Williams was hardly a match made in heaven, but it was politically potent."

Joyce was well aware that good ideas alone do not change public policy, that one needs to organize, and that effective organizing requires money. Using his national connections and his Bradley money, Joyce used Wisconsin as his personal laboratory for social policy, and in turn helped propel Milwaukee's voucher supporters into the national limelight. "In Milwaukee, success [on vouchers] required a multiracial, bipartisan coalition of lawmakers, educators, business leaders, parents, and philanthropists—and Michael Joyce played a key role in bringing them together," Miller noted in his analysis.[31]

One of the essential connections was Joyce's friendship with William Bennett, whose career has included education secretary, drug czar, chair of a for-profit Internet-based education company, and CNN commentator. Joyce had served on President Reagan's transition team in 1980, and some even credit Joyce with helping Bennett land his job as Reagan's secretary of education.[32] Bennett once described Joyce as "the kind of guy you think about when you're in a really tough jam. . . . When I've needed his advice, he has returned my calls saying: 'This is Coach Joyce and this is what I want you to do.'"[33]

From 1988 to 1989 Bennett served on the Bradley Foundation's board of directors. Among other things, he brought with him his experience a few years earlier promoting a national voucher initiative while Reagan's education secretary. Known as the Equity and Choice Act, the ultimately unsuccessful bill called for vouchers for low-income students taking part in remedial, federally funded programs. The rhetoric behind the program extolled the benefits of choice for minorities in urban areas, in particular African Americans.

A similar rationale was presented in January 1988 when Republican governor Thompson presented the first voucher bill to the Wisconsin state legislature. The bill called for publicly funded vouchers for low-income Milwaukee children to attend private schools, including religious schools, anywhere in Milwaukee County. The bill was proposed with little groundwork within Milwaukee, however, and carried the stigma within the African American community of being a partisan, Republican proposal. "My proposal was met with a resounding thud," Thompson admits.[34]

It was clear that Milwaukee's black power brokers needed to be brought on board if a publicly funded voucher program for Milwaukee was to pass

the state legislature. One of the most significant efforts to do so was a conference on education reform in March 1989 at the Milwaukee Area Technical College. "The highlight of the conference, attended by several hundred
black parents, was a debate over school choice," notes African American
journalist and activist Mikel Holt.[35] Panelists included two local education
activists: Fuller, a voucher supporter who at the time was dean of general
education at MATC; and University of Wisconsin–Milwaukee education
professor Walter Farrell, a voucher critic. There were also the two Bradley-
supported national school voucher proponents, Chubb and Moe. "Many
believe it was this forum that served to establish school choice in the minds
of black activists as a major educational reform strategy," notes Holt.[36]

The following year, in the spring of 1990, Williams introduced a voucher
bill and helped shepherd its passage by the Wisconsin legislature. The bill
was more narrowly crafted than Thompson's earlier plan and focused on
helping community schools. (A number of the original voucher schools had
their start as Catholic schools, transforming themselves into independent,
nonreligious community schools in the late 1960s after the Milwaukee
archdiocese withdrew its subsidies of several inner-city parishes. The
community schools enjoyed a reputation for good academics and parental
involvement.)

Williams's proposals limited the publicly funded vouchers to low-income
children. Only private schools within Milwaukee were eligible, and only
nonreligious schools. In addition, the vouchers were to be accepted as full
tuition, and vouchers could only be used by up to 49 percent of a school's
students; the rest had to be private-paying students. The program was limited to one thousand students and was to last only five years, but Thompson
vetoed the five-year limit.[37] (Wisconsin's governor has the broadest veto
power in the country, with a line-item veto on budget bills allowing the governor to rewrite sections by selectively crossing out words.)

Gwen Moore, a state representative at the time who went on to become
Wisconsin's first African American representative in the U.S. Congress,
recalls how voucher supporters initially packaged their program to both
legislators and the public. "The program was small, it was totally secular,
it was an experiment, and it was for kids who the Milwaukee Public
Schools couldn't serve for a variety of reasons," she recalls. She voted in
favor.

"Of course this is a vote I deeply regret," she now says, "because I allowed vouchers and then I saw what it came to be. I never was the kind of voucher person who wanted to destroy public education."[38]

A national media campaign praised the about-to-begin Milwaukee program of public dollars for private voucher schools. The George H.W. Bush administration and the *Wall Street Journal* were among those heaping accolades on Williams and on Milwaukee's program even before the school year started. A *Wall Street Journal* editorial, meanwhile, likened the state's school superintendent, who opposed vouchers, to arch-segregationists such as George Wallace. The newspaper argued that criticism of vouchers was little different from the actions of white supremacists who blocked schoolhouse doors to black students.[39] It was a rhetorical tactic that voucher supporters would perfect in the following years as they framed publicly funded vouchers for private schools as a civil rights issue.

In Milwaukee, the reaction to vouchers was generally restrained, in line with the program's modest size. Most attention was focused on the roughly 100,000 children in the Milwaukee Public Schools. It did not take long for problems to surface in the voucher program, however, foreshadowing difficulties that would grow as the program expanded. In the middle of the first school year, Juanita Virgil Academy went bankrupt and closed, and its voucher students were sent back to the Milwaukee Public Schools.[40] By the second semester other private schools had dismissed fifteen voucher students for disciplinary reasons or because they had learning problems.[41] The following fall, almost half of the nongraduating voucher students did not return to a voucher school.[42]

One of the many contradictions of Milwaukee's voucher program is that it relied on bipartisan support in the Wisconsin legislature to gain a foothold. Over time, however, vouchers have increasingly been identified as integral to a Republican strategy that folds together disdain for the public sector, diversion of public dollars into privately controlled institutions, antiunionism (the National Education Association is the country's largest union, considerably larger than the Teamsters, the largest private sector union), and use of the phrase "compassionate conservatism" to woo African American and Latino voters and undermine the Democratic Party.[43] As Grover Norquist, the influential conservative and head of Americans for

Tax Reform, said in a 1998 interview with *Insight*, the magazine of the con-servative *Washington Times*: "School choice reaches right into the heart of the Democratic coalition and takes people out of it."

Backed by deep-pocket funders and skilled at legislative lobbying, pro-voucher forces have made considerable inroads. But the public at large re-mains skeptical. Any time that vouchers have been put to a popular vote, such as in statewide referendums in Michigan, Utah, and California, they have been resoundingly defeated.

18.

VOUCHER CROSSFIRE: FIGHTING FOR THE SOUL OF PUBLIC EDUCATION

Schools are the public nurseries of our future, and their wanton neglect entails a kind of silent social suicide.

—Benjamin R. Barber, *An Aristocracy of Everyone: The Politics of Education and the Future of America*[1]

Monticello, Thomas Jefferson's five-thousand-acre plantation, is nestled in the foothills of the Blue Ridge Mountains. Jefferson's gravestone, a short walk from the Monticello mansion, is inscribed: "Here was buried Thomas Jefferson, author of the Declaration of American Independence, of the Statute of Virginia for Religious Freedom, and father of the University of Virginia."

Jefferson chose not to mention his two terms in the presidency among his top accomplishments. He took more pride in the lesser-known fact that in 1819 he established the University of Virginia. A publicly supported institution and the first nonsectarian university in the country, the University of Virginia was dedicated to educating leaders in public service.

Jefferson believed in an inherent link between strong democratic institutions and a citizenry educated not just in the three Rs but also in their civic responsibilities. Like the history of democracy in this country, however, Jefferson was rife with contradictions. He penned some of the most famous words in U.S. history—"We hold these truths to be self-evident, that all men are created equal"—yet owned hundreds of slaves during his lifetime. It would be almost a century after the Declaration of Independence before the phrase "all men are created equal" would apply to African Americans. As Jefferson's contradictions make clear, democracy and equality in the United States are not fixed ideals but are redefined through struggle.

Public schools have long been an essential arena where such struggles either advance or are pushed backward.

The "public" in public education is not "an accident of infelicitous speech," political scientist Benjamin Barber writes.[2] In a free society, he argues, "education must be both public and democratic if we wish to preserve our democracy's public spaces."[3] Indeed, every state constitution in the country enshrines the right to a free and public education—an honor that is not bestowed on other requisites for life, liberty, and the pursuit of happiness, from housing to employment to health care.

John Dewey, an early-twentieth-century philosopher whose name is synonymous with progressive education reform, titled his groundbreaking work *Democracy and Education*. Then as now, some viewed education for the masses primarily as a matter of preparing workers and pouring data into children's minds. Others called for educating the entire person and instilling both a sense of individual discovery and a conception of broader civic responsibilities. Then as now, there was a gulf between the ideals of public education and the realities in the classroom. But the answer, Dewey insisted, lay not in abandoning the broader purposes of public education. Instead, the way forward was to demand that public schools live up to their promises and potentials. "The ideal may seem remote of execution," Dewey wrote, "but the democratic ideal of education is a farcical yet tragic delusion except as the ideal more and more dominates our public system of education."[4]

Just as the Declaration of Independence called for equality yet left unquestioned the institution of slavery, the connections binding democracy, equality, and education are often frayed. The power of *Brown v. Board* flowed from its demand that the institution of public education extend the promise of equal opportunity to a group of people so glaringly excluded for so long. The relationship between education and democracy was forcefully underscored as the *Brown* decision not only affected public schools but also played an essential role in undermining the entire edifice of Jim Crow.

In more recent decades, rather than demanding that public education fulfill its promise, the debate has shifted dramatically. "Choice"—which in education now is code for private-school vouchers and privately controlled charters—has become the guiding principle. One chooses with little regard for how one's decision might impact others. As for the schools, they often get to do the choosing. When a publicly financed commodity such as education is provided through a private entity, as is the case with vouchers, the public essentially has no voice in decision-making and minimal power to demand accountability or transparency. As the Milwaukee-based education publication *Rethinking Schools* noted in a special issue warning of the dangers of vouchers and a marketplace approach to public education:

> It's not that our society doesn't know how to teach children well, but that we do so unequally. It's not that we don't have good schools, but that they are clustered in affluent communities. It's not that we refuse to spend lots of money on children, but that it is disproportionately showered on already privileged children.
>
> How will this country confront these inequalities? That should be the central issue in education reform.
>
> Yet the conservative movement has tried to transform the issue from one of inequality to one of "choice."[5]

In the current debates on vouchers, there is strikingly little discussion of the relationship between democratic values, the common good, and public education.

Wisconsin's voucher schools are defined as private schools, and therein is the heart of the problem. They are privately controlled, have limited public accountability, and operate under far different rules than public schools—even when every student at the private school receives a taxpayer-financed voucher. A look at the many differences between public and private schools is daunting.

Wisconsin public schools, for instance, must abide by the state's open meetings and records law. They must make publicly available data on staff pay and certification, student suspensions and expulsions, graduation rates, student and staff demographics, and so forth. Meetings are open to the public. Private schools do not have to adhere to Wisconsin's open meetings and records law.

Public schools must provide special education services to all students who require them. Private schools are not required to meet a student's special needs beyond what can be provided with minor adjustments.

Public schools must honor constitutional rights of due process when students are suspended or expelled. They must also respect students' and employees' constitutional right of equal protection, rights of free speech and association, and right against unreasonable search and seizure. Private schools do not have to honor these constitutional rights.

Regarding state law and students' rights, Wisconsin public schools may not discriminate against students in a range of areas, including sex, pregnancy, marital or parental status, or sexual orientation.[6] (Private schools do not have to follow Wisconsin law on students' rights. Private voucher schools, however, are subject to federal prohibitions against discrimination on the basis of race, color, or national origin. They also are required to admit students on the basis of a lottery, and are not to screen students on the basis of academic performance. However, there are no safeguards preventing expulsion if a student does not meet the private voucher school's academic or behavioral expectations.)

Including religious schools in voucher programs further complicates matters—and in Milwaukee, some 85 percent of voucher students attend a religious school.[7]

Under the First Amendment's separation of church and state, government is not to "entangle" itself in the oversight of a religious institution. The prohibitions against "entanglement" in a private religious school involve both curriculum and employee rights. For example, the U.S. Supreme Court ruled unconstitutional a Louisiana law that forbade the teaching of evolution unless accompanied by the teaching of "creationism," saying the law was an endorsement of religion.[8] The court's ruling does not cover religious schools, however. Religious schools may also teach, for instance, that homosexuality is a sin or that abortion is murder.[9]

As for employee rights, Wisconsin law bars discrimination in employment, including in private schools, in a variety of areas, from age to disability, marital status, and sexual orientation. However, exceptions are made for religious institutions. Most recently, in 2009 the Wisconsin Supreme Court dismissed the case of a first-grade teacher who claimed age discrimination when she was fired from a Catholic school in La Crosse. The Court said the complaint unconstitutionally restricted the school's religious freedom.[10]

Finally, federal law and Wisconsin state law provide protections for staff at both public and private schools to engage in concerted, protected activity—to join together, for instance, to protest working conditions. These protections do not extend to most religious institutions.

* * *

For two decades, voucher advocates have tried to blur the many differences between private and public schools. Instead, they have consistently framed the issue as a matter of "choice." It was a shrewd move.

Individual choice has long been considered a component of liberty, so ingrained in our national psyche that it is as American as apple pie. In education, every parent wants the flexibility to choose the best school for his or her child. Used appropriately and in moderation, there is no doubt that choice can help ensure that public education is sensitive to the varying needs and preferences of this country's 50 million public school students. Many social policies, such as school desegregation initiatives that relied on parents choosing integrated magnet schools, have depended on the appeal of choice.

"Choice" is a fluid concept that is not limited to one particular vision, however. In recent decades, it has increasingly been used by conservatives to promote individual, free-market reforms and to stifle regulations serving the broader good. Indeed, the homage to choice reached such a level of absurdity in 2011 that Representative Michele Bachmann (R-Minn.), a Tea Party star who briefly harbored presidential ambitions, introduced the Light Bulb Freedom of Choice Act to repeal a federal initiative to promote conservation and increase energy efficiency in the typical 100-watt bulb.

Within education, the concept of "choice" has moved beyond accommodating individual preferences or implementing agreed-upon priorities. It is now a guiding policy, promoted as a free-market alternative to the egalitarian, democratic responsibilities of public education. What's more, the mantra of "choice" has been used to stifle much-needed discussions of the policies being promoted. Voucher proponent and former Milwaukee mayor John Norquist, for instance, dismissed concerns about public taxpayer support for a religiously based curriculum by extolling parental choice and arguing, "If a family in Milwaukee believes that their child should go to this Lutheran school that teaches creationism that's okay with me because at least they learn how to spell creationism."[11]

Within Milwaukee, the debate over public dollars for private voucher schools has focused on costs (are private voucher schools cheaper?) and standardized tests (who gets better scores?). The fundamental issue—what is the role of public education in a multicultural democracy—has been ignored.

Warren Furutani, president of the Los Angeles City Board of Education in the 1990s, when vouchers were being proposed throughout California, spoke eloquently to the issue at hand. Paralleling the concerns of Dewey, he said: "When we talk about choice . . . we are talking about a mortal battle for the fundamental soul of public education in a democratic society. That is what the fight is about."[12]

19.

MULTICULTURAL CROSSFIRE:
REDEFINING THE PUBLIC SCHOOL CURRICULUM

We're worried when Johnny can't read. We're worried when Johnny
can't add. But shouldn't we be worried, too, when Johnny tramples
gravestones in a Jewish cemetery or scrawls racial epithets on a dormitory
wall?

> —Henry Louis Gates Jr., professor of African
> and African American studies,
> Harvard University[1]

When Gwen Moore walked into Milwaukee's North Division High School
in September 1965 on her first day as a student, she was terrified. "North
was seen as this jungle," she explains. "All black, segregated, inferior."

Moore had wanted to attend West Division High School, a "white"
school closer to home. When she tried to register at West, school officials
told her she had to go to North Division. "My mom was in Texas at a Baptist convention, and I talked to her and said, 'Mom, they wouldn't let me go
to West,'" Moore tells the story.

"Gerrymandering," her mom muttered.

"Gerry who?" Moore asked.

"Never mind. Go on to North, and when I get back we'll straighten this
out," her mom answered.

Moore laughs at the story's irony. By the time her mother returned,
Moore had fallen in love with North Division. "I begged my mom to let me
stay," she recalls.[2]

In 2004, Moore became the first African American from Wisconsin
elected to the U.S. Congress. As a state legislator, she initially supported
the voucher program, but over the years her concerns grew. The final straw

was when it was discovered that a man convicted of raping a woman at knifepoint had been allowed to start a voucher school. Moore was livid.

Moore speaks forcefully about the need to defend public education. Talking about her own education within the Milwaukee schools, Moore comes alive. She energetically gestures with her hands, her smile broadens, her eyes light up, and she shows in full force the fire and passion that are her political trademark. She can't say enough good things about her time at North Division, and she uses her personal experience to underscore that no school should ever be judged merely by test scores or its reputation in the media.

"North ended up being one of the best experiences I ever had," Moore says, tapping her fingers on the table for emphasis. "In terms of social development and leadership skills, North was the most significant part of my life."

Moore had always been proud to be black. But, the eighth of nine children in a financially struggling family, as a child she had felt the stigma of poverty. Not at North, however. No one looked down on her because she didn't have the right clothes or hairdo, or because her skin color was especially dark. "People appreciated me for being intelligent," she explains. Finding both acceptance and courage, Moore was surprised to learn that she had leadership skills. Students listened to her. She went on to become vice president of an organization known as Black Organized Youth, and then president of the student council at North Division.

Along with several other Milwaukee high schools at the time, North Division was a center of black pride. Moore remembers in particular Jake Beason, an African American social studies teacher who talked with students about the contributions of Malcolm X, H. Rap Brown, Bobby Seale, and Martin Luther King Jr. Moore loved the discussions, and she became involved with student-led demands for textbooks reflecting the contributions of African Americans. In early 1968, students at the North, Rufus King, and Riverside high schools increased their pressure on the administration. "We kept walking out over and over, until we got them to buy *Before the Mayflower*," Moore recalls with a laugh, referring to a well-known history of black America by Lerone Bennett.

Moore did not realize it then, but she was part of a broader, loosely organized movement that would, over time, challenge the established school curriculum. The movement—which reached its apex in the early to mid-1990s and remains influential to this day, although more as an orientation than as a movement—was known as "multicultural education." It's a catchall term to describe the belief that in a multicultural democracy, schools must respect and appreciate diversity, and must acknowledge the contributions of those too often relegated to curricular obscurity.

In Milwaukee, as in many urban areas, the movement for multicultural education had its roots in high school and university student protests of the 1960s. By the 1980s and 1990s, many of those students were themselves teachers—people such as Kathy Williams, who as a ten-year-old got her first dose of an antiracist curriculum when she attended a Milwaukee Freedom School in 1964.

Unlike Moore, Williams lived in the North Division neighborhood. But her mother wanted her to attend Riverside University High School, because North did not have a full array of college preparatory classes. Just as Moore valued North Division, Williams speaks highly of her experience at Riverside. When Williams entered Riverside, in 1967, the school's mix of black, white, and Latino students roughly paralleled the city's overall racial demographics. "There was a lot of conversation going on about human relations and integration," Williams recalls. "And the administration was quite proud, thinking that our school's diversity was preparing students for our community and the larger society."

Williams was also inspired by her brother's experiences at the University of Wisconsin–Oshkosh, and still remembers the title of one of his term papers she read as a seventh grader: "The Opposing Philosophies and Ideologies of Booker T. Washington and W.E.B. Du Bois." When she got to Riverside, Williams jumped into the controversies of the day, from demanding multicultural textbooks to integrating the school's cheerleading squad. She credits Riverside with giving her a strong educational grounding. "I thought Riverside was an excellent school," she says. "Not just a good school, but an excellent school."

While Moore chose a career in politics, Williams entered public education. Along with a multiracial group of teachers, in the late 1980s and early 1990s she was involved in the Multicultural Curriculum Council. It was one of several efforts within the Milwaukee Public Schools to address the question of how best to educate a diverse student body and prepare youth for the global realities of the twenty-first century.

The multicultural movement was a reflection of the times. On one hand, the civil rights and black power movements had raised issues of access, equity, and pride, and demands grew to encompass the school curriculum. On the other hand, the movement took place before standardized testing seized control of the curriculum and constrained teachers' ability to stray off-test. Political factors also provided the breathing space and funding necessary to innovate. In the late 1980s and early 1990s, Milwaukee had not yet abandoned its public schools. Except for those ideologically committed to privatization and public funds for private voucher schools, most people maintained hope that the public schools could and would rise to the challenges they faced.

In 1988, Milwaukee's hope for its public schools was reflected in the school board's unanimous selection of forty-three-year-old Robert Peterkin as superintendent. With experience in both the Cambridge and Boston schools, Peterkin was an outsider without established loyalty to any particular group of Milwaukee politicians or power brokers. He was also the first African American hired to head the Milwaukee Public Schools.[3] It was a sign of broader changes, as Milwaukee's public schools and the city and county government became the main source of middle-class jobs for the African American community. Within the Milwaukee Public Schools, for instance, 35 percent of principals were black by 1990.[4]

The final years of Superintendent Lee McMurrin's eleven-year reign (1976–87) had been sluggish. A sense of inertia had settled over the district. McMurrin was given high marks for a desegregation plan that headed off violence by whites, but low marks for the plan's undue burden on blacks. Metropolitan desegregation, meanwhile, had been pushed as far as politically and legally feasible. Whites had increasingly left for the suburbs, while the black community was increasingly beset by long-standing problems of unemployment and poverty, and unexpected repercussions of the AIDS and crack cocaine crises. Between 1981 and 1991, the number of high-poverty census tracts in Milwaukee had tripled, more than in any other city in the country.[5] The schools faced new realities, and it was time to move on with new ideas.

The city was undergoing its own political changes, with fresh leaders at both the city and county levels. Most important, John Norquist was elected mayor of Milwaukee in 1988, ending the twenty-eight-year mayoral reign of Henry Maier. (Unlike Maier, who was interested in educational issues but did not meddle in school affairs, Norquist had strong and vocal opinions on how the city's public schools should be run.)

Peterkin's hiring as Milwaukee's superintendent increased the expectations of transformation. "If anyone can lead [Milwaukee Public Schools] out of the wilderness, it would seem to be Peterkin," the *Milwaukee Journal* editorialized.[6] The business community was similarly upbeat. A few months after Peterkin's arrival, the Greater Milwaukee Education Trust was formed to encourage the private sector to support the public schools. "There are big problems, but they are solvable," said Vaughn Beals Jr., head of the trust and also the CEO of Harley-Davidson, Inc., one of the city's leading manufacturers. "We are very optimistic, but the key to change is marshalling the forces of this community."

With the hindsight of more than twenty years, the Peterkin era is generally remembered as an example of trying to do things right. The business community partnered with the public schools. The administration and school board had good working relations. The central office viewed teachers as necessary participants in educational change. Board members supported a variety of innovations: La Escuela Fratney, which had an explicit multicultural, antiracist perspective and was the state's first two-way bilingual school; two African American immersion schools based on an Afrocentric curriculum and geared toward the specific needs of young black men; and the country's first public Waldorf school, Milwaukee Urban Waldorf School, founded in 1991.

The Milwaukee district's innovation both precedes and succeeds Peterkin's time as superintendent. The district is also home to the country's second public International Baccalaureate high school—Rufus King, which began its IB program in 1979 as an integrated "specialty school" as part of desegregation; the first public high school in the world to offer an IB diploma using the methods of Montessori education—Montessori High School, founded in 2006; and the country's first "gay friendly" middle school—the Alliance School, which began in 2003 as the country's second gay-friendly high school and in 2009 expanded to include middle school students.

In one of the many contradictions surrounding education in Milwaukee, these innovations received little attention locally even as media outlets across the country highlighted such initiatives. The Milwaukee media instead focused on legitimate concerns to unrelentingly condemn the public schools as incapable of reform.

Most of Peterkin's challenges were on a broad policy level—desegregation, budgets, busing. On the classroom level, it was a time when multicultural education came to the fore, spearheaded by educators who believed that desegregation meant not only changing the racial mix of students, but also transforming the curriculum.

The district's approach to multiculturalism was noteworthy not just because of the educational goals but also because of the inclusion of teachers and parents at the grassroots level and the support of a school board and administration that provided funding, staffing, and professional development. "We felt that the world was changing, Milwaukee was changing, and the school district was changing," former school board member Joyce Mallory recalls in explaining the board's support. "We wanted to make sure our children weren't getting left behind in connection to the larger society."[7]

One of the efforts involved curriculum councils funded by the district and led by teachers. The Humanities Council, for instance, expanded the traditional canon, in particular in the high schools. The Early Childhood Council focused on early elementary grades. The Multicultural Curriculum Council played a leading role, and involved schools across grade levels.

The multicultural council started with about a dozen schools and, by 1995, involved teachers from about two-thirds of the district's schools. One of the council's many issues was how to define multicultural education. Did that mean focusing on tolerance? The content of textbooks? Issues of race and power? Williams, co-chair of the council, argued for a comprehensive approach. "Multicultural education is not just including perspectives and insights and information from various cultures or groups," she argued. "It's an ongoing process that empowers students to view the world from multiple perspectives and to understand the ongoing dynamics of this rapidly changing world."[8]

The school board, meanwhile, was also rethinking curricular approaches. Three women played a key role in that era—Mallory and Jeanette Mitchell, who were African American, and Mary Bills, a white liberal. Despite the different paths they would take later in life, the three worked well together and approached issues on the basis of children and education, not partisan politics or strict ideology. In fact, it was Mallory, a strong supporter of desegregation, who was a leading force in the board's recommendation to transform two all-black schools into African American immersion schools. Peterkin supported that measure, which was popular with many in the black community but not without controversy. The NAACP, for instance, was opposed. Most people viewed the effort as a small experiment, not as a district-wide shift in policy, and had little problem with giving the two schools a try. As Mallory argued, "We're just saying that we have to try something to see if we can't improve the academic performance of black boys."[9]

For a district whose school board fifteen years earlier had done all it could to derail desegregation, perhaps the most unexpected development was what became known as the K–12 Teaching and Learning Initiative. The initiative began under Peterkin with meetings of hundreds of teachers and parents during the 1990–91 school year; that summer, a group of parents and teachers met for three weeks to finalize a curricular strategic plan. The initiative defined curriculum to include not only what was taught but how it was taught, and encompassed the entire school environment, from posters in the hallways to announcements on the PA system. Consisting of ten goals, the initiative made its orientation clear with its very first goal: "Students will project anti-racist, anti-biased attitudes through their participation in a multi-lingual, multi-ethnic, culturally diverse curriculum."

The Peterkin era came to an early and unexpected end, however. In November 1990, slightly more than two years into the job, Peterkin announced he was leaving the following June to take a prestigious job at Harvard University as director of the Urban Superintendents Program. Throughout Milwaukee, there was disappointment bordering on anger that the man who had promised so much and had received such widespread public support would leave so soon. As a *Milwaukee Journal* columnist wrote, "Two years ago, Peterkin gave as much hope to Milwaukee as, on Monday, he gave it despair. . . . Peterkin came to town with a confidence and competence that inspired hope, and that's what puts the pain in his departure."[10]

The K–12 curriculum councils did not die with Peterkin's departure, but it was a definite blow. The councils continued to meet, but every year there was less support from a central administration focused on decentralization and beset with budget cuts. In the spring of 1996, the district eliminated the councils' budgets. With no money for speakers or materials, forced to rely on volunteer efforts to maintain the networking, the councils died out.

At the same time, conservatives were attacking the very concept of multicultural education. Conservative policy analyst Lynne Cheney, six years before her husband became vice president in the administration of George W. Bush, penned a *Wall Street Journal* op-ed, "The End of History." The October 20, 1994, opinion attacked proposed U.S. history standards because they were insufficiently patriotic, devoting too much attention to "obscure" figures such as Harriet Tubman and to political embarrassments such as the Ku Klux Klan and McCarthyism. The U.S. Congress, meanwhile, took up "English-only" legislation—foreshadowing a backlash that reached new heights in 2010 when Arizona passed unprecedented legislation requiring that immigrants carry their documents at all times or risk arrest, and that banned Mexican American studies in the public schools.

Within K–12 schools, the most prominent pushback against multicultural education in the 1990s was in New York City. Given New York's prominence as a media center, the controversy received national attention and shaped the future of multicultural initiatives across the country.

In 1989, the New York City Central Board of Education called for curricular efforts to help counteract discrimination on the basis of race, religion, physical abilities, and sexual orientation. The city was a magnet for people from across the globe, and it seemed logical to promote respect for diversity within the city's one thousand schools and one million students, instilling in children the tolerance needed to make the city work.

A rather innocuous multicultural guide was developed. Its very title, *Children of the Rainbow*, underscored its low-key approach. Among other things, the guide urged "respect for the diversity of families," including gay and lesbian parents. Intolerance toward gay people was particularly strong at the time, both because of long-standing discrimination based on sexual orientation and also because of irrational fears linked to the escalating AIDS epidemic. In the fall of 1991, after two years of development, school board chancellor Joseph Fernandez adopted the guide. There was little notice. Public controversy at that point centered on the development of an HIV/AIDS curriculum that advocated both abstinence and safe sex practices and which developed policies for making condoms available at the high schools. *Children of the Rainbow* seemed destined to be another well-intentioned manual collecting dust on the shelf while teachers coped with day-to-day survival. In fact, most schools and teachers had never heard of the guide until Community School Board #24 in Queens launched a crusade.[11]

Board #24 was known as conservative, Catholic, and a stronghold of middle-class whites. Mary Cummins, head of Board #24, was already angry over the HIV/AIDS curriculum. Catholic Church leaders, including Cardinal John O'Connor, encouraged Board #24 to oppose *Children of the Rainbow*, even providing legal assistance. Cummins also reportedly consulted with the Family Defense Council, a national group aligned with what was known as the religious right. Cummins began a campaign against the multicultural curriculum, saying: "We will not accept two people of the same sex engaged in deviant sex practices as 'family.'" She also linked the multicultural curriculum with the AIDS curriculum and broadened her attack: "The victims of this AIDS scourge are homosexuals, bisexuals, intravenous users of illicit drugs and the innocent people they infect by exposing them to their tainted blood and other bodily fluids."[12]

Before long, the campaign spread to boards across New York. Community meetings turned ugly, with accusations hurled and obscenities exchanged. The *Wall Street Journal* entered the fray, using the controversy to critique public schools in general and to argue that *Children of the Rainbow* "all adds up to more fuel for the burgeoning school-choice movement." Fernandez proposed changes in the curriculum, for instance referring to lesbian and gay families as "same-gender parents," and broadened the ability of local schools to modify content. The controversy did not die, however. In February 1993, largely as a result of the upheaval over *Children of the Rainbow*, the Central Board voted 4–3 not to renew Fernandez's contract. The message to superintendents across the country was clear: proceed with extreme caution when tackling issues of prejudice and intolerance.

Although the term *multicultural education* is a bit of a historical anachronism, public schools continue to be a battleground over what we, as a society, want our children to learn. In Milwaukee, controversy erupted in 2008 over new social studies textbooks. Teacher activists analyzed the textbooks, in particular the fifth-grade text. They found no mention of racism or anti-Semitism, and little mention of discrimination or social movements such as the women's movement or the environmental movement. Working with community members, they forced the district to provide supplementary materials, and set up an ongoing initiative encompassing professional development and Internet-based resources.

Nationally, there have been any number of controversies over curricular content. In March 2010, for instance, the Texas Board of Education approved a social studies curriculum "stressing the superiority of American capitalism, questioning the Founding Fathers' commitment to a purely secular government and presenting Republican political philosophies in a more positive light."[13] At the other end of the political spectrum, a year later California became the first state to require public schools to teach about the contributions of gays and lesbians, a move propelled in part to counter the bullying of students who do not conform to heterosexual expectations. "We are failing our students when we don't teach them about the broad diversity of human experience," noted Mark Leno, the bill's sponsor and California's first openly gay man to serve as a state senator.[14]

In Milwaukee, calls for multicultural education never reached the explosive level they did in New York City in the early 1990s. In 1993, Milwaukee education politics were dominated by a different yet ever-present controversy: money. This time, the controversy involved a referendum to raise $366 million in bonds to relieve overcrowding, upgrade facilities, and build new schools.

20.

1993–95: WHITE VOTERS REJECT NEW SCHOOLS FOR BLACK CHILDREN, AND THINGS FALL APART

All our children ought to be allowed a stake in the enormous richness of America.

—Jonathan Kozol, *Savage Inequalities*

The weather in February is thoroughly unpleasant in Milwaukee, dominated by gray skies, freezing temperatures, and icy sidewalks. Partly because of the weather and partly because February is reserved for primary elections for local races, voter turnout in this month is embarrassingly low.

In terms of the weather, February 16, 1993, was no different. The temperature didn't make it above freezing, and pockets of ice and snow remained throughout the city. Politically, however, this February was different. The ballot included a referendum on a $366 million bond issue to build new public schools and relieve the overcrowding that had led to children being taught in cramped closets or dismal basement hallways. The money was also to be used to reduce class sizes, upgrade rooms for the arts and vocational ed, and allow all eligible children to attend kindergarten. Nearly 125,000 people voted on February 16, 1993, dwarfing the figure of 15,962 voters in the February primary two years earlier.

The voters' message was unequivocal: they rejected the building plan by a two-to-one margin.

Like any multimillion-dollar referendum, many factors were at play. Was the plan too ambitious? Did voters adequately understand the issue? Did key power brokers sit on the sidelines? In the final analysis, however, the defeat hinged on two issues: race and property taxes. "Ultimately, the referendum came down to the question of whether White property owners were willing to pay for improved public education for African-American and Latino children," the education publication *Rethinking Schools* editorialized. "The answer was a resounding 'no.'"[1]

The referendum had been central to the agenda of Superintendent Howard Fuller, an African American hired in 1991 to replace Peterkin. With his abundant charisma and energy and strong connections to both the African American community and the white business and political establishment, Fuller had seemed the one person who could lead the building plan to victory. But it was not to be.

Mayor John Norquist was the most vocal and influential critic of the building plan. Norquist had long argued that good schools were essential to attracting and retaining city residents and businesses. Rather than focus on improved education, however, Norquist emphasized how the building plan would raise property taxes. The plan, he said, "is not in the best interests of our city."[2]

Norquist, while a Democrat, was steeped in libertarian beliefs and embraced marketplace solutions for social problems. The year before the referendum, for instance, he specifically argued against urban areas looking to the federal government for assistance, arguing, "No more tin cups."[3]

Within the black community, the most vocal opponent was Polly Williams, a state legislator from Milwaukee. The referendum, she said, was "another plan to colonize, to control the black community," a claim that reflected concerns that Fuller was too close to the white business community and that the new schools were part of a plan to gentrify black neighborhoods.[4] Williams's comment made it possible for opponents, particularly on the predominantly white South Side, to say that criticisms had nothing to do with race. But it was a tortured argument. As *Milwaukee Journal* columnist Joel McNally wrote after the vote, "You hardly needed to raise the race issue at all. That's the beauty of having a black superintendent advocating nice, new schools for the black community just like those that white suburban kids get. No one had to mention race. It was understood."[5]

At that time, only 26 percent of students in Milwaukee's public schools were white. Yet 68 percent of the city's voting-age population was white. The higher the percentage of white voters in city wards, the higher the number of no votes. In two overwhelmingly white wards on the South Side, voters cast

92 and 93 percent no votes. By contrast, the referendum passed in every ward that was predominantly black.[6]

A multiracial coalition had formed to support the referendum, but it couldn't overpower the double punch of taxes and race. "There's no question that the call to fear, prejudice and distrust worked once again in Milwaukee," a key player in the referendum noted.[7]

Fast-forward two years to 1995, when the Milwaukee Brewers desperately wanted a new stadium. That spring, the Brewers successfully pushed for a statewide referendum on a proposed Wisconsin sports lottery that would provide necessary funding. Voters, however, resoundingly rejected the proposal. In stark contrast to the response after the defeated school referendum, business and political leaders rallied behind the Brewers. Governor Tommy Thompson quickly pieced together a bill that called for an increase in the sales tax to fund the stadium and that would not need voter approval. Even though the tax would be limited to southeastern Wisconsin, where Milwaukee was the most populous city, Thompson still needed to sell the idea to legislators across the state.

In the final days of summer 1995, Thompson began what was to be a low-key, three-day trip in northern Wisconsin, riding a borrowed Harley-Davidson motorcycle and stumping for his bill. For the media, it was to be typical summer fill: lots of color and little of substance. But the ride was more difficult and tiring than Thompson anticipated. What's more, the media were tired of made-for-TV photo ops. While "up north" on his Harley, Thompson made a mistake and spoke what he thought. The media pounced.

In Wisconsin, "up north" is an all-encompassing, almost mythical name for northern Wisconsin that refers as much to a state of mind as to a specific location. When you say you've been "up north," it means anywhere north of Madison and Milwaukee, anything rural where deer hunting and fishing reign supreme, anyplace where "the city" is used as a pejorative and a code for crime, black and Latino people, overpriced restaurants, and crazy downtown traffic. And there was Thompson "up north," in front of reporters and camera crews, telling the "up north" residents to pass his bill because, after all, the sales tax would affect only Milwaukee and surrounding counties.

"Stick it to 'em," he said.

Thompson's message was clear—stick it to those city folks before someone crafted a plan to tax the entire state.[8]

Thompson's stadium bill passed in October 1995. By the time the stadium tax ends at some point between 2015 and 2018, taxpayers in southeast Wisconsin will have paid as much as $530 million for the privilege of hosting a major league baseball team—some $164 million more than Milwaukee's failed school-building referendum.[9]

Thompson's "stick it to 'em" comment was a slip of the tongue. But the political instincts behind the comment were nothing new. Back in 1986, he had learned the power of turning "up north" voters against Milwaukee.

In the early months of 1986, Thompson seemed destined to end his political career as it had started two decades earlier, as a Republican legislator from the small town of Elroy in central Wisconsin. But he ran for governor in 1986, telling voters around the state he would cut welfare. The policy's subtext was clear: he would take action against freeloading blacks in Milwaukee. Thompson won the governor's race, stunning political experts. As governor, he oversaw Wisconsin's experiment in welfare reform, successfully promoting it as a national model. He was rewarded with an appointment as secretary of health and human services in the George W. Bush administration in 2001.

As with vouchers for private schools, Thompson says he thought up his welfare reform using common sense. As with vouchers, it was a policy change grounded in the conservative view that society's ills were the result of the nanny state's social programs. Government, rather than being responsible for providing a safety net, was seen as a negative force that fostered dependency and laziness. As with vouchers, Wisconsin became a laboratory for making conservative policy dreams come true. Jason DeParle, in his groundbreaking work on welfare reform, *American Dream*, focused on Milwaukee because, he says, it was "the epicenter of the anti-welfare crusade."[10]

This wasn't an accident. The Lynde and Harry Bradley Foundation, as with publicly funded vouchers for private schools, played a pivotal role in promoting Wisconsin's welfare reform. There was also a strong ideological link between the two initiatives, both of which branded government as the source of the problem and looked to the free market and "individual choice" to promote the common good. The reforms, notes political reporter John J. Miller, "were the result of much hard work and thinking—a good deal of it made possible through the philanthropy of the Bradley Foundation."[11]

In 1984, when Thompson was still a state legislator and a decade before Charles Murray would co-author *The Bell Curve*, Murray wrote *Losing Ground*. The book became the bedrock of conservative ideology toward welfare. Always one for bold statements, Murray argued that Aid to Families with Dependent Children—which had its beginnings as a New Deal program during the Great Depression—was an evil that spawned other evils associated with poverty, from crime to single-parent families. In *The Bell Curve*, Murray expanded his antiwelfare argument. "Of all the uncomfortable topics we have explored," he writes in *The Bell Curve*, "a pair of the most uncomfortable ones are that a society with a higher mean IQ is also likely to be a society with fewer social ills and brighter economic prospects, and that the most efficient way to raise the IQ of a society is for smarter women to have higher birth rates than duller women. Instead America is going in the opposite direction."[12] Referring to welfare, Murray argues that the United States "subsidizes births among poor women who are also disproportionately at the low end of the intelligence distribution. We urge generally that these policies, represented by the extensive network of cash and services for low-income women who have babies, be ended."

Thompson shepherded various welfare experiments through the Wisconsin legislature in the 1990s, culminating in the 1997 Welfare Works (W-2) program. Hallmarks consisted of time limits for receiving welfare benefits and requiring that women work as a condition of assistance. (In response to concerns raised by Milwaukee archbishop Rembert Weakland, Thompson fell back on the stereotype that poor black women are looking for easy money, complaining about "these women [who] won't do their end of the deal by working.")[13]

Thompson was not the only person who rose to national fame on the basis of Wisconsin welfare programs. Jason Turner, hired by Thompson in 1993 to implement Wisconsin's reforms, went on to lead New York City's welfare initiative. A prep school graduate from the rarefied world of Darien, Connecticut, Turner had an almost religious belief that once welfare women started working, they would reach the promised land of orderly homes, high-achieving children, and personal fulfillment. He once argued on television that women on welfare would find a job liberating because "it's work that sets you free." He did not realize this was the motto on the gates of Auschwitz.[14]

In 1992, Bill Clinton campaigned for president on a promise to "end welfare as we know it." Four years later, looking over his right shoulder after the Republican Party's 1994 capture of the House for the first time in forty years, President Clinton ended welfare. On August 22, 1996, he signed the Personal Responsibility and Work Opportunity Act. It was a mouthful of a name, but it wonderfully captured welfare reform's underlying ideology.

Milwaukee was a model for welfare reform, and the welfare rolls did indeed diminish. But poverty remained. In Milwaukee, the figures got worse every year. In 1975, just before the federal courts ordered desegregation, 35 percent of elementary school children in the Milwaukee Public Schools were eligible for free or reduced-price lunch. In 1996, just after Clinton's welfare reform, the figure was 69 percent. By 2010, the figure was 82 percent.[15]

At the same time welfare was being replaced/reformed, conservatives called for reinventing public education. Paul Hill, a RAND consultant brought in by Superintendent Fuller to lead decentralization planning within the district, even called his report "Reinventing Public Education." Invariably, the reinvention became embroiled in issues of privatization, teacher unions, bureaucracy, and budget cuts. More often than not, the reinvention promoted a marketplace orientation including public and private schools in which "students and teacher would choose and be chosen by schools." As with welfare and vouchers, Milwaukee was at the center of such debates.

After the failed 1993 building referendum, reform had stalled. The broad, multiracial coalition that had formed to support the building plan fell apart, unable to paper over strategic differences among its members. It didn't take long for differences to dominate, ending the relative unity of the Peterkin era and the first two years of Fuller's administration.

Some referendum proponents advocated reform of the state's funding of public education, with more equitable treatment of Milwaukee and other hard-pressed districts. They also wanted to target proposals by Governor

Thompson to freeze local property taxes, which would severely hamper local education spending. Superintendent Fuller was cool to such a focus, and increasingly aligned himself with business community reforms. Fuller went so far as to oppose a 1994 proposal from the state's Department of Public Instruction to fund smaller classes in the early elementary grades. (The proposal ultimately passed, becoming one of the most popular education reforms within the city's schools.)

After the failed referendum, and as calls for privatizing public education increased, tensions escalated between Fuller and the Milwaukee teachers union. An unexpected issue, staffing at the district's two African American immersion schools, developed into an iconic struggle that shaped public discussion for years to come.

The African American immersion schools were proposed during the Peterkin era. The elementary school, renamed after Martin Luther King Jr., opened in 1991, and the middle school, renamed Malcolm X Academy, opened in 1992. Given the schools' Afrocentric curriculum and black student body, additional black staff were assigned to the school. There was a stumbling block, however. As part of the federal court's desegregation orders from the 1970s, the contract between the district and the teachers union set a minimum and maximum number of African American teachers at every school. The African American immersion schools exceeded the maximum. Even though no white teacher who wanted to teach at either school was denied a placement, and even though the African American positions were filled on the basis of seniority, the contract was technically broken. The union filed a grievance.

In March 1993, an arbitrator's ruling upheld the union view that the staffing violated the contract. In the court of public opinion, however, the union lost. The union was denounced for placing the interests of white teachers above those of African American children, and the union became a lightning rod for all that was wrong with Milwaukee's schools. As Greg Stanford, an African American columnist for the *Milwaukee Journal*, wrote, "The Milwaukee teachers union likes to say its interests are the kids' interests. Baloney . . . In fact, the Milwaukee Teachers' Education Association is a big reason why the schools are in sad shape."[16]

For not the first or last time, the union was criticized as an entrenched bureaucracy trying to preserve privileges for its members, not, as union lore had it, a champion of the little guy against the rich and powerful. Nor did the union learn needed lessons from the controversy over the African American immersion schools. In the spring of 1993, a slate of progressive teachers running for union office was defeated by "old guard" candidates whose main concerns were protecting wages and benefits, getting disruptive students out of the classroom, and eliminating a requirement that teachers live in the city of Milwaukee.

At the time, the union was led by proponents of bread-and-butter unionism who argued that it was the administration's job to oversee educational quality and teacher performance, and that the union's job was to protect teachers' rights. The contract was their bible, and the union was quick to file grievances for any infraction. The school board and administration were viewed as bosses and, in the union leadership's view, adversaries. It didn't help that the union's full-time paid staff was dominated by white men. In 1990, for instance, there was only one African American and four women among the union's twenty-two full- and part-time field staff.[17]

"I will defend teachers, and many of them were performing magic in the classroom," notes Mary Bills, a white liberal who was school board president from 1993 to 1996. "But the union is another matter. We knew the union was critical to reform. We made overtures, but we always hit a brick wall. We all bear some responsibility for what has happened in Milwaukee, but the union more so than most."[18]

In 1997, progressives were elected to leading positions within the teachers union, and African American educator Paulette Copeland became president. She pulled no punches in her criticism of the old guard in both the staff and elected leadership. She called the union's paid staff an "ingrown group of friends" and criticized previous leaders for advocating merely for teachers, not for teachers *and* students.[19] The progressive slate, while winning the presidency and secretary positions, remained a minority on the executive board.

In coming years, under pressure both from union progressives and from public opinion, the union changed some of its most controversial positions—relaxing seniority rules by agreeing to school-based hiring during the spring, and developing partnerships with the administration to deal with ineffective teachers. But as old issues were resolved, new ones emerged. More often than not, the union reluctantly followed the curve of reform rather than being in the lead. Complicating matters, some principals and administrators were known for top-down, authoritarian directives. At the same time, antiunion, free-market forces were insistently pushing privatization proposals. Bread-and-butter union traditionalists used these realities to justify their focus on the contract and their circle-the-wagons approach. A dynamic of opposition over collaboration was established, which ultimately undermined both the teachers union and public education.[20]

At the same time that tensions were increasing between Fuller and the union, Fuller was realizing that reform was difficult. The media continued to treat Fuller with kid gloves, with a few exceptions. "Fuller's vision for the schools is increasingly blurry," *Milwaukee Magazine*'s Bruce Murphy argued in January 1994. "He's a great communicator, yet it's not clear just what the master plan is."

Fuller, with strong support from the business community, found his way forward by focusing on privatization, in particular a plan to bring in charter companies such as the for-profit Edison Project. The privatization issue came to the fore in the spring of 1995. The union-based candidates opposed privatization, and won four of five board seats up for election.

Fuller had enjoyed good relations with the board, which had backed his major initiatives. After the 1995 elections, however, Fuller's agenda was sure to receive increased scrutiny. Two weeks later, on April 18, 1995, Fuller announced he was leaving. Once again, as with Peterkin, a leader who had been initially greeted as a unifying reformer unexpectedly left for a university-based position. Fuller's resignation was doubly painful. He spent the remainder of his political career promoting publicly funded vouchers for private schools.

Shortly after his resignation, but with a few months left as superintendent, Fuller publicly reiterated his support for vouchers. It was a longstanding position, but he had previously honored the school board's request that he not publicly promote vouchers while superintendent. Shortly afterward, he announced the formation of the Institute for the Transformation of

Learning at Marquette University in downtown Milwaukee, with the Bradley Foundation providing significant financial support.[21]

In the summer of 1995, with Fuller's backing, the Wisconsin legislature expanded Milwaukee's voucher program to include private religious schools. It was a strategic advance toward the conservative goal of universal vouchers.

21.

1995: VOUCHERS FOR RELIGIOUS SCHOOLS, ABANDONMENT ADVANCES

Question: So, you're not for vouchers?

Answer: Only if you want to kill public education. That sucking sound you hear is the sound of public schools collapsing with the voucher system.

—Interview with former schoolteacher Frank McCourt,
author of *Angela's Ashes*[1]

David Behrendt was editorial page editor at the *Milwaukee Journal* during the 1990s. As is customary in the media, certain people's phone calls bypass the secretary and go straight to influential editors. In 1990, when the voucher controversy was first surfacing in Milwaukee, Behrendt got a call from "a prominent Milwaukee business executive" who wanted to speak off the record.

"He said some well-connected Powers That Be had concluded that it was finally time to pump taxpayer dollars into the Catholic schools because that was the only way to save them," Behrendt explained years later. "The push would be framed as an effort to help impoverished black children get a better education (Polly Williams's agenda), but that saving the Catholic schools was the driving force. Apparently it was expected, correctly, that the Supreme Court *of this state* would never strike vouchers down as unconstitutional. To coin a phrase, the rest is history."[2]

It took five years, but in 1995 Catholic-school supporters reached their goal. Wisconsin passed legislation expanding the voucher program to pay for tuition at private religious schools. Milwaukee, already home to the country's oldest and biggest voucher program, continued to make educational history.

Despite the contention that expanded vouchers would, above all, help poor black children escape failing public schools, the reality was different. In the 1998–99 school year, legal challenges had been exhausted and the expansion to religious schools was allowed to proceed. Voucher enrollment immediately quadrupled to some six thousand students. Only 25 percent had previously been enrolled in the Milwaukee Public Schools.[3] Most had already been attending a private school. That year, 67 percent of the voucher students attended religious schools.[4] (By 2010, the figure had increased to almost 85 percent, with the voucher worth $6,442 a student.)

When I talk to my friends back in New York City, they are amazed that Milwaukee's voucher program provides public money to religious schools and religiously based instruction—and, furthermore, that this has become the program's dominant feature. Having lived in New York, I appreciate the sensitivity that comes from living in a multiple-religion, non-Christian-centric world. It is precisely the experience of growing up in Milwaukee, however, that helps me understand why there was so little debate over publicly funded vouchers for private religious schools. Religious education in Milwaukee historically has meant two things: Catholic schools and Lutheran schools. Neither group was known for proselytizing, instead rooting their evangelism in good works. Catholics had a well-established and well-respected system, one that in the mid-1960s enrolled some 46,000 students in Catholic elementary schools in Milwaukee County.[5] As for the Lutherans, they were so self-effacing (yet hardworking) that few non-Lutherans realized they had a system of schools.

The Catholic Church is particularly influential in Milwaukee. Partly it's because so many Milwaukeeans were raised Catholic, from Polish, Irish, and Italian immigrants to more recent Latinos. But the Catholic Church also oversees a vast network of institutions, from hospitals to social services and schools. When it comes to education, there are not only the archdiocesan schools but also the more prestigious schools run by the Jesuits. Marquette University, a Jesuit university in downtown Milwaukee, has always been the city's most esteemed school of higher education. Marquette also is home to the city's only law school, and more than one joke has been made about the Marquette mafia's hold over the city's legal institutions.

My brothers attended the all-boys Marquette University High School, while I attended Holy Angels Academy, the elite all-girls school nearby. My first husband attended Marquette High, where we met at a basketball game. Because I was raised Catholic in Milwaukee, there were things I knew in my bones, for instance that Catholics were better than Protestants and Catholic schools were better than public schools, but that it would be a sin of pride to make such boasts publicly. It was also an unspoken rule that one never criticized the parish priest or archbishop, let alone questioned the church's teachings. The pedophilia scandal notwithstanding, that culture still shapes civic discourse in Milwaukee. Publicly criticizing the Catholic Church is not for the faint-hearted.

In 1990, school board member Mary Bills found that out the hard way. In an opinion in the *Wall Street Journal* she noted how several of the non-religious community schools receiving vouchers had originated as Catholic schools, and she referred to Catholic school closings over the years as the church's white ethnic base moved to the suburbs. "The Catholic Church got out of the business of educating poor children in Milwaukee in the 1970s," Bills wrote. Before long, her mailbox was filled with letters from outraged and influential Catholics. As John Stollenwerk, head of the Allen-Edmonds Shoe Corporation and a leading Milwaukee businessman, wrote to Bills, "You are the real problem along with the entire bureaucracy at Vliet Street [the school district's central offices] and none of you can see this. Educating students has nothing to do with your agenda."[6]

The Catholic Church and its influence formed the foundation of support for religious-school vouchers in Milwaukee. But it was the changing political climate that made it possible for the necessary legislation to pass.

On November 9, 1994, the national Democratic Party woke up to a new reality. In elections the day before, Republicans had captured fifty-four seats in the U.S. House, leading to a Republican majority for the first time in forty years. President Bill Clinton's administration spent the next six years responding to a resurgent right. Wisconsin also faced a new reality as Republicans took control of the assembly. Republicans already held the senate and Republican Tommy Thompson was governor, so the victories meant clear sailing for the conservative agenda in Wisconsin. (Sixteen years later, there was a disturbing replay of the same political dynamics: a Republican/Tea Party surge during the November 2010 elections allowed Wisconsin governor Scott Walker to launch his attacks on public education and public sector unions.)

In education, Thompson moved quickly. That February, his proposed state budget expanded the publicly funded voucher program to include private religious schools. Conservatives successfully sold the expansion as "choice" rather than "paroch-aid" for religious schools, a formulation that had never gained political traction. "The repackaging and new spin of this old idea was brilliant politics which totally reshuffled the political deck," noted Mordecai Lee, a political scientist who served twelve years in the Wisconsin assembly and senate.[7]

Developing a game plan that would be perfected by Walker in 2011, Thompson's educational measures were a Republican wish list. Thompson not only expanded vouchers but instituted a permanent cap on public school spending and reconfigured education funding in order to lower property taxes while letting stand the inequities between rich and poor school districts. Thompson had thrown "everything in but the kitchen sink," complained Mary Bills, the school board president. "It all leads to the fundamental conservative position, which is to reduce the cost of education now and into the future."[8]

Thompson enjoyed strong business community support for his education agenda. The Metropolitan Milwaukee Association of Commerce, in particular, had increasingly moved toward private school vouchers as the solution to problems within public education. Gone were the sentiments of two years earlier, when the CEO of Harley-Davidson optimistically called on the business community to work shoulder to shoulder with the public schools.

In mid-February 1995, the association of commerce met with the new editorial board of the about-to-be combined *Milwaukee Journal* and *Milwaukee Sentinel*. Eager to influence the new editorial board and reflecting a disdain toward the Milwaukee Public Schools that had become the modus operandi in the business community, the chair of the association's education committee said that the voucher program needed to include religious schools because the public schools were creating "an army of illiterates with no skills." The committee chair was Richard Abdoo, CEO of Wisconsin Energy Corp., a major employer in the city. Abdoo went on to extol the benefits of Catholic schools and to praise students at Messmer High School. "In the [Milwaukee Public Schools] system, they'd be in a gang somewhere," he said.[9]

The head of the commerce association, Peter O'Toole, took a softer approach and said that an expanded voucher program would be good competition that would force the public schools to improve. Milwaukee Public Schools have "had no competition because every year their budget goes up," said O'Toole, who was CEO of A.O. Smith, a major Milwaukee corporation.

Both arguments were essential to the voucher expansion, allowing pro-voucher forces to build a formidable coalition. The "army of illiterates" argument appealed to those who, susceptible to negative stereotypes of poor black people, had already given up on the city's public schools. The competition argument appealed to those who, while supporting public education, were swayed by the drumbeat of criticism—often exaggerated but also grounded in legitimate problems—that the public schools were incapable of reforming themselves. The most ardent supporters of public education, meanwhile, found themselves on the defensive. They had no equally compelling vision of reform. They relied instead on long-standing views that good schools were based on good teaching, a challenging curriculum, adequate resources, respect for diversity, and an economically viable community—a formula that did not lend itself to media sound bites.

The Republican Party "has captured the public perception that it is the party of 'new ideas,'" Mordecai Lee noted. "Whether this is substantively true or not is irrelevant. In politics, perception is reality. Naturally, the corollary of that image is that groups on the other side are viewed as opposing change, being defenders of a 'bad' status quo."[10]

On July 27, 1995, Governor Thompson signed legislation expanding publicly funded vouchers to religious schools and increasing the cap on private voucher school enrollment to about fifteen thousand students—15 percent of the enrollment in the Milwaukee Public Schools. More than a hundred private schools, mostly religious, immediately applied to become part of the voucher program.

At the same time, the private religious schools did not want to abandon their culture of independence from public oversight and accountability. While the initial program in 1990 called for an annual study evaluating student performance, that oversight was eliminated when religious schools came on board. (The studies had found the private voucher schools and the Milwaukee Public Schools performing at roughly the same levels.)

Given the momentous step of providing public money for religiously based instruction, few were surprised when the courts delayed implementation until First Amendment issues were resolved. In 1998, however, the Wisconsin supreme court ruled that the expansion was constitutional and could proceed in the 1998–99 school year. The U.S. Supreme Court did not accept an appeal, allowing the decision to stand.

That summer, a controversy erupted over whether the private voucher schools would be required to follow state law prohibiting discrimination against students in public schools. Critics of vouchers had long argued that if private schools were receiving public money, they should follow the same rules as public schools. With the inclusion of religious schools, the issue took on added importance. Six of the religious schools applying for admission to the private voucher school program were single-sex schools.[11]

As part of the application process to become a voucher school, the state Department of Public Instruction included a letter outlining the rights of students in public schools, and noted that it believed the private voucher schools should follow the measures. The rights ranged from nondiscrimination on the basis of sex, sexual orientation, and pregnancy status to provisions for following constitutional due process when students were suspended or expelled. The controversy stemmed not just from the actual antidiscrimination measures but also from the voucher schools' desire to maintain their status as private institutions. "No one here is pro-discrimination," John Norris, superintendent of schools for the Archdiocese of Milwaukee, told the *Milwaukee Journal Sentinel*. "The debate is, what kind of schools are we talking about? Are they private schools or public schools?"[12]

The issue was resolved when the Wisconsin Department of Public Instruction said the private voucher school principals or administrators merely had to sign a letter acknowledging that they had received the letter in which the department outlined the student rights. The letter was modified to state: "This acknowledgment is not to be construed as an agreement between DPI and the school or as an admission that the student rights provisions attached hereto apply to private schools participating in the choice program."

Representative Polly Williams, known as the "mother of school choice," was upset with the expansion to religious schools, and complained that the business community was hijacking the program for its own purposes.[13] "We've got our black agenda and they have got [their own] agenda," Williams said. "I didn't see where their resources really were being used to empower us as much as it was to co-opt us."[14]

It's a hot summer day in 2010, with the midday sun beating down. The Atkinson Library in Milwaukee's central city is supposed to open at 1:00 P.M., but it's 1:10 P.M. and the doors are still locked. An impatient group of African Americans paces the sidewalk. The library finally opens and people rush in to grab seats at the computer tables. Polly Williams, who often uses the library as an informal office, has agreed to meet me there, and we are among the waiting crowd. We are ushered into an air-conditioned meeting room, the cooler air helping to ease our nerves. We are both unsure how the interview will unfold.

Williams had previously announced she would retire in the fall after thirty years in the Wisconsin legislature. Never one to mince words, her pending retirement makes her blunter than usual. "I see things in terms of black and white," she announces shortly after the interview begins.

Williams has always been up-front that she is a black nationalist with a focus on the black community. She'll work with whites when she needs to, but she doesn't trust them. Now seventy-three years old, she has come, quite literally, to embody her practice. Her short and stylish hair has, over the years, become a salt-and-pepper mixture. Even her glasses are black and white, the black frames highlighted with black-and-white zebra patterns.

A former welfare mom and single mother of four (and now with seven grandchildren and two great-grandchildren), Williams came to Milwaukee in 1946 from Belzoni, Mississippi, when she was ten years old. Her father worked at a tannery, and her cousin Monroe Swan was elected to the Wisconsin state senate in 1972. Williams herself was elected to the state assembly in 1980. Above all, she is identified as the founding mother of the Milwaukee voucher program. But it has become a bittersweet legacy. "In no way was it our intent, in any way, to harm the Milwaukee Public Schools," Williams says of the private school voucher program. "Our intent was always to show the Milwaukee Public Schools that, see, if parents had more say, see how much better off the student would be. And to replicate that in the public schools."

Williams has long had a love-hate relationship with the public schools. It's not unusual for political leaders to take policy positions that deviate from their choices as parents; Williams is no exception. As a politician, she opposed metropolitan-area-wide desegregation; as a parent, she tried (unsuccessfully) to sign her daughter up for a suburban school as part of the Chapter 220 program. As a politician, she supported efforts to maintain North Division, her alma mater, as a neighborhood school; as a parent, she fought to make sure her daughter went to Riverside University High School, known for its college prep program.[15]

Williams has consistently argued that she wanted the private voucher school movement to serve the needs of black parents and the black community. For a few years, when she felt an alignment between her goals and the voucher movement, Williams was the star of the national voucher movement. She was featured in the *Wall Street Journal* and appeared on CNN and *This Week with David Brinkley*. She spoke before conservative gatherings across the country—including "An Evening with Polly Williams" in 1990 with luminaries such as Vice President Dan Quayle and the up-and-coming Newt Gingrich. Between 1990 and 1997, she earned more than $163,000 on the conservative talk circuit. She was even flown to New Zealand to promote her voucher initiative.[16]

The schism began with the 1995 expansion that included public dollars for religious schools and eliminated requirements that the voucher schools have at least 35 percent private-paying students. Williams started publicly complaining. "The conservatives made me their poster girl as long as it appeared I was supporting their case," Williams told *USA Today*. "And now I am the odd person out. They want the religious schools to be tax-supported. Blacks and poor are being used to help legitimize them as the power group." Before long, the schism could not be papered over and Williams was persona non grata in the national voucher movement. "She's off the conservative circuit," one close observer told *Milwaukee Magazine*.[17]

Although she has deep criticisms of how the voucher program has evolved, Williams is reluctant to let go of her legacy. "If I had to do it all over again, I would," she says during our talk at the Atkinson Library. "But I would be wiser, knowing what I know now, the things that are happening now that I don't agree with." In particular, she would try to make sure the private voucher schools hire more experienced teachers of color, that schools adopt a multicultural curriculum, and, above all, that the black community, not whites or white-controlled schools, would benefit.

Williams is also perplexed about the way forward for education reform. Asked what she would do if she were magically named superintendent, she is stumped. "Oh, boy," she says. "I don't know where to start, I really don't. The problems are so great." She shakes her head, purses her lips. We move on to new topics. As she talks, she increasingly focuses on the overarching problem of racism in Milwaukee. Whether you talk about teachers unions, the private voucher schools, the public schools, or charter schools, Williams steers the conversation back to that constant. "As long as you have white people with power making decisions about people of color, it is never going to work the way it should," she says.

For now, Williams is turning her attention toward the Milwaukee Public Schools, where most black children still go to school, especially low-income black students with special education needs or those who, for disciplinary or educational reasons, are not welcome at the private voucher schools. In 2010, Milwaukee hired Philadelphia native Gregory Thornton as the first African American superintendent in fifteen years. In our interview at Atkinson Library, Williams said her main focus is on protecting Thornton's political back. "I know people have the knives ready for him," she says.

Just as Williams was distancing herself from the voucher movement, conservative foundations and think tanks had a new African American spokesman from Milwaukee to promote publicly funded vouchers for private schools. In 1995, Howard Fuller seamlessly segued from Milwaukee superintendent to national proponent of vouchers.

Fuller himself doesn't speak much about his meteoric rise as national spokesperson for the voucher movement. Michael Joyce, when still head of the Bradley Foundation, explained it this way: "[Williams] was poised to be and could have been the leader of school choice. But she stepped aside and Fuller became the leader."[18] Williams has a different version: she didn't step aside but was pushed aside because she disagreed with the conservative, free-market vision of vouchers. "Howard . . . is the person that the white people have selected to lead the choice movement now because I don't cooperate," she said.[19]

While there are sharp differences in people's evaluations of Fuller's role in educational politics, some appraisals are universal: he is charismatic, articulate, handsome, self-confident, hardworking, politically shrewd. He has gained levels of achievement rare for an African American man in Milwaukee: member of the governor's cabinet, school superintendent, head of a university institute, presidential adviser, nationally prominent speaker. Even those who disagree with him are awed by his preacher-like sensibilities of performance and persuasion—with an uncanny ability to adapt his cadence, diction, and arguments to accommodate his audience and win them over.

A convert to Catholicism at a young age, a Marxist radical in the 1960s, and an educational consultant to George W. Bush, Fuller is filled with contradictions that have allowed him to re-create himself and nimbly respond to changing political dynamics.

Fuller, for instance, was a proponent of black separatism and a separate black school district, yet he himself found success at integrated or all-white schools his entire life—St. Boniface grade school (where he was the only black in his third-grade class), an integrated North Division (where he helped lead the basketball team to the state finals), Carroll College (where he was the first black male to graduate), and Marquette University, where he earned his doctoral degree. Able to quote Malcolm X, Frederick Douglass, and W.E.B. Du Bois with ease, he finds his most consistent and strongest support from conservative foundations and influential Republicans, in particular the Walton Family Foundation of Wal-Mart fame and the Bradley Foundation of *Bell Curve* fame. Though he was an opponent of metropolitan desegregation in the 1980s, two decades later he did not publicly oppose an expansion allowing Milwaukee voucher students to attend school anywhere in the state. An unrelenting critic of low academic achievement in the Milwaukee Public Schools, he admitted in 2011 that he found running even a single school "sobering." (The voucher school he helped found seven years earlier had some of the lowest scores of any school, voucher or public, when voucher school results were released publicly for the first time.)[20]

Through it all, Fuller has maintained an almost blessed relationship with the media. A longtime political reporter in Milwaukee once dubbed him "a reporter's dream. There's nothing more deadly to a news story than a dull source with lackluster opinions." Fuller, in contrast, "is endlessly quotable: He's frank, opinionated, down-to-earth and always, always articulate."[21] In the media, as in basketball and politics, Fuller likes to be on the winning side.

Fuller's successes belie difficult childhood years. Born in Louisiana in 1941, he lived with his grandmother until he was six years old, then moved to Milwaukee to join his mother and stepfather. He didn't know his father, and his stepfather drank himself to death. "Because of the drinking, there were a lot of physical things that happened between him and my mother," he related in a *Milwaukee Magazine* feature in 1988. "So I always hated him for it."[22] At the same time, Fuller has fond memories of Milwaukee in the 1950s, a time when most people did not lock their doors and few people knew they were poor. He doesn't remember ever being denied anything as a child.

During the tumultuous 1960s, Fuller was gone from Milwaukee. After receiving a master's in social work at Case Western Reserve University, he worked briefly for the Urban League in Chicago and then moved to Durham, North Carolina, for a community organizing job. He quickly rose to become a leader in the black power movement. In 1969, then going by the name Owusu Sadaukai, he helped found Malcolm X Liberation University. In 1971, he spent a month with Marxist guerrillas in Mozambique. Shortly afterward, Malcolm X University was beset with factionalism and closed. Fuller was briefly a union organizer, and in 1976 he helped organize a national meeting of the Revolutionary Workers League. Details are murky, but the experience left him physically exhausted and close to a breakdown. "Without telling anybody, Fuller left his public life and family in North Carolina [he had a wife and children] and limped home to Milwaukee," *Milwaukee Magazine* recounts. He recovered, sold insurance, and after a year became involved in politics around education and police brutality. Before long, he was a household name in Milwaukee.

By the 1990s Fuller had settled on what would be his lasting claim to fame: publicly funded private school vouchers, marketed as parental choice. He supported the idea in the late 1980s but refrained from public comments while superintendent. After his resignation in 1995, he devoted the rest of his career to "choice" initiatives, encompassing private school vouchers, charter schools, and tuition tax credits. His single-minded focus was such that publicly funded vouchers for private schools became a litmus test. In 1999, he became an educational adviser to George W. Bush during his campaign for president. "There is no room for someone like me with someone like Al Gore," Fuller told the *Milwaukee Journal Sentinel*. He went on to note that he had visited Bush in Texas and was pleasantly surprised. "I ended up liking him a lot," Fuller said. "It was supposed to be a half-hour meeting and ended up lasting an hour and a half."

In 2008, meanwhile, Fuller took presidential candidate Barack Obama to task for not supporting private school vouchers (although he publicly supported Obama over McCain). "He sends his kids to private schools, but yet questions the value of vouchers because there is 'no proof that they work,'" Fuller said in a press release two weeks before the presidential election. "I don't know what he means when he questions whether or not they work. The vouchers 'work' if they give parents the option to choose."[23]

Fuller's support of vouchers has been well rewarded by conservative foundations. The Institute for the Transformation of Learning at Marquette University, which Fuller founded shortly after resigning as superintendent, has received almost $14 million in grants, much of it from conservative foundations.[24] The Bradley Foundation, for instance, granted almost $4 million to Fuller's institute from 1995 to 2010.[25]

In 2000, the institute launched the Black Alliance for Educational Options, a national organization with chapters throughout the country that has been Fuller's main organizing base. Providing a budget of around $3 million in recent years, the alliance's funders have been a veritable who's who of conservative foundations. The most significant support has been from the Walton Family Foundation (which provided $900,000 in start-up funds in 2000) and the Bradley Foundation. Between 2001 and 2008, Walton reportedly donated almost $7 million, and Bradley another $2 million.[26]

From the beginning, the black alliance's strategy has rested on framing publicly funded private school vouchers as a civil rights issue, even though the group's main financial support has been from conservatives aligned with the Republican Party. Its first national ad campaign began soon after the group's founding, in November 2000, with print ads in national newspapers such as the *Washington Post* and *New York Times*, and in black community newspapers across the country.[27] The campaign escalated the following spring. The *Christian Science Monitor* reported in July 2001 that the alliance's ad buys were worth as much as $3 million—an enviable feat for an organization that was only a year old. A subsequent study by the Annenberg Public

Policy Center found that the alliance's 2001 ads in Washington, D.C., alone cost $4.33 million. During the 2001–2 period studied, the alliance's spending made it the fourth-largest spender in that market, surpassing the AARP and Lockheed Martin.

The media blitz was part of a strategy to shape public opinion for upcoming political and legal battles. The main obstacle confronting the voucher movement at that point was the U.S. Constitution. Did publicly funded vouchers for religious schools violate the First Amendment's separation of church and state?

"We pledge allegiance to the Christian flag and to the Savior for whose Kingdom it stands, One Savior crucified, risen and coming again with life, liberty for all those who believe."

Students at Calvary Center Academy in Cleveland recited this pledge every day of the 2001–2 school year—with the support of public tax dollars. That fall, the U.S. Supreme Court agreed to decide whether Cleveland's program of publicly funded vouchers for private and religious schools violated the First Amendment and was thus unconstitutional.

The Court took up a federal appeals court decision that the Cleveland program violated church/state separation. At the time, Cleveland's and Milwaukee's were the only voucher programs in the country providing money for religious schools. Some 4,250 students received vouchers in Cleveland, compared to about 10,500 students in Milwaukee. There was also a two-year pilot program in Florida involving about fifty students.

Everyone knew that the Court's decision would reverberate far beyond Cleveland, which instituted its program in 1995 after Republicans, just as in Wisconsin, took control of the Ohio house. Lawyers on both sides compared the case's significance to *Brown v. Board*. When the nine justices gathered to hear the case on February 20, 2002, protesters on both sides gathered near the august columns of the U.S. Supreme Court.

Inside, the justices extended the oral arguments beyond the usual sixty minutes. Justice Antonin Scalia most aggressively questioned the view that the program constituted government aid to religion, noting that the money was allocated on the basis of the individual choices of parents. "Unless there is an endorsement of religion involved here, I don't see why the fact that some of the money, even most of the money, goes to religious schools, makes any difference," he said. (As in Milwaukee, the voucher check was made out to individual parents but sent directly to the voucher schools, where the parent endorsed the check and handed it to the school.) Justice Scalia also embraced the voucher proponents' argument that the Cleveland schools were a monopoly and that this monopoly was the source of public school failures in the city.[28]

Justice David Souter seemed most disturbed by the religious nature of the Cleveland voucher program, with 96 percent of the voucher students attending religious schools. "At the end of the day," he said, "the effect is a massive amount of money into religious schools."[29] Voucher advocates meanwhile argued that the program was neutral toward religion because there was a variety of publicly funded options for parents in Cleveland, from traditional public schools to public magnet schools, public charter schools, and the voucher program.

That June, on the final day of the 2002 term, the justices ruled 5–4 that the Cleveland program did not violate the constitutional separation of church and state. "We believe the program challenged here is a program of true private choice," wrote Chief Justice William Rehnquist. "The Ohio program is neutral in all respects toward religion. It is part of a general and multifaceted undertaking by the State of Ohio to provide educational opportunities to the children of a failed school district."

The U.S. Supreme Court decision resolved concerns about the constitutionality of Milwaukee's voucher program, and the Milwaukee program grew significantly. But cracks began to appear in the free-market foundational belief that the hidden hand of parents would provide sufficient accountability because, in theory, parents would leave a failing voucher school. Accountability, not constitutionality, soon became the center of controversy.

While I was managing editor at *Rethinking Schools*, I would often get phone calls from reporters around the country. They would ask me for a thirty-second sound bite on academic quality at Milwaukee's voucher schools. I replied that voucher schools varied even more than public schools. There were some good voucher schools, especially those that predated the voucher program. There were lots of average schools. And there were some not-so-great schools.

None of the not-so-great schools, however, compared to the problems at Alex's Academic of Excellence.[30]

On May 3, 2000, the CEO of Alex's Academic of Excellence, forty-eight-year-old James A. Mitchell, stood before a circuit court judge and was sentenced to six months on charges of tax fraud unrelated to the voucher school. It wasn't the first time Mitchell had been sentenced to jail. Three decades earlier he had been convicted of rape after he and a friend slapped, threatened to kill, and raped a woman at knifepoint.[31] He was sentenced to thirty years, paroled in 1980, and then returned to prison until 1984 for a burglary that violated parole. In 1991 he founded a treatment center for juveniles, but it went out of business.

In 1999, Mitchell started Alex's Academic of Excellence. Parents and staff had raised concerns about the school, but the state's Department of Public Instruction had limited authority to regulate the private voucher schools. The school moved several times after building inspectors found numerous code violations. Mitchell, meanwhile, was paid about $58,000 by the voucher school, which was owned by Mitchell's girlfriend, Diane Anthony. (When a court investigator asked Anthony the address of the school, she couldn't remember it.)

The tax fraud conviction led to increased scrutiny of Alex's Academic of Excellence. When circuit judge Elsa Lamelas sentenced Mitchell, she said the case "raises so many questions about what is going on at that school." Lamelas also criticized the voucher program overall. "It seems that it's easy pickings for people who are not inclined to be honest," she said.

The state Department of Public Instruction had minimal ability to close a private voucher school as long as it met city occupancy permits and submitted regular financial audits. In 2003, Alex's again made the news when teachers, landlords, and bus companies said they were not paid, former administrators said there was illegal drug use at the school, and a school employee physically threatened two reporters who visited the school that September. At the time, there were growing calls for accountability, but voucher supporters fought back. "Many of the people who will use Alex's as a poster child are not interested in improving the program, but destroying it," Fuller told the *Milwaukee Journal Sentinel*.[32]

A few years later, in 2005, there was a disturbing rash of voucher school horror stories. At that time, nearly fourteen thousand students received vouchers to attend private schools, at a cost of $83 million to the taxpayers. In line with the free-market view of voucher proponents that parental choice was a sufficient safeguard, public oversight was minimal. "Few people, even state officials, know what is going on inside all 115 schools in the program," the *Milwaukee Journal Sentinel* noted.[33]

The first scandal to surface that year was in January. The Milwaukee County district attorney's office investigated Academic Solutions Center for Learning following a fight at the school that police said "included over 100 students, chaotically fighting among themselves." The school, which had more than seven hundred voucher students, was ordered closed on grounds that it was unsafe. Students told police there were not many teachers at the school because they were not getting paid. A month later, the Milwaukee County district attorney's office was asked to investigate another voucher school, the Louis Tucker Academy. Among other things, the school falsified attendance records and student applications. The school, which started the school year with seventy-six students, subsequently closed.

Problems continued in the summer and fall. In August, the former chief financial officer at Harambee Community School was found guilty of fifteen charges related to embezzling up to $750,000 from the school.[34] In October, the founder of the Mandella School of Science and Math was convicted of stealing $330,000 from the state via the voucher program. Among other things, founder David Seppeh used the money to buy two Mercedes-Benzes, including a $43,000 convertible titled in the school's name. Teachers, meanwhile, went unpaid.[35] (The school was supposed to be named after antiapartheid leader Nelson Mandela, but Seppeh spelled the name wrong.) That same month, state officials ordered the Ida B. Wells Academy out of the program because it did not meet minimum standards even to be considered a school (it had only twenty-three students). In December, Northside High School was ordered closed because it did not provide a minimum number of hours of instruction and the school had no developed curriculum.

Even schools that were not closed had questionable practices. In an investigation of voucher schools published in the summer of 2005, *Milwaukee Journal Sentinel* reporters estimated that about 10 percent of the schools they visited demonstrated "alarming deficiencies," without "the ability, resources, knowledge or will to offer children even a mediocre education." Some schools were nothing more than refurbished, cramped storefronts, such as a former tire store. Some did not have any discernable curriculum. Some did not teach evolution or anything that might conflict with a literal interpretation of the Bible. One school kept lights off in order to save money. Another used the back alley as a playground. At the Sa'Rai and Zigler Upper Excellerated Academy, principal Sa'Rai said she opened the school after she had a vision from God. She said that the word *upper* referred to "the upper room where Jesus prayed." The word *excellerated* was a fusion word combining *accelerated* and *excellent* and was "spelled wrong on purpose."

By 2006, with entrepreneurs rushing in to start voucher schools, the program was reaching its fifteen-thousand-student cap. Voucher proponents wanted a further expansion. But concerns over the lack of public oversight and accountability had become widespread.

Republicans controlled the state assembly and senate, but Democrat James Doyle was governor. Legislative initiatives required compromise. The year before, the state budget had added the provision that teachers at voucher schools be high school graduates.[36] But Doyle wanted to take accountability further. He wanted voucher schools to be accredited, which was an essential step in preventing fly-by-night schools from receiving voucher money. He also wanted voucher students to take nationally normed standardized tests.

Voucher proponents unleashed a media campaign attacking Doyle and framing vouchers as a civil rights issue. Radio spots compared Doyle, the adoptive parent of two African American sons, to southern governors Orval Faubus and George Wallace and their refusal in the 1960s to allow black children to enter white schools. It was a long-standing tactic among voucher supporters, going back to comments in 1990 against then Wisconsin state superintendent Herbert Grover. In the fall of 2003, when the U.S. Congress was debating vouchers for Washington, D.C., the pro-voucher campaign compared Senator Edward Kennedy, a voucher opponent, to segregationist Eugene "Bull" Connor, who had used police dogs to attack civil rights demonstrators in Birmingham. (As recently as August 2010, Fuller used the tactic, this time against teachers unions. Speaking before a national conference of the KIPP charter school chain and referring to Randi Weingarten, head of the American Federation of Teachers, Fuller said: "People like her, with all due respect, they are standing in the way of progress for our children. And these people believe, like one time George Wallace stood at the

door trying to keep our kids from getting in, and people like her are standing at the door keeping our kids from getting out.... Until we confront
these people, and quit talking to them like they really want to do so much
for our kids, we are not getting anywhere.")[37]

The 2006 voucher expansion ultimately passed, as part of a broader compromise. The cap was increased to 22,500 students, and any student, whether
or not he or she had ever attended a public school, could receive a voucher. In
addition, income eligibility was modified. Previously, voucher students were
to be members of families with incomes at or below 175 percent of the poverty level. Under the expansion, once a student was in the voucher program,
family income could increase up to 220 percent of the poverty level.

In return for the expansion, voucher schools faced Doyle's new, if limited,
accountability measures. This included the requirement that the voucher
students be required to take standardized tests. At the same time, the private
voucher schools did not have to release the test scores publicly; they were required only to provide the scores to a national group of researchers as part of
a longitudinal study. In addition, voucher schools were to be accredited.
(There is no accreditation process for new private schools in Wisconsin, nor
any requirement that teachers or administrators be licensed. It wasn't until
2010 that teachers in the private voucher schools were required to have a
bachelor's degree from an accredited college.)[38]

After the 2006 expansion, it became increasingly clear that the voucher
program, rather than providing an option for public school students, was
primarily a subsidy of private, religiously based education. When vouchers
expanded in the fall of 2006–7, some 60 percent of the new voucher students had already been in private school.[39]

Interestingly, in 1989, the year before the voucher program began, there
were 29,988 students in private schools in Milwaukee.[40] In 2010, the number was almost exactly the same—29,528 students.[41] The difference was
that most of the students (20,996) received publicly funded vouchers to pay
the tuition.[42] Roughly 85 percent of those voucher students attended a religious school, in particular a Catholic or Lutheran school.[43]

The expansion to religious schools put the Milwaukee voucher program on
a new trajectory. What had started as an experiment to help a couple of
hundred students became a system of state-funded private schools whose

size rivaled the state's largest school districts—but with minimal public accountability.

The false promise of vouchers also provided a rationale to further abandon Milwaukee's public schools; vouchers meant there was a private system that could step into the breach. To confound problems, before long policy makers adopted initiatives for the public schools that mimicked rather than challenged free-market policies and diminished educational options for low-income students and students of color.

The era of neighborhood schools and open enrollment was about to begin.

22.

1999: (RE)SEGREGATION DÉJÀ VU—NEIGHBORHOOD SCHOOLS AND OPEN ENROLLMENT

Tonight marks the end of forced busing and the beginning of
real reform.
> —Board president Bruce Thompson, on the Milwaukee school board's
> 1999 return to neighborhood schools

You're raising your kids, sandwiching in family dinners, visits with Grandma, after-school events, and parent-teacher conferences, and through it all hoping that some worksheet-obsessed teacher hasn't assigned too much homework. Months fly by, the blur that is the life of a working parent. Who has time to follow school board proceedings? It's only when you have the time to look back that you realize the extent of the changes, and how seemingly disparate developments fit together.

Such were the 1990s in Milwaukee. The move to expand the program of publicly funded vouchers to include private religious schools became the bedrock for other strategic shifts. By the decade's end, the vision of a public school system balancing the needs of all children had essentially vanished. The free-market consumer mentality dominated. Parents focused on their individual child, principals on their individual school. Voucher schools defended their right to be funded by the taxpayer yet remain private schools. Charter schools arrived and soon protected their particular niche.

The developments were shaped by the broader political context not just in Milwaukee but also across the country. Desegregation was passé, and Martin's Luther King Jr.'s vision of a color-blind society had been twisted to mean that policies enhancing racial balance were un-American. Issues of class intersected with race, and people who were both poor and black or Latino became the new unwelcome.

As poverty increased, the mission of Milwaukee Public Schools expanded. Over the years the district has become the city's largest social services agency. It oversees a breakfast and lunch program serving tens of thousands of children, and after-school programs from pre-kindergarten through high school. School-based nurses, psychologists, and social workers provide direct services and also act as liaisons with agencies throughout the city. The Milwaukee Public Schools are also a major employer, with some ten thousand employees and a budget surpassing $1 billion.[1]

Throughout all the changes and controversies of the last half century, the Milwaukee Public Schools have remained the educational home for the city's children—the place where, when you knock on the door, they let you in.

One quote came to symbolize the philosophy of the powers that be in the 1990s. Fittingly, it happened in the new public commons: the coffee shop. Not the coffee shop of the 1950s, with its meat loaf and mashed potatoes, but the coffee shop of the twenty-first century, with its lattes and biscotti.

On February 21, 2000, at a Starbucks near Marquette University, divinity student and doctoral candidate Elijah Mueller stopped in for a coffee and some quiet study time. School board members John Gardner and Bruce Thompson happened to be at the Starbucks talking about the district's decision to return to neighborhood schools. Gardner was a self-described progressive whose libertarian, free-market beliefs led him to consistently refer to public schools as "government schools." He was known for his pontifications, delivering his pronouncements in a bombastic voice. His remarks easily traveled in Starbucks' small confines. Mueller, who had a three-year-old son whom he was hoping to enroll in the public schools the following fall, found it impossible not to pay attention. Trained by decades of schooling and with a master's degree in biblical languages, Mueller began to take notes. He captured verbatim Gardner's view of the essential conundrum facing the Milwaukee school district. "We need to insulate wealthy and white students from the floaters," Gardner said.[2]

Thompson and Gardner were upset when word got out of their Starbucks tête-à-tête, with Thompson writing a letter of complaint to university officials. Gardner did not deny the veracity of Mueller's account.

In that moment of seeming privacy, Gardner articulated what many people had suspected—that the neighborhood schools initiative was, at its core, a rationalization for resegregating the schools by race and class. "We should all be grateful to have the racial intent of the Neighborhood Schools Initiative out in the open," political commentator Joel McNally said of the incident.

It wasn't the first time Gardner's blunt statements made news. A year earlier he had opposed a proposal to provide laptop computers to high school students unless "there isn't some process to make sure kids aren't selling them for cocaine."[3]

The return to neighborhood schools was a conscious decision to abandon racial integration as the guiding process in school selection and assignment. Harking back to a 1950s mind-set, school board members said that housing patterns, this time between city and suburb rather than within city neighborhoods, made integrated schools impossible.

Unlike the struggle to desegregate, which took a fourteen-year court battle, the return to neighborhood schools happened quickly. It was proposed by Republican governor Tommy Thompson in his 1999 state budget, passed by the legislature, supported by a newly elected school board majority, subjected to widespread but perfunctory community meetings, and given final approval in 2000.

As with many policy turnarounds, the media shaped the debate. The battle centered on sound bites of "neighborhood schools" versus "forced busing," the very terms creating an imbalance. For many, the phrase *neighborhood school* evoked nostalgic 1950s visions of children happily walking to school, perhaps with Mom and the family dog. Within the black and Latino communities, some equated the phrase with a vision of community-controlled schools honoring the input of parents and families. All things being equal, why wouldn't one want a school grounded in one's neighborhood?

The phrase *forced busing*, meanwhile, conjured up negative images of young children dragged unwillingly onto a bus by government bureaucrats. It became an emotional catchall for everything that seemed to be wrong with urban education.

Fundamentally, however, the Milwaukee Public Schools' neighborhood schools initiative was based not on memories of an idealized past but on politics. And the politics were simple: segregated neighborhood schools were deemed preferable to integrated schools, especially given the overwhelming poverty within Milwaukee's African American community and the double stigma of being both black and poor.

The federal court order mandating desegregation of the Milwaukee schools was, in part, the result of Milwaukee's refusal to integrate its housing. But much of Milwaukee's power elite had never been comfortable with desegregation, and their main concern had been that there be no violence as in Boston. Over the years, as worries of violence subsided, other concerns came to the fore. Desegregation cost a lot. It was complicated. It relied on racial quotas and admissions lotteries. It exacerbated white flight to the suburbs, a key factor in Milwaukee's status as one of the most segregated districts in the country.[4] In the black community, meanwhile, many still smarted from the fact that blacks bore the brunt of busing for desegregation.

On a practical level, the neighborhood schools initiative was promoted as a way to build more schools in black neighborhoods, an enticing argument after the failed building referendum of 1993. Money saved on busing was to be used to build new schools and build additions onto existing K–5 schools as part of a move toward K–8 schools—which was popular with some principals because upper elementary students received higher per-pupil funding.

Ultimately, however, the rhetoric of ending forced busing was a way "to force children to stay in their neighborhood schools," argued McNally. Interestingly, the people promoting neighborhood schools were also ardently supporting voucher schools, whose bedrock principle was "choice."

"It's ironic that at a time when the new cliché in education is choice—public school choice, private school choice, religious school choice—the one group of parents and children who are seeing their choices being taken away are those attending Milwaukee Public Schools," McNally noted.

The return to neighborhood schools was a particular priority of Mayor John Norquist, who had long railed against desegregation's "social engineering" and who was keenly interested in wooing middle-class whites back to the city. The neighborhood schools plan seemed to fit—too conveniently, some thought—with a long-standing desire by some city leaders to make Milwaukee "safe" for white people by gentrifying certain neighborhoods and reestablishing neighborhood schools.[5]

The *Milwaukee Journal Sentinel*, forgetting the segregationist/white-supremacist origins of the "forced busing" slogan, repeatedly used the phrase in its headlines and stories—and conveniently ignored that parents liked the bus. For many, busing solved the question of how to get their child to school given complicated work schedules and the rampant problem of neighborhood safety. Others liked the bus because it was free transportation to the school of their choice, which didn't necessarily correspond to the closest school. At the time of the reform, fewer than 20 percent of public school families were choosing their neighborhood school as part of the district's three-choice selection process.[6]

Over the years, choosing a school had become ingrained in the city's educational culture. What's more, parents had come to like the concept of specialty schools, developed during desegregation, whether for arts, language immersion, or programs such as Montessori or Waldorf education. "Despite much of the rhetoric, . . . busing today is mostly voluntary," noted a 1999 analysis by the Public Policy Forum, a civic, nonpartisan research organization.[7] In the 1999–2000 school year, 82 percent of Milwaukee public school students got their first-choice school, and 89 percent got one of their top three preferred schools. Everyone knew that busing cost a lot. But it had become the price paid for Milwaukee's unwillingness to desegregate housing and to develop a more rational and equitable desegregation plan that included mandatory busing of both whites and blacks.

Like publicly funded vouchers for private schools, the neighborhood schools reform passed primarily because of an alliance between unlikely interests, including black nationalists, the white business community, and a varied grouping of those who felt that money spent on busing and desegregation could be better spent elsewhere. The plan was approved by the state legislature in the summer of 1999, with the school board to work out the details. A cross section of parents and community groups spoke up against the neighborhood schools plan, with concerns centered on resegregation, the plan's lack of details, its hasty approval, and a limiting of educational choices (especially for those without a car). They pointed out, for instance, that not only did there remain a significant white population within the public schools, but also Latinos and Asian Americans were a fast-growing population. Desegregation, they stressed, was not just a black-white issue.

Why not view the city's growing diversity as a strength rather than a weakness, and embrace the twenty-first century's multiracial reality? But their arguments were never seriously addressed. The return to neighborhood schools was on the fast track.

Ten days after the final neighborhood schools plan was released to the public in August 2000, the school board unanimously approved the measure. "Tonight marks the end of forced busing and the beginning of real reform," school board president Thompson said.[8]

The Public Policy Forum provided a more sober assessment. "If all Milwaukee Public School attendance area schools were to enroll only students from the neighborhoods, the number of racially balanced schools would decline sharply, while the number of schools with majority white student bodies would increase," it noted in its 1999 report.[9]

Ten years later, the alleged advantages of the neighborhood schools initiative had yet to come true. Academic achievement had not increased, neighborhoods remained economically distressed, and many parents still looked beyond neighborhood boundaries for their child's school. Because of unanticipated parental support for the specialty schools developed during desegregation, the school district maintained both neighborhood and citywide specialty schools. "The percent of students attending neighborhood schools remained just about the same in 2007–08 as it was before the initiative was launched," noted a *Milwaukee Journal Sentinel* analysis eight years after the reform passed.

The lack of support for the neighborhood schools initiative from on-the-ground parents also reflected the fact that many families, especially in poor neighborhoods, tend to move frequently. They do not necessarily develop an allegiance to the closest school. Overall, about 30 percent of all students enroll in a new school every year, according to district data for the period 2007–10.[10]

Doris Mays, the mother of ten children, reflects the twenty-first-century realities that run counter to idealized, 1950s-style images of neighborhoods. Mays, forty-five, grew up in the Riverwest area of Milwaukee and attended two nearby public schools: Fratney Street School and Riverside University High School. At a neighborhood barbecue on a summer day in 2011, she explained that her mother still lives in the family home, and has for more than forty years. But as an adult, Mays has never stayed long in one area.

She has moved to seven or eight different neighborhoods—"all over the city," she laughs. Over the years, her children have gone to so many different public, charter, and voucher schools that she can't easily remember them all. At the time we talked, she lived on the city's far northwest side and her school-age children attended three different schools. One was at Bradley Tech on the city's South Side, about ten to twelve miles away. She liked having choices and didn't mind if her children needed to take a bus to get to school.

On a district level, it's not clear how the neighborhood schools initiatives will affect racial balance in Milwaukee schools over the long run. One unanswered question is whether the city's white population will continue to decline or, as in some major cities, whites will find new interest in urban living.

The case of the two Montessori schools, both close to downtown, underscores how schools can evolve along segregated patterns. MacDowell Montessori, an integrated specialty school, dropped to 9 percent white students by 2010. Maryland Avenue Elementary, re-formed as a Montessori school as part of the neighborhood schools initiative, rose to 59 percent white during the same time.[11]

The greatest disparities, however, remained between Milwaukee and surrounding suburban school districts. As Justice Thurgood Marshall had predicted three decades earlier, the country's metropolitan areas had become divided into two different realities. In 2009–10, whites accounted for 12 percent of the students in the Milwaukee Public Schools, and 81 percent of district students were eligible for free or reduced-price lunch. In Elmbrook, a nearby suburban district, whites were 80 percent of the student body, and 11 percent of district students qualified for free or reduced-price lunch.[12]

Neighborhood schools were not the only significant policy change in the 1990s. Open enrollment, under which Milwaukee students could enroll in nearby suburban districts, also became official district policy, as did admissions policies for high schools.

The admissions policy, like the neighborhood schools initiative, was an about-face. During the desegregation era, the Milwaukee Public Schools had instituted a policy that admissions to citywide specialty schools would be based on a lottery, while still adhering to racial guidelines. The policy not only was based on the view that all children should be treated equally but also was grounded in Milwaukee's egalitarian, blue-collar ethic. Milwaukee, after all, was a city of beer and brats, not champagne and caviar. Over the years, several citywide Milwaukee high schools had developed long waiting lists, especially Riverside and two specialty schools developed during desegregation, Milwaukee High School of the Arts and Rufus King.

In line with Gardner's infamous view that the public schools needed "to insulate wealthy and white students from the floaters," middle-class parents from both the black and white communities increasingly pressured the school board to allow admissions standards for high schools with waiting lists. Free-market arguments of choice and competition dominated the controversy. Who supported and who opposed admissions standards, however, did not fall neatly along ideological lines.

The first step toward admissions policies was taken in the summer of 1996, when the board allowed high schools to give preference to students with a record of good attendance in eighth grade. School board member Gardner, a leading proponent of admissions policies, was especially relentless in arguing against the lottery system. In a letter to the *Milwaukee Journal Sentinel*, he argued that the lottery "prevents schools and students from choosing each other." Attendance preferences, he said, were "a small but significant step in replacing random lottery assignments with public school choice." Others saw the matter quite differently. As Michael Sonnenberg, principal of Pulaski High School, noted, "What this policy will potentially result in is a two-tiered educational system in high schools in this system."[13]

A year later, the school district broke with past practice and solidified the move toward the tracking and sorting of students. During an emotional school board meeting, the board voted 5–4 to approve an admissions policy that allowed high schools to screen students on the basis of not only attendance but also behavior and academic achievement.

Board member Sandra Small, who voted in favor, argued that the public schools needed to better compete with private and suburban schools. "Public schools must change," Small said. "We must hold students accountable in order for public education to survive." Board member Chris Sinicki, usually an ally of Small, disagreed. "This is a slap in the face of public education and everything I believe in," Sinicki said.

* * *

The same year that the Milwaukee school board adopted admissions standards, the state legislature passed a policy of "open enrollment." Like admissions requirements, open enrollment was promoted under principles of
choice and individual preference.

Open enrollment was a statewide policy. It allowed students to apply
to attend a public school in another district under certain conditions—
for instance, if there was space in the receiving district. In Milwaukee,
the school board initially restricted open enrollment options for students
wanting to attend suburban schools. It realized that this seemingly race-
neutral policy would be used primarily by whites in Milwaukee, and it
did not want to exacerbate segregation. In addition, the board was committed to the metropolitan-area-wide desegregation program Chapter
220, which was a race-specific policy targeted at helping blacks and Latinos attend suburban schools.

Once again, school board politics became embroiled in racial politics
that too often tiptoed around issues of race. Once again, board elections
became a battleground as proponents of open enrollment cited the school
board's restrictions as yet another example of the district's resistance to
change. Money came to play a significant role.

Before the 1990s, Milwaukee school board elections had been low-key
affairs. An involved parent or community activist gathered signatures,
knocked on doors, and maybe printed up a leaflet or two. But then Milwaukee became ground zero in the movement toward marketplace-based reforms, in particular publicly funded vouchers for private schools. The school
board races became tumultuous and expensive, closely watched by national
publications such as the *Wall Street Journal* that realized the national implications of Milwaukee's educational controversies. The first indication of
things to come was in 1991, when attorney David Lucey spent the then unheard-of sum of $50,000 to win his race. It was also the first time a candi-
date extensively used television ads, and professional political consultants
turned Lucey into a polished campaigner. Lucey supported vouchers for
private schools and promised "to take back our schools from forced busing,
violence and wasteful spending."[14]

In the spring of 1999, during the legislature's debate on neighborhood schools and tensions over the school board's restrictions on open

enrollment, there was a particularly crucial election involving five seats. John Gardner, a supporter not only of neighborhood schools but also of vouchers and open enrollment, was running as an incumbent for the influential citywide seat. He spent over $190,000 on the race, more than four times what was spent by his opponent, retired African American principal Theadoll Taylor. Gardner received donations from across the country, including from prominent conservatives such as Wal-Mart heir John Walton and Betsy DeVos of the Michigan-based Amway Company. While winning only 31 percent of the vote in districts with African American aldermen, Gardner handily won in white districts. It was enough to win the election.[15]

All five candidates supported by the mayor and business community won, giving them a majority. The new board immediately changed course. It dropped its opposition to the voucher program, endorsed Governor Thompson's budget proposals for voucher schools, and backed the neighborhood schools initiative.

In April 1999, emboldened by the school board elections, Mayor Norquist called for the Milwaukee school district to end "racial quotas" and to allow white students to enroll in suburban schools regardless of the effect on desegregation. Nine days later, at a meeting packed with cheering whites, the school board agreed to do so.

Unlike Chapter 220, open enrollment was allegedly color-blind. But in practice it privileged those with more money—an issue closely correlated with race in Milwaukee. Chapter 220, for instance, provides transportation for students. Under open enrollment, students need to get to school on their own—a problematic situation for those wanting to attend suburban schools beyond the reach of the Milwaukee County bus system. In addition, at the time more than 21 percent of all Milwaukee households did not own a car, with percentages much higher in the central city.[16] As in the 1950s, seemingly race-neutral policies eased the way for whites to transfer to predominantly white schools.

Finances also worked in favor of open enrollment, with the suburban districts financially better off if they accepted open enrollment students over Chapter 220 students.[17] Within a decade of the 1999 school board elections, open enrollment had edged out the Chapter 220 desegregation program. In the 2000 school year, some 5,000 Milwaukee students took part in Chapter 220. By 2010, the number was 2,250. Meanwhile, some 5,750 Milwaukee students took part in open enrollment, and 61 percent were white. The Milwaukee district's enrollment was 15 percent white.

"It's a new form of white flight," the *Milwaukee Journal Sentinel* wrote of open enrollment.[18]

Milwaukee broke new ground in another arena in the 1990s: charter schools. In August 1998, the City of Milwaukee approved three charter schools—the first in the nation to be chartered by a city government.

The charter school movement began in the 1990s, with the first charter school in Minneapolis–St. Paul in 1992. Charters have carved out a niche in education as public-private partnerships. They are considered public schools and are publicly funded, but are generally run by independent boards of directors who, unlike school board members, are not subject to voter approval. Charters vary significantly from state to state. Even within states and districts they can differ, depending on the requirements of the chartering agency. In general, charters are approved by the local school district.

In Milwaukee, for-profit charters had tried to win contracts with the district in the mid-1990s, but widespread opposition defeated the plans. Viewing the charter movement as a Trojan horse for privatization and dismantling of the public schools, the school board remained skeptical of the charter school movement. Charter supporters then inserted a measure into the state budget, where controversial issues become muted because they are part of an omnibus bill. The measure singled out Milwaukee and was designed to circumvent the Milwaukee district's authority to oversee charters; it specifically allowed charters to be approved by the city, the University of Wisconsin–Milwaukee, and the Milwaukee Area Technical College. By national standards, it was an unusual move, heralding future initiatives by other states to establish charters beyond the control of local school boards.

In Milwaukee, one of the first issues was who would oversee the city's charter schools. The aldermen weren't thrilled with the idea. They had their hands full with the police and fire departments and services such as snow plowing and garbage collection. They acknowledged that they knew nothing about running schools. The city turned to voucher proponent Howard Fuller to chair its Charter School Review Committee.

Before the city charter schools even opened, they were embroiled in controversy. The Charter School Review Committee wanted to define its charter schools as a new entity, neither public nor private. If this happened, the Milwaukee Public Schools would be responsible legally and financially for special education services for charter school students. Wisconsin superintendent of public instruction John Benson disagreed with Fuller and the mayor and accused them of discrimination against children with disabilities. "I can only think that both men have forgotten their days as civil rights activists, as defenders of those who are disadvantaged or underserved," Benson said.[19] The city threatened to sue over the matter, but Benson held firm. The city ultimately agreed its charter schools were public schools and, reluctantly, agreed to provide special education services.

The University of Wisconsin–Milwaukee, with its School of Education, was better positioned to oversee charters. But when it approved two charters the following year, it also created controversy. Although state law prohibited giving charters directly to for-profit education companies, the university circumvented the law's intent and approved charters to a nonprofit that then subcontracted to the for-profit Edison Project.

Both the university and the City of Milwaukee, meanwhile, came under criticism for the lower percentage of special education students in their charter schools. Percentages have increased in recent years but still remain significantly lower than in the Milwaukee Public Schools. One of the university's charters, Urban Day School, did not have any special ed students among its 633 students in 2010.[20]

For its part, the school district responded to the charter competition by jumping into the movement. It soon promoted charters as an option within the school governance structure, which had long included partnership schools involved in what traditionally was known as alternative education. In some cases, new charter schools were formed. In others, Milwaukee public schools converted to charter status, often to better control their budget and to win federal and state grants earmarked for charter schools. By 2003, the Milwaukee district had twenty-five charter schools and another twenty-two were applying. Before long, charters were widespread: city charters, university-approved charters, district instrumentality (unionized, public school) charters, district non-instrumentality (nonunion public-private partnership) charters. Some charters were for-profit, some were nonprofit, some were union, most were nonunion. Even education policy wonks found it hard to keep up with the many charter school permutations.

Despite the growing array of charters, the movement failed to deliver on its fundamental promise: that freedom from bureaucracy and union contracts would allow educational excellence to flourish. "You can have great charter schools and great public schools, and Milwaukee is a perfect example," notes Spence Korte, Milwaukee's superintendent from 1999 to 2002. "But you have the same distribution of great charter schools, lousy charter schools, and completely dysfunctional charter schools. All we have done is taken the problem and diffused it across another illusion called governance."[21]

Of all the reforms that proliferated in the 1990s, the charter school movement is the most ideologically and educationally complicated. Like traditional public schools, charters come in many varieties. They are shaped by a state's charter school laws, by the motivations and capabilities of the charter school's founders, and by the broader local, state, and national political climate. (Notwithstanding the City of Milwaukee controversy described above, charters are considered public schools; the confusion often erupts because, unlike traditional public schools, many charter schools operate as private or semiprivate entities.)

Several legal requirements are common to all publicly funded charter schools. They are to be nonreligious and are not to charge tuition. They must obey the same civil rights regulations and nondiscrimination guidelines as public schools. As for special education, charter schools may not discriminate in terms of admissions, but the responsibilities to provide and pay for special education services can vary depending on a state's charter school legislation.[22] Charters are not to be confused with publicly funded voucher schools. By definition, the voucher schools are private schools—even if 100 percent of their students receive publicly funded vouchers. Private voucher schools operate under far less stringent requirements regarding civil rights, nondiscrimination, public transparency, and public oversight. Voucher schools also include religious schools.

Philosophically, charters have their roots in a progressive agenda that viewed charters, as one early advocate noted, as "an important opportunity for educators to fulfill their dreams, to empower the powerless, and to help encourage a bureaucratic system to be more responsive and more effective."[23] Early proponents viewed their reform not as a cure-all but as one of many vehicles to improve public schools, particularly in urban areas. They also viewed charter schools as laboratories of curricular experimentation, with lessons to be shared with other public schools.[24]

The charter concept, however, also appealed to traditional conservatives and to a new generation of billionaire philanthropists who chafed at regulatory oversight and who preferred efficient decision-making by a self-selected elite rather than the often messy deliberations by publicly elected officials. For-profit entrepreneurs, meanwhile, knew that public education was a multibillion-dollar industry, and they quickly saw the financial possibilities in charters as a way to tap into those billions. Over the past decade, these forces have seized the upper hand in the charter school movement. Rather than a vehicle to help improve all public schools, charters in many cities are a semiprivate alternative and have adopted an entrepreneurial, go-it-alone mind-set that values privacy and competition over transparency and collaboration. Rather than pioneers in innovation, many charters are stalwarts of convention and a stalking horse for privatization and decreased public control over public schools. While a few charters are governed by a board with strong community ties and value democratic input, most charters have adopted a corporate model of well-connected boards that operate behind closed doors.

Nationally, most charters are nonunion, with some charters beset by high teacher turnover due to long hours at low pay. The disparity between the highest- and lowest-paid employees tends to be greater in charter schools, even nonprofit ones, than in traditional public schools. As one education activist summed up the charter movement, trying to balance its progressive roots with the privatization and anti-public-school orientation of key financial backers: "It's a great idea controlled by the wrong people for the wrong reasons."

Overall, studies have found relatively little difference in the standardized test scores of students in charter schools and traditional public schools, although charters tend to enroll fewer students with special education or language needs. Other markers of success, such as graduation rates, tend to be unhelpful because there are few charters at the high school level.

As for segregation, charters have tended to exacerbate matters—not sur- prising, since the movement coincides with the country's retreat from con- fronting institutional racism. Charter schools "enroll a disproportionate share of black students and expose them to the highest level of segregation," notes Gary Orfield of the Civil Rights Project. "Almost a third end up in apartheid schools with zero to one percent white classmates, the very kind of schools that decades of civil rights struggles fought to abolish in the South. Many have no policies for transporting students from their segre- gated neighborhoods. There are large concentrations of charter schools in some of the nation's most hypersegregated metropolitan areas, including Chicago and Detroit, and they too often create the illusion of real choice without providing the slightest challenge to the color and class lines that usually define educational opportunity."[25]

The charter movement has received significant bipartisan political sup- port and impressive financing from foundations and corporate philanthro- pists. With publicly funded vouchers for private schools highly controversial in most states, charters have evolved to become the main vehicle for privatiz- ing public education and decreasing democratic oversight.

From only a handful of schools in the early 1990s, by 2009 charter schools enrolled more than 1.4 million students in forty states and the Dis- trict of Columbia. In some urban districts, charters dominate. In New Or- leans, for instance, charter schools outnumbered traditional public schools by a two-to-one margin in 2011. In Washington, D.C., 35 percent of public school students were in charters.[26] Overall, by 2010 there were more than seven hundred public K–12 schools nationwide managed by for-profit com- panies, and all but a few were charters.[27] One of the pioneers, Edison Learn- ing, worked with partners to help educate 450,000 students in schools in twenty-five states, the United Kingdom, and countries in the Middle East.[28] (Edison's founder and board chair, Chris Whittle, planned to open a for- profit private school in New York City in 2012 as part of an international chain, charging an estimated $40,000 a year in tuition.)[29]

Despite the substantial and increasing power of for-profit and privately controlled charters, the fundamental question remains in play: will the charter school movement be used to improve public education and serve the needs of those too often left at the educational margins? Or will it be a vehicle for further segregation of students, undermining of teachers unions, entrepreneurial opportunities to make money, and privatization of an institution fundamental to our democracy? As with many education issues, the answer varies from district to district and state to state. Nationally, however, there is no doubt. The trend is not encouraging.

Throughout the debates of the 1990s, in line with a Milwaukee mind-set that is constantly playing catch-up with reality, Milwaukee policy makers viewed education through a black/white lens. Yet Milwaukee was changing. It had become home to immigrants not just from Mississippi and the rest of the South but from all over the world.

23.

MILWAUKEE'S GREAT MIGRATION #3: GLOBAL IMMIGRANTS MAKE MILWAUKEE THEIR HOME

This problem with illegal immigration is nothing new. In fact, the Indians had a special name for it. They called it "white people."

—Jay Leno, comedian

On a brisk fall morning, I join police officer Manny Molina on his rounds on Milwaukee's near South Side. The son of a Mexican mother and a Tejano (Texan-Mexican) father who worked at a Milwaukee tannery, Molina has walked and bicycled his South Side beat for more than four years. As we walk along, we pass Mexican restaurants and stores, a day care center run by African Americans, a Buddhist temple, Phan's Garden Restaurant (Molina calls their Vietnamese beef soup "out of this world"), a Native American social service agency, a Middle Eastern food mart, and a Korean-owned hip-hop clothing store.

Forty years earlier, the South Side was infamous as the center of white opposition to Milwaukee's civil rights movement. Today, the area has a new reputation: the city's most culturally and racially diverse neighborhood. It is not without tensions and challenges, from poverty to gangs to crime. But it does its best to be a good home. For Milwaukeeans who know their history, the South Side is a testament to the power of change.

Although home to immigrants from around the world, the near South Side is particularly known for its Latino population. In 1970, there were an estimated 15,589 Latinos in Milwaukee, about 2 percent of the population. Three decades later, more than 100,000 Latinos live in Milwaukee, constituting more than 17 percent of the population and almost a quarter of public school students. Many have legal papers. Many do not. Both groups are welcome at the Milwaukee Public Schools.

*   *   *

Denis Rodriguez left Vera Cruz, Mexico, in 2002.[1] He was eleven years old and did not speak a word of English. More problematic, neither he, his mother, his father, nor his younger brother had legal papers. When immigrants from Europe traveled across the ocean a century earlier, passports and legal documents were not required to pass through Ellis Island and enter the United States. Not so anymore.

Undocumented people rarely call attention to themselves. Rodriguez, with the confidence of youth, has decided he will not live in fear and he refuses to hide his undocumented status. "Fear is a mind killer," he says during a recent interview at the dining room table in his family's upper flat on Milwaukee's South Side. "I truly believe we need to do what we need to do, and to realize that we have options and choices."

Rodriguez didn't always feel that way. While at South Division High School, which has a significant percentage of Latino students, he and many of his friends thought there was little reason to do well academically because an undocumented person had little future beyond washing dishes or mowing lawns. He got poor grades, failed biology, and was told to take an after-school makeup class.

One day the biology teacher was called to the office. There were only two students in the after-school class that afternoon, and the teacher asked them to accompany him. On the way, they walked past a book sale sponsored by the school librarian. That book sale changed Rodriguez's life.

Rodriguez was an avid reader, and his bilingual classes in middle and high school had allowed him to maintain his Spanish while learning English. The Harry Potter series had been some of his favorites in English. In Spanish he had moved on to more difficult books, including works by Gabriel García Márquez and Pablo Neruda.

"I'm kind of nerdy," Rodriguez recounts with a laugh, "so I was excited when I saw the book sale. I asked the librarian what would be good to read. She pointed to one book, explaining it was by a psychologist talking about his experiences during the Holocaust." Rodriguez explains the book was *Man's Search for Meaning* by Viktor Frankl, and talks of its powerful message.

"I pick up Frankl's book, and underneath is a book with a bright orange cover and this guy with wild hair and big darting eyes," Rodriguez continues, using his hands and facial expressions to underscore the cover's craziness. "The librarian said the book was by Nietzsche. She wasn't sure if she should recommend it, because she knew it was hard to read. But that cover was so eye-catching!"

The books were only a couple of dollars. Rodriguez bought them. "It took me forever to get through the books, especially Nietzsche," he says "But they made me realize that I don't have to settle for what is here and now. I can build my own life. I mean, here's Frankl, this man who lost so much and went through so much suffering. Those books were a life changer, completely."

Currently a student at the Milwaukee Area Technical College, Rodriguez gives the public schools credit for ensuring his fluency in both English and Spanish. (To this day, his mother does not speak English. His father, who now works at an auto body shop, has limited English skills.) When he first came from Vera Cruz, Rodriguez was put in a bilingual program at Mitchell School, one of twenty public elementary and middle schools offering Spanish/English bilingual programs with an emphasis on developing proficiency in both languages. (Over the years, the Milwaukee school district has developed one of the country's strongest networks of bilingual, dual immersion, and language immersion schools.)[2] By the time Rodriguez got to South Division he didn't need to stay in a bilingual program, but chose to do so depending on the subject. "I like to learn in both my languages," he explains. "I could have seen myself going through a lot of issues if I had been forced into an English-only class in middle school."

Rodriguez is active with YES! (Youth Empowered in the Struggle!), formed by the immigrant and workers rights group Voces de la Frontera. Voces, as the group is often called, has taken up a mantle that is part Joe Hill, part Cesar Chavez, and part Martin Luther King Jr. Through YES! Rodriguez is working on immigration issues and is also a mentor to high school students. "I'm trying to help them realize that they can't let the anti-immigrant factors in society control them," he says. "They have options out there on how they choose to live their lives."

In his own life, Rodriguez walks a thin line, acutely aware of his undocumented status yet wanting to live his life as if that did not matter. We talk about the various restrictions on undocumented people—no in-state tuition at the state's universities, no ability to get a driver's license, no Social

Security card. How is it, for instance, that he drives to school at the technical college? "I drive vee-e-ery carefully," he says with a comedian's sense of timing and delivery. "I go five miles over the speed limit—not too fast, not too slow. The last thing you want to do is stick out."

While Mexicans and other Spanish speakers have been the most significant immigrant group in recent decades, Milwaukee has also become home to people from countries spanning the globe, from Somalia to India, Palestine, and the mountain regions of Laos where the Hmong ethnic minority live. The Hmong are most prominent, and the Milwaukee Public Schools have Hmong/English bilingual programs at two elementary schools. The school district also oversees the Hmong American Peace Academy, the first Hmong charter school in Wisconsin.

The office of Chris Her-Xiong, the charter school's principal, is cluttered with books, bulging manila folders, and oversized three-ring binders. It's the typical office of an overworked principal. What stands out are the exquisite, handmade Hmong tapestries. Others hang throughout her school. Most depict the Mekong River and scenes of warplanes and people fleeing—beautiful, almost soothing artwork that belies the deadly seriousness of the events reenacted. The artwork, like the school, exists in two worlds.[3]

About forty thousand Hmong live in Wisconsin, the third-highest number after California and Minnesota. Milwaukee has been their cultural center, and the Peace Academy embraces a dual vision of both preparing students for life in the United States and sustaining Hmong culture within an increasingly Americanized generation. Her-Xiong explains how they chose the school's name, the Hmong Peace Academy.

"The Hmong people have been fighting wars as long as we can remember," Her-Xiong says. "We want to teach our children to learn you don't have to fight wars to get what you want."

24.

2002–10: NO CHILD LEFT BEHIND. REALLY?

Now what I want is, Facts. Teach these boys and girls nothing but Facts. Facts alone are wanted in life. Plant nothing else, and root out everything else.

—the opening lines of *Hard Times*, by Charles Dickens

On Monday, February 18, 2002, Jennifer Morales took her first and most important trip to Washington, D.C., as a member of the Milwaukee school board. Just a few weeks earlier, President George W. Bush had signed what became his signature domestic initiative—the No Child Left Behind educational reform. Board members and staff from the nation's largest urban systems had been invited to help hammer out implementation details.

The 1,100-page bill, weighing over ten pounds, had passed a few months after the 9/11 attacks on the World Trade Center, when the country's attention was focused on Al Qaeda and Osama bin Laden. The bill was promoted as an effort not only to raise standards for all children but also to narrow the achievement gap between white and African American students. Promising progress in these all-important areas, the bill received significant bipartisan support in Congress. It was particularly championed by President Bush, who sought to bolster his abysmal standing among African Americans by decrying "the soft bigotry of low expectations" and by promoting himself as a "compassionate conservative."

Morales, thirty-two at the time, had been elected to the school board shortly after Bush assumed the presidency. The first Latina school board member, she had two young sons in the Milwaukee Public Schools, and worked as an educational researcher and grant writer. She took her school board responsibilities seriously and saw the Washington, D.C., trip as a way to dig in and help reform public schools.

The urban representatives gathered at the Willard Inter-Continental, a block from the White House and billed as "the crown jewel of Pennsylvania Avenue." A beautiful hotel blending luxury and historic charm, the Willard existed worlds apart from the bare-bones, nitty-gritty reality of most urban schools—a not uncommon phenomenon when top-down policies are formulated. A staff person from the Council of Great City Schools briefed those present at the Willard, in preparation for the next day's meeting with U.S. secretary of education Rod Paige. The staffer turned on his PowerPoint presentation and started with the law's fundamental requirement: by 2014 every student in America would be proficient in math and reading.

"At first everyone just laughed," Morales recalls. "We knew it was impossible for 100 percent of all students to be proficient by that time. That had never happened in any country, at any point in history, let alone in twelve years."[1]

The laughter was soon followed by a stunned silence, and then protest. "We explained that the goal was statistically impossible, especially given the resources available to urban schools," she says. Instead of a dialogue, however, the PowerPoint presentation continued.

Schools were expected to make "adequate yearly progress" toward that 2014 goal. Progress would be determined by standardized tests. Test results would be broken into forty different subgroups if there was a sufficient number of students in each subgroup (for example, special education students, English-language learners, African Americans, Hispanics, and so forth at various grade levels). Urban schools and districts, with their broader diversity and larger student populations, were more likely to include all subgroups. Inadequate progress in any subgroup could trigger sanctions for the entire school and/or district. Every year of additional "failure" upped the sanctions, with a fifth year leading to "restructuring" that could include takeover by a private management company.

Morales returned from Washington deeply troubled—not by the legislation's rhetorical goals and stated mission of improving education for all, but by what had become an on-the-ground reality of unrealistic expectations, punitive sanctions, and a narrow focus on standardized test scores. "The diversion of resources from the classroom to what I call the compliance machine is hard to imagine," she says. "We created an oversight bureaucracy whose sole function was to generate data and send it to Washington, D.C., in order to label schools as failures."

Morales served eight years on the school board and did not run for a third term so that she could devote more time to her children and return to school for a master's degree. She wishes her time had not so closely overlapped with the Bush administration. It was eight years of trying to keep the Milwaukee school district afloat in the face of increased urban poverty, school privatization, and an almost obsessive focus on English and math standardized tests that edged out time for other curricula and even for recess. To this day, she gets upset when she remembers that Washington, D.C., meeting. "No Child Left Behind became a function of control," she says. "It was known from the start to be statistically impossible. That's the part where I start getting bitter."

No Child Left Behind (NCLB) dominated education reform throughout the Bush administration and set the stage for President Barack Obama's Race to the Top initiatives. At a time when "reform du jour" was in full swing— from small schools to teacher-led schools—no other reform had such national impact. Taking off from the public's commonsense understanding that schools need both accountability and standards, No Child Left Behind equated that with high-stakes, fill-in-the-bubble standardized tests.

The initiative also rested on the assumption that student failure is overwhelmingly the result of incompetent and/or insufficiently caring teachers. As with the call for high standards, the assumption went unquestioned in part because there was a slice of truth in it. At some point in their life, everyone has put up with a lousy teacher. NCLB, however, focused on teachers not merely as an important factor but as the main cause of low scores on standardized tests. In doing so, it sidestepped decades of studies showing that family income most reliably predicts test scores.[2] It also failed to address the well-documented fact that underperforming schools, especially in urban areas, tend to have less-experienced teachers and teachers who are not certified in the subject they are teaching.

After No Child Left Behind became law, standardized tests—and teaching to the tests—molded the parameters of what was preferred, permissible, and possible at the local, state, and national levels. Higher scores on standardized tests, not student learning, became the overarching focus throughout American education.

Much to the dismay of some on both the right and the left, NCLB vastly increased the federal government's role in K–12 education. At the same time, it has its roots in federal education legislation that was part of President Lyndon Johnson's Great Society antipoverty program.

Historians Robert Lowe and Harvey Kantor note that both No Child Left Behind and its predecessor are in contrast to New Deal initiatives, which had a wide-ranging emphasis on jobs programs, protecting the right to unionize, promoting efforts such as a minimum wage, unemployment insurance, and Social Security, and developing income/taxation policies that helped redistribute income in order to prevent gaping disparities. The Great Society of President Lyndon Johnson began the shift away from such a New Deal emphasis and instead "favored the provision of services—especially education and job training—that were designed to improve opportunities for those on the margins by enabling them to help themselves," Lowe and Kantor argue. No Child Left Behind passed during a post–civil rights, pro-marketplace era that took the retreat a step further: the federal government no longer felt the need to even protect existing social benefits. "The dominant view today seeks to free the market from any social encumbrances and to limit federal responsibility for social welfare by privatizing it or eliminating it altogether," Lowe and Kantor write.[3]

Grover Norquist, head of Americans for Tax Reform and a leading conservative, summarized the approach with a bit more flair. In a 2001 interview he said, "I don't want to abolish government. I simply want to reduce it to the size where I can drag it into the bathroom and drown it in the bathtub."[4]

Public schools—the only social, political, or economic institution given a mandate to close racial gaps, and already battered in urban areas by segregation, poverty, institutional inequities, and lack of resources—were unable to shoulder the unrealistic expectations of No Child Left Behind. They failed.

Labeling the schools as failures was an essential step in abandoning and dismantling public education and easing the way for privatization, whether through voucher schemes or charter schools. Not surprisingly, the dismantling occurred primarily in urban districts, where no one could reasonably defend the status quo because the problems were so persistent and so glaring.

No Child Left Behind, in line with other social analyses, ignored the relationship between inequality and intense segregation. In the twenty-first century, that segregation was far more complicated than in the Jim Crow era. It involved not only issues of race but also factors such as class and language. In a paradox explained partly by political expedience and partly by public weariness, the more such segregation increased, the more it became a taboo topic.

A similar paradox emerged in discussions of the "achievement gap" in test scores results between whites and African Americans or Latinos. The more the stated concern with the gap, the less the recognition that at one point this country significantly narrowed the gap—during the desegregation era. As historian James Anderson notes: "As is well known by now, scores on national reading and math tests for blacks and Latinos rose steadily between 1970 and 1988, and gaps in scores that separated minority students and whites narrowed. These results, although heartening, received virtually no national publicity."[5]

The link between a "failing" school and a high-poverty school became increasingly clear over time. (In urban areas, high-poverty schools more often than not served mostly students of color.) In 2009, at schools with 75 percent of students receiving free or reduced-price lunch, 1 percent of eighth graders scored "advanced" in math and 12 percent scored "proficient." In schools with 25 percent or less of students receiving lunch subsidies, 15 percent were "advanced" and 35 percent were "proficient."[6]

Interestingly, before the mid-1990s, the term "failing schools" was all but nonexistent. It certainly, for instance, was not applied to Jim Crow–era segregated black schools in the South that could not even afford desks. After the election of George W. Bush in 2000, use of the term and its variations reached new heights, applied to schools and districts alike.[7] It became part of the established educational lexicon—by politicians and, in the 2002 U.S. Supreme Court case allowing vouchers for religious schools, by Chief Justice William Rehnquist in his reference to Cleveland's "failed school district."

It wasn't long before Milwaukee was labeled. By 2004–5, the district as a whole missed "adequate yearly progress," by then uniformly and fearfully known as AYP. As the failure and sanctions continued, other dreaded acronyms became common: AMO (annual measurable objectives), SIFI (school identified for improvement), DIFI (district identified for improvement), CAR (corrective action requirements), and DIP (district improvement plan). The Milwaukee Public Schools missed AYP for two consecutive years in 2006, becoming a DIFI Level 1. By 2010–11, the Milwaukee district was at DIFI Level 5. A DIP was developed. According to a district document explaining the plan, "Implementation of DIP is supported and monitored by the Regional System of Support core teams; which consists of the Regional Executive Specialist, who provides an accountability check for principals, the Special Education Leadership Liaison, who provides an accountability check for special education, and the School Improvement Supervisor, who provides an accountability check for corrective action."[8]

On June 15, 2004, a few years into No Child Left Behind, my mother attended my daughter Mahalia's graduation from the Milwaukee High School of the Arts. My mother had gone to any number of Mahalia's school events and performances over the years. She was well aware of how the Milwaukee Public Schools had helped further Mahalia's overarching interest in dance.

I'm not sure what strings were pulled, but school officials were able to hold the graduation at the Pabst Theater in downtown Milwaukee. An opulent theater built in 1895, the Pabst is known for its marble staircase, its two-ton crystal chandelier, and a stage adorned with thick maroon curtains and gold leaf decorations. My mother was impressed.

The graduation had its traditional moments—the processional was Pachelbel's Canon in D Major and the recessional was "Pomp and Circumstance." But overall, it turned out to be a raucous affair. The theater, while beautiful, was too small, and the crowd's energy bounced off the walls. The school's art students have a tradition of bringing an over-the-top panache to all they do, and they were not in the mood to be subdued. During the ceremony, several parents shrieked in delight when their child walked across the stage. Culturally, it was light-years away from the high school graduations of my mother and me from a Catholic all-girls academy; you could have heard a pin drop during our graduations.

I worried that my mother might find the noise indecorous and physically taxing; she was eighty-six years old, and her health was not great. But she thoroughly enjoyed herself. She was proud of Mahalia, and completely understood the boisterous pride of other parents, uncles, cousins, and grandparents. "I just wish other people could see this," she said at one point. "They're just too negative about the Milwaukee schools." I had been hearing such comments ever since my mother first came to Fratney Family Fun Day on a snowy February some fifteen years earlier and, for what I imagine was the first time in her life, ate a tamale.

My mother attended Catholic schools and was always thankful for the scholarships that helped her be the first one in her family to graduate from college. Until the day she died, she regularly attended Mass and contributed to various Catholic schools in the area. But she was a child of the Great Depression and had an innate distrust of people who thought they were better just because they had more money, lived in fancy homes, or had an address in the "right" neighborhood. That distrust led to a respect for Milwaukee's public schools.

Some of my mother's friends thought that by sending my daughters to a public school in Milwaukee, I was sacrificing my children on the altar of my ideals. But my mother knew they were wrong. She understood that I sent my children to the Milwaukee Public Schools because I believed they provided the best educational opportunities in the entire metropolitan region—both academically and in so-called soft educational areas of respect for art, cultural difference, and bilingualism.

Were there public schools in Milwaukee that failed their students? Undeniably. The data were too strong to deny. In the 2002–3 school year, for example, only 33 percent of African Americans were proficient in reading, compared to 63 percent for whites. That same year, the district's high school graduation rate for African Americans was 56 percent, compared to 71 percent for whites. Overall, high school attendance was just short of 80 percent. The student suspension rate for middle school grades was 36.6 percent. Some 202 students were expelled (mostly for weapons or drugs).[9]

At the same time, such aggregate figures masked a reality common in most urban districts: there are a few schools that excel, many that are okay, and some that serve as warehouses. No urban district has found a way to guarantee success and rigor throughout all its schools, just as no suburban school has been able to guarantee success for all its students.

At the very time the Milwaukee Public Schools were making local headlines for their failures, predominantly black high schools such as Riverside and Rufus King were receiving recognition nationally for their academic achievements. Riverside, for instance, has long had one of the state's strongest offerings of Advanced Placement courses. King, meanwhile, was ranked by *Newsweek* as the top high school in Wisconsin every year from 2006 to 2010.[10]

Unfortunately, educational policy in Milwaukee was propelled by media-fueled perceptions of the public school system as an abject failure, rather than the reality of a complicated system with weaknesses and strengths. The tragedy of No Child Left Behind was not that it set standards but that it set the standards so narrowly and used them to label and punish an entire district.

No Child Left Behind has been described as a "post-desegregation" policy. Five years after the law began, the U.S. Supreme Court went beyond policy and legally ended racial desegregation—in the name of preventing racial discrimination.

On June 28, 2007, in a 5–4 decision, the Court overturned desegregation plans in Seattle, Washington, and in Jefferson County, Kentucky (metropolitan Louisville), even though the plans had been voluntarily adopted by the local school boards and involved significant parental choice.[11] While the decision did not outright overturn *Brown v. Board*, it came close. During oral arguments, Justice Ruth Bader Ginsburg pointed out that the voluntary plan in Jefferson County was an outgrowth of court-mandated desegregation in the 1970s. With an understated irony conjuring up images of *Alice in Wonderland*, Justice Ginsburg noted: "What's constitutionally required one day gets constitutionally prohibited the next day? That's very odd."[12]

The majority opinion was written by Chief Justice John G. Roberts Jr., named to the court by President George W. Bush in 2005 in what was the crowning achievement of a long-term conservative goal of dominating the court. Chief Justice Roberts, invoking *Brown* and citing the Fourteenth

Amendment, argued that public schools may not achieve or maintain integration programs by taking into account a student's race, but must instead be color-blind. "The way to stop discrimination on the basis of race is to stop discriminating on the basis of race," he wrote.[13]

The decision was criticized as a rewriting of both the history of desegregation and the equal protection clause of the Constitution's Fourteenth Amendment, passed after the Civil War to protect the rights of former slaves. Justice John Paul Stevens was most explicit in lamenting the court's turn to the right, noting that the majority opinion "rewrites the history of one of this court's most important decisions."

Justice Stephen G. Breyer, who wrote the main dissent, took the unusual step of speaking from the bench when the decision was released. As the *New York Times* reported, "Justice Breyer made his points to a courtroom audience that had never seen the coolly analytical justice express himself with such emotion. His most pointed words, in fact, appeared nowhere in his seventy-seven page opinion. 'It is not often in the law that so few have so quickly changed so much,' Justice Breyer said."[14]

The 2007 Supreme Court decision all but removed race as a permissible topic in school reform initiatives, even as race remained a dominant reality in urban education. Special education is not dissimilar. Like race, special education is complicated, controversial, absolutely integral to the vision of educating all children—and rarely at the core of educational discussions. Few policy makers are willing to talk about special education with any depth or complexity. So when Spence Korte was willing to discuss the subject, I listened.

Korte was a well-known principal before becoming Milwaukee superintendent in 1999 for three years. During our interview, we talked mostly about special ed. Months later, one particular story stays with me.

In the 1990s, Korte was principal at HiMount, a K–8 school in an integrated neighborhood. Like most school leaders, he spent an inordinate amount of time making sure that an everyday occurrence—a late bus, a cancelled field trip, a fight on the playground—didn't turn into a full-blown crisis. On this particular day, he knew it was an emergency the minute he received word: a severely depressed student on the third floor of the school was threatening to jump out the window. He rushed out of his office and bounded up the three flights. The student was convinced not to jump and the story ends well. But it's a day Korte has never forgotten.

"I'm up there talking to this student, and I realize, I'm not trained to do this, nor is the teacher," he recalls. "This was a child who was so injured that he needed to be protected from himself—some combination of psychotherapy, medication, and family counseling. But how is that supposed to happen in a school?"

In fact, Korte had a significant amount of special education training. Long before he was a teacher, principal, or superintendent, Korte was doing an internship in Washington, D.C., while finishing his doctorate, working for the Council for Exceptional Education. He was involved in efforts that later became codified in landmark federal legislation in 1975 requiring schools to provide students who had a broad range of disabilities with a "free appropriate public education." He supports the goals of special education and is thankful that the days are over of warehousing severely disabled children or shunning those who, through no fault of their own, may have mental health problems. But Korte also knows the day-to-day realities of how special education has been allowed to evolve. He has seen what happens when a fundamental right and much-needed reform is undermined through inadequate financing and support, or when untrained teachers are expected to solve complicated medical and social problems. "The greatest teacher on earth cannot compensate for brain damage, or fix bipolar disorder, by merely changing the curriculum," Korte says.

In Milwaukee, special education has become a new way to segregate, stigmatize, and abandon those deemed difficult to educate. Schools and policy makers know that the best way to get a good reputation is to control a school's enrollment and get rid of "problem" students. Within Milwaukee Public Schools, as in other large districts, some schools have become skilled at keeping low their enrollment of special ed students, especially those with complicated problems. By federal law, however, a district must find services in one of its schools for all special education students.

The biggest disparity in special education in Milwaukee is not among the district schools, however, but between the public schools and the publicly funded voucher schools. By virtue of being private schools that do not have to provide the same level of special education services, the voucher schools have become particularly adept at avoiding the responsibility of educating all children. In the 2010–11 school year, the private voucher schools in Milwaukee enrolled almost 21,000 students. Approximately 1.5 percent required special education services, most of a limited nature. The Milwaukee Public Schools, in contrast, had almost 20 percent of their roughly 81,000 students classified as requiring special education services in 2010–11.

"All together, the 102 voucher schools are serving a special education population that is equal to what the Milwaukee Public Schools serves in *just one* of its district schools: Hamilton High School," noted Milwaukee superintendent Gregory Thornton.[15]

On Tuesday, June 6, 2011, civil rights groups asked the U.S. Justice Department to investigate the publicly funded private voucher school program, on the grounds that the voucher schools' exclusion of children with disabilities had led to a segregated environment and violated the rights of children with disabilities. "Wisconsin's creation, implementation and expansion of a private school voucher program in Milwaukee has resulted in a dual system of education in the city," the complaint argues. "There is essentially one option for students with disabilities: Milwaukee Public Schools."[16]

The complaint describes how the private voucher school Messmer told a mother that her eight-year-old son could attend the school only if he received medicine for his attention deficit hyperactivity disorder—even though his doctor had not prescribed medication. Another voucher school, meanwhile, expelled an eighth grader with a mental health disability after she had an argument with another student. The school was aware of the student's history when she transferred in from the public schools, but failed to make any accommodations for her disability. After the voucher school expelled the student, she returned to the Milwaukee Public Schools.[17]

At the time of the civil rights complaint, most of the voucher schools were dependent on public tax dollars to operate. About half of the private voucher schools had 94 percent or more of their students receiving publicly funded vouchers, and twenty-two schools had 100 percent of their students receiving tax-funded vouchers.[18]

At the beginning of the twenty-first century, Milwaukee was home to two realities. It was a midwestern mirror image of New Orleans.

Before Hurricane Katrina, New Orleans was beloved as the city of Mardi Gras—a festive celebration of music, street festivals, and Cajun food. When

Katrina inflicted its wrath in 2005, the city's racial divides were portrayed on television screens across the country. New Orleans became the shame of the country.

Milwaukee lives in a similar limbo, caught between two worlds. Its *Happy Days* image remains strong—a family-friendly city on a beautiful lake, with world-class museums, a major-league baseball stadium, and its annual Summerfest, an eleven-day party along Lake Michigan billed as the world's largest music festival. All of those attributes remain a source of understandable civic pride. But, thanks in part to the interstate system that allows easy access in and out of the city, Milwaukee's flip side is hidden. The blocks with two, three, or four boarded-up homes. Forsaken strip malls with weed-filled parking lots. Empty factories. Swaths of "food deserts" without any major grocery store. If, by chance, a Katrina-type disaster struck Milwaukee, that abandonment would become clear.

On August 30, 2005, the day after the levees were breached in New Orleans, the U.S. Census Bureau released a report showing that Milwaukee's poverty rate of 26 percent was the seventh-worst of any U.S. city—and higher than the New Orleans rate of 23.2 percent. Milwaukee's child poverty rate of 41.3 percent compared to 38 percent in New Orleans. A post-Katrina report by the Brookings Institution, a Washington think tank, found that conditions of concentrated poverty in Milwaukee's African American neighborhoods closely paralleled those in the black neighborhoods of New Orleans. As Bruce Katz, director of the Brookings report, said, "Milwaukee looks exactly like New Orleans did before the hurricane."[19]

Overall, however, the metropolitan Milwaukee region was doing quite well. The nearby and predominantly white counties of Waukesha and Ozaukee were among only nineteen counties in the entire United States with poverty rates below 5 percent.[20]

Of all the dual realities in Milwaukee, two are particularly striking: the disparities in incarceration and in infant mortality.

In 2008, Wisconsin had the country's highest rate of black incarceration, surpassing law-and-order states such as Texas. Milwaukee, with the majority of the state's African American population, drives the statewide figures. In 2007, an estimated 40 percent of African American males ages twenty-four to twenty-nine in Milwaukee County had spent time in jail. The percentage was even higher for those thirty to thirty-four years old.[21]

Milwaukee's infant mortality rate has received attention in part because the city had been known for its public health accomplishments. From 1979 to 1981, Wisconsin's black infant mortality rate averaged third-best in the nation. By 2003 to 2005, it was the second-worst. In the 53210 zip code in Milwaukee's central city, the infant mortality rate was worse than that in the Gaza Strip.[22]

Long before key Milwaukee power brokers gave up on the public schools, they abandoned entire neighborhoods. The plight in hard-pressed Milwaukee neighborhoods was of such long standing that it had stopped making headlines. The media, meanwhile, more often than not bolstered racial stereotypes that allowed people across Wisconsin to distance themselves from the city's problems.

But, as Wisconsin was soon to find out, the abandonment of social responsibility for the common good in Milwaukee was just a harbinger. Milwaukee, the state's largest city, had been a testing ground for conservative policies that would be imposed throughout Wisconsin.

25.

2011: THE HEARTLAND RISES UP, AND A NEW ERA OF PROTEST BEGINS

O, yes,
I say it plain,
America never was America to me,
And yet I swear this oath—
America will be!

— "Let America Be America Again" by Langston Hughes

On February 6, 2011, Wisconsin was ecstatically happy. The Green Bay Packers, recovering from the loss of legendary quarterback Brett Favre, were guided to a Super Bowl victory by Aaron Rogers in a 31–25 win over the formidable Pittsburgh Steelers.

Within a week, the glow of that victory was gone. Newly elected Wisconsin governor Scott Walker, taking the lead in an increasingly aggressive national Republican agenda, introduced legislation to eviscerate collective bargaining rights for most public sector unions.[1] For the first time in years Republicans controlled all three branches of the state government, and Walker called for the bill's passage within days.

Walker's timeline was upended, however. His no-holds-barred attack unleashed a populist upsurge that was unprecedented in Wisconsin history. Across the country, meanwhile, progressives grasped the national repercussions of the events in Madison and embraced the slogan "We Are Wisconsin." Even Green Bay Packers players joined the struggle, an almost unheard-of development in the sports world. "Thousands of dedicated Wisconsin public workers provide vital services for Wisconsin citizens," cornerback Charles Woodson said in a statement, joining other current and former Packers in proclaiming support. "These hardworking people are under an unprecedented attack to take away their basic rights to have a voice and collectively bargain at work."[2]

Walker unveiled his 144-page union-busting bill on Friday, February 11, under the guise of repairing a budget shortfall. At the news conference announcing the bill, he warned that he had put the National Guard on alert to quell unrest or illegal strikes. "I don't have anything to negotiate," he said.

There had been rumors about Walker's plans, but no one was prepared for the bill's scope. It took a few days for its full significance to sink in. Teachers and educators, who account for the largest percentage of public sector workers in Wisconsin, quickly came to play an essential role in the organizing.

The first public hearing on Walker's bill was on Tuesday, February 15, at the state capitol in Madison. More than ten thousand protesters gathered, with thousands filling the capitol's corridors and demanding they be allowed to speak. No one, neither union organizers nor police nor legislators, had anticipated such an outpouring of anger. That night, protesters began camping out overnight at the capitol, with the UW-Madison Teaching Assistants' Association as the lead organizer. In the Milwaukee suburb of Wauwatosa, teachers union activists organized a demonstration of thousands of people outside Walker's residence.

It was day one of what became twenty-six days of nonstop, round-the-clock protests involving hundreds of thousands of people from across Wisconsin and unheard-of collaboration between private and public sector unions, teachers and firefighters, police and student radicals.[3]

On day two, Wednesday, February 16, the Madison protests grew to tens of thousands of people. The Madison schools were forced to close as teachers and students marched at the capitol, realizing it was a time to make history, not study it. Late that afternoon, the state teachers union, the Wisconsin Education Association Council, called on its 98,000 members to come to Madison Thursday and Friday. "If you can't walk up to the Capitol, get as far as you can and sit down," the e-mail urged, couching its call to action as a peaceful demonstration rather than as a teachers' strike or sick-out, which are illegal in Wisconsin. The teachers union—the largest union in the state, public or private—was known for its behind-the-scenes lobbying and power brokering, not for its grassroots mobilizing.[4] If there had been any doubt, there was now none: Wisconsin politics on both the right and the left had irrevocably changed.

On day three, Thursday, February 17, the avalanche of protest escalated. Both public sector and private sector unions ramped up their organizing, and demonstrators descended from across the state. School districts across Wisconsin were forced to close because so many teachers were in Madison. The normally quiet capitol was in upheaval. People marched in the streets, crowded the capitol's corridors, and pounded on closed legislative doors while chanting, "Kill the bill! Kill the bill!" It wasn't just seasoned activists, union organizers, university students, or concerned clergy who were in motion. Walker's attack on collective bargaining struck a nerve with people who had never before been to a demonstration in their lives.

On day four, Friday, February 18, Traci McKean woke up shortly before 6:00 A.M. She immediately checked the news. A thirty-four-year-old kindergarten teacher with the Milwaukee Public Schools, she had spent the previous evening texting as many co-workers as possible and encouraging them to call in sick and get to Madison. When she went to bed Thursday night, it was still unclear whether Milwaukee district officials would be forced to cancel school for the day. The day before, even though hundreds of teachers had called in sick and demonstrated at the capitol, the schools remained open. But McKean had decided that on Friday, she would go to Madison no matter what. It wasn't just a question of unions and what might happen to her paycheck. She worried about the long-term effect on children's education if good teachers were forced out of the profession.

"It was a big deal for me to call in sick and go to Madison," McKean recalls. "I felt very torn. Do I go to school for the children, or go to Madison for the children? Because both were for the children and their future."

By five o'clock that Friday more than six hundred Milwaukee teachers had, like McKean, called for a substitute. District officials finally succumbed to reality and closed the schools. McKean immediately called several of her friends. "We have to go to Madison. Bring your kids along," she told them. She put on her warmest jacket and mittens, and threw a pair of gloves in her backpack for good measure. She grabbed a couple of granola bars, a banana, and a few bottles of water, and met up with her friends at a nearby park-and-ride. Two hours and ninety miles later, she found herself among tens of thousands of protesters. She particularly remembers the pride she felt when she found out that the state's fourteen Democratic senators, emboldened by the protests, had left the state in order to prevent the votes necessary for passage of Walker's bill.

"I knew something big was happening, even if I wasn't sure what it all meant," McKean recalls. "It was all so overwhelming."

The Friday protest was one of four or five trips McKean made to Madison that spring, a time when events unfolded so fast and intensely that one day's memories melded into another's. "Every time I went to Madison, I wanted to just hug and thank everybody," McKean recalls. "Like the people who spent the night in the Capitol, or the people who had lost their voice because they had been chanting so long. Or the people who were freezing and couldn't feel their toes anymore, and the people who were supporting us even though it didn't affect them."

More than seven months later, on a sunny afternoon, McKean is cleaning up in her kindergarten classroom after the students have left for the day. Her writing, science, health, and craft centers are all neatly organized. Blue plastic chairs, child-sized, are stacked on top of tables. The school's air-conditioning is turned off at 2:00 P.M. in order to save money, and the air is becoming stale. This week she is concentrating on helping children understand the days of the week and the months in a year. Going just by months, February seems long ago. But February 2011 in Madison, Wisconsin, left a lasting impact on McKean. She knows she's not always successful in expressing her thoughts. Like many others, she finds it hard to articulate the deep-seated, widespread, and visceral response to Walker's union busting.

The Madison demonstrations were McKean's first taste of popular protest. Born in 1977, she was the only child in a working-class family that lived in various inner-ring suburbs adjoining Milwaukee. Her parents were not particularly political, nor were they involved in any church. Visiting her relatives in northern Wisconsin as a child, they were as likely to talk about Jell-O recipes as who was running for president. Asked what guides her political views, she mentions only her father's insistence, from the time she was a young child, that she treat people fairly and consistently. She became involved in the teachers union several years earlier, after the principal had asked teachers to work during the lunch hour. "How does not having lunch or time to go to the bathroom help children to learn?" she asks.

McKean is a classic kindergarten teacher: kind, firm but understanding, and indefatigably energetic. She views her students as her extended family and therefore deserving of the extra hours she puts in before and after school, the trips to Target to buy school supplies, the unpaid summer weekends preparing her classroom. She has difficulty understanding how teachers became public enemy number one, the cause of social problems ranging from low test scores to budget deficits.

When Walker demanded immediate passage of his union-busting bill, McKean was appalled. "It was all moving so fast, and that's what was infuriating," she says of Walker's bill. "That's one of the main reasons I went to Madison, to stop this madness and ask people to stop and think before we start putting things into law without thinking of the ramifications."

The emotional impact of spring 2011 in Madison was felt most strongly by the hundreds of thousands of people who set aside their everyday lives and protested despite snowstorms and freezing temperatures. But across the country, the political repercussions were widely understood. Governor Walker's attack on unions, the public sector, and working people was particularly harsh, but it was in line with a newly invigorated national Republican strategy following the November 2010 elections.

A classic middle-American state, both geographically and politically, Wisconsin represents the much sought-after heart of U.S. politics. Beginning in 1988, it has voted for the Democratic Party candidate in every presidential election, but there has been only one Democratic governor in that time. Home to Senator Joe McCarthy and the John Birch Society, Wisconsin was also a pioneer in workers' compensation, unemployment insurance, and public employee rights. A century ago, its role in the progressive reform movement led Teddy Roosevelt to call Wisconsin a "laboratory for democracy."[5]

"Wisconsin has become ground zero," said Jonathan Williams of the American Legislative Exchange Council, a conservative group that develops templates for state legislation. "What happens could serve as a domino, win or lose, in either direction."[6]

The other end of the political spectrum agreed. "Madison has become ground zero in the battle for democracy in this country," noted *Nation* editor Katrina vanden Heuvel. "Don't fall for the dodge that this is about money, the pay and perks of public employees. This is about basic democratic rights, and the balance of power in America."[7]

Although Walker promoted his bill as a necessary fiscal measure, progressives recognized it as an attempt to cripple organized labor's influence on wages, working conditions, and social policy, and to undermine the base of the Democratic Party.

The bill unfolded within the context of the conservative movement's long-term goal of shrinking social services and public institutions—defunding and dismantling them while promoting the marketplace and privatization as the alternative. With advances on these fronts in Milwaukee, it was only a matter of time before such an agenda would be rolled out across the state. The southern strategy, first applied to northern electoral politics in the 1970s, was now being applied to public institutions, collective bargaining, and workers' standard of living. (Interestingly, the head of the Bradley Foundation, Michael Grebe, chaired Walker's gubernatorial campaign and led the transition team. Within days of his election, Walker and his wife dined with the foundation's board and senior staff at one of Milwaukee's most elite restaurants.)[8]

Wisconsin had been the first state in the country to allow collective bargaining by public sector unions, in 1959. Walker knew that if he could bust the public unions in Wisconsin, it would have nationwide impact and bolster his credentials as a rising star in the conservative movement. In the now infamous twenty-minute talk with a blogger posing as David Koch, the billionaire donor to conservative causes, Walker fawned over the man he presumed to be Koch and talked of his ambitions. He explained that on the day after the Green Bay Packers' Super Bowl victory, he had called his cabinet to his home for dinner. He had already made plans for his legislation, and noted how the dinner "was kind of the last hurrah before we dropped the bomb." He'd then taken out a picture of Ronald Reagan and said that Reagan "had one of the most defining moments of his political career, not just his presidency, when he fired the air-traffic controllers."

Walker went on to say: "In Wisconsin's history, I said this is our moment, this is our time to change the course of history."[9]

Walker's original rationale for his bill—to solve an immediate fiscal crisis—became inoperative after unions agreed to increase their health care and pension payments. Even after that concession, Walker rejected any compromise. It became clear the bill was essentially a blueprint for decimating public sector unions, the strongest sector within organized labor given the decline of manufacturing, and a bulwark of the state's middle class. (Under the bill, public sector unions were required to be recertified every year by a majority of union members, not just a majority of those voting. In addition, the unions could no longer be funded through dues check-offs as part of workers' pay. The bill also stipulated that contracts could cover only wages, not working conditions or hiring/firing, sick leave, overtime, seniority, performance pay, and so forth. Finally, any wage increase beyond the cost of living would have to be approved by public referendum.)

On March 1, 2011—with the bill still stymied and protests in Madison continuing unabated—Walker expanded his attack. He unveiled his budget for the next two years, detailing extensive cuts in public education, Medicaid, and social and environmental programs big and small. Walker, for instance, cut aid to mass transit systems by 10 percent and also eliminated $5 million in funds for bicycle and pedestrian paths. Both were in line with a cars-at-any-cost transportation philosophy that led him, in one of his first acts as governor, to reject almost $810 million in federal funding for high-speed rail in Wisconsin.

The cuts to education were the most disturbing. State funds to elementary and secondary public education were cut by $840 million, amounting to $635 per student from fiscal 2011 to fiscal 2012 and the second-biggest cut on a dollar basis of any state in the country.[10] Walker also reduced the amount of money districts were legally able to raise at the local level without going to a referendum, with the reduction varying from about $500 to $1,100 per pupil.[11] Funding to several specific programs was cut completely, such as state grants for nursing services, Advanced Placement courses, and science, technology, engineering, and math programs. In addition, Walker's budget cut $250 million from the state university system and eliminated in-state tuition for undocumented students who had graduated from a Wisconsin high school. Funding for the state's technical colleges was cut by $72 million.

Wisconsinites had long taken pride in their public schools and universities, regarded as some of the best in the country. It seemed unfathomable
that, at a time when a good education was uniformly recognized as essential to success in the digitalized global economy, Walker would slash education budgets more than any other governor in state history.

At the same time that Walker and his Republican allies reduced money
for public schools, they proposed an unparalleled expansion of the state-
funded private school voucher program. The voucher initiatives made clear
that conservative ideology and the privatization of public institutions, not
fiscal due diligence, were guiding their agenda.

For more than twenty years, supporters of vouchers for private schools had
a chance to prove their assertion that the marketplace and parental choice
were the bedrocks of educational success, and that unions and government
bureaucracy were the enemies of reform. In the end, their claims failed the
test of reality.

The publicly funded private voucher schools reflected a virtual wish list
of conservative reform: no unions, no central bureaucracy, minimal government oversight, the ability to hire and fire teachers at will, and wide
latitude to institute just about any innovation desired, from the length of
the school day to curricular reform.

In the fall of 2010, for the first time, students at voucher schools were
required to take the same tests as public school students. What's more, the
results were released on a school-by-school basis, providing a level of detail
and reliability that had been missing in voucher school analyses for more
than two decades.

The results? Students in the private voucher schools performed significantly worse in math than comparable students in the Milwaukee Public
Schools, and about the same in reading. When special education students
are factored out of the test results, voucher schools' low performance is
even more striking. In the fifth-grade reading results, 68.7 percent of non-
special-ed students in the public schools were proficient, compared to 55.5
percent of non-special-ed voucher students.[12]

The test results were not the only bad news for voucher proponents that
year. In the summer of 2010, data showed that only 40 percent of the
voucher students selected for an independent long-range study were still in a

voucher school three years later, with about a third having transferred to the public schools. Within the Milwaukee Public Schools cohort, meanwhile, almost 78 percent were still in the public schools after three years; only 7 percent had transferred to a voucher school.[13] The exodus of voucher students, as state officials noted, undermined the reliability of the long-range study.

No longer able to claim that parents preferred voucher schools and that the schools were academically superior, voucher supporters emphasized a different rationale: voucher schools were cheaper. As *Milwaukee Journal Sentinel* conservative columnist Patrick McIlheran wrote in defending the voucher schools, "They're teaching those students for much less money." McIlheran also came up with a new rationale, albeit one with an extremely low bar: "The experiment does no harm to any children."[14]

Against this backdrop, the debate over vouchers gained new urgency in the early months of 2011. The governor originally proposed an unprecedented expansion of the taxpayer-supported private voucher schools, while cutting funds for public schools. Under Walker's plan, Milwaukee was slated to become the first city in the history of American education where taxpayers would pay for all children, even the children of millionaires, to attend a private secular or religious school. As *Milwaukee Journal Sentinel* columnist Ricardo Pimentel noted: "Walker is close to achieving in Milwaukee a long-held dream on the right: universal choice to opt out of the social contract to fund the public schools that most children attend and will continue to attend long after every middle-class dollar has flown the coop for a private school."[15]

In line with abandoning the program's initial focus on low-income African American students in community schools, Walker called for private schools outside Milwaukee to accept voucher students. His unprecedented expansions caused a public uproar. Polly Williams, the African American legislator who had shepherded the initial voucher program through the state legislature two decades earlier, organized a public meeting with other African American educators under the slogan "Stop Scott Walker's plan to give the wealthy private school vouchers! Taking funding from the needy and giving it to the greedy." Even longtime voucher supporter Howard Fuller labeled Walker's expansion "egregious" and "outrageous." Ever the shrewd politician, Fuller successfully promoted a plan that deflected the public

uproar while allowing the voucher program to expand. He called for families to be eligible for vouchers if their income did not exceed 300 percent of
the federal poverty level ($67,050 for a family of four), up from the existing
threshold of 220 percent but less than Walker's universal voucher proposal.
Republican legislators, seeing the widespread dismay over Walker's plan,
quickly embraced Fuller's 300 percent solution.

Significantly, however, the Republican-controlled legislature maintained
or expanded the voucher program in other ways. First, it lifted the cap on
the number of voucher students. Second, it added a provision that should
a voucher family's income increase—regardless of how much—already
enrolled students could still receive vouchers. Third, while Walker's initial
legislation limited voucher school expansion from the City of Milwaukee
to Milwaukee County, the final bill allowed any private school anywhere
in the state to apply as a voucher school. Finally, and most significant, the
legislature expanded vouchers beyond Milwaukee, beginning with Racine,
the state's fifth-largest city. It also developed statewide criteria (such as
poverty levels and per-pupil spending) under which vouchers would automatically be allowed in a district without the need for specific legislation or
a chance for local input. Cities and small rural districts throughout the
state were potentially eligible. There were no public hearings on the statewide
expansion.[16]

Most revealing was that the expansion abandoned the program's long-
standing focus on lower-income students and the requirement that the private schools accept the voucher payment as full tuition. High schools, where
per pupil costs tend to be more, had been particularly concerned that the
voucher payment ($6,442 in 2010) was insufficient. Under the adopted legis-
lation, high schools were allowed to charge extra tuition to families earning
between 220 and 300 percent of the poverty level.[17] It was another blow to
American democracy's belief in a system of free public education open to all
children, and a seemingly small but important strategic advance for the
voucher movement.

Wisconsin's voucher expansion was in line with the rebirth of a movement that many people had erroneously dismissed as a passing fad. In Indiana, another stronghold of the Republican offensive in 2011, Governor Mitch
Daniels established a statewide voucher program. Nationally, pro-voucher
advocates boasted that more than fifty-two bills had been introduced to

allow publicly funded vouchers or other tax-funded benefits for private schools.

The voucher movement's abandonment of public education that had begun in Milwaukee two decades earlier was moving to a new and unpredictable stage. Supporters of public funds for private schools were so emboldened that they dropped their rhetoric of concern for poor children in urban schools and openly promoted universal vouchers as the alternative to public education. As Teri Hall, a national Tea Party supporter who backed voucher bills in New Jersey and Pennsylvania, said: "We think public schools should go away."[18]

A well-funded network of free-market ideologues provided national coordination as the voucher movement expanded its attack. In Wisconsin, voucher supporters were active not just in lobbying around educational issues but also in promoting Governor Scott Walker and his overall agenda. "The new 800-pound gorilla—actually it's more of a 1,200-pound gorilla—is the tax-funded-voucher groups," says state representative Mark Pocan (D-Madison). "They've become the most powerful lobbying entity in the state."[19]

The American Federation for Children was particularly involved, as is true in voucher battles across the country. The federation is led by Betsy DeVos, an heir to the Amway fortune, a major Republican contributor, and the former chair of the Michigan Republican Party. (DeVos is perhaps most infamous as the sister of Erik Prince, founder of the private mercenary group Blackwater Worldwide, which was the leading subcontractor for privatized U.S. military efforts in Iraq and Afghanistan.)

It is sometime around 3:00 A.M., February 22, 2011, and I slowly walk around the dimly lit yet still stunningly beautiful capitol rotunda in Madison. An architectural wonder, the rotunda contains marble from Greece, Algeria, Italy, and France, limestone from Minnesota, syenite from Norway, and red granite from Waupaca, Wisconsin. The rotunda's dome extends up hundreds of feet, with the outside dome only three feet shorter than that of the nation's capitol in Washington, D.C.

In 2001, the capitol was named a National Historic Landmark. The public usually marvels at the building as part of an architectural or legislative tour. But in the spring of 2011, the rotunda became the epicenter of the protests. People had the rare opportunity to view the rotunda's majesty at all hours of the day or night.

That particular Monday night and Tuesday morning, in a pattern established on day one of the protests, hundreds of protesters huddled in sleeping bags in every imaginable space: out-of-the-way nooks and crannies, spacious hallways, offices of Democratic legislators. Many had brought their protest signs with them—"Democracy Is Better in Person," "Screw Us and We Multiply," "This Is What Democracy Looks Like." Months later, the almost surreal memories of that night will come to mind as I ponder the many unpredictable, spontaneous, and inspiring events that took place during the spring of 2011.

The sleepover did not dominate the national news, but it was an essential part of the Madison uprising. Just a few days into the protests, it was clear that the battle was about more than just respect for workers' rights in Wisconsin. Democracy—especially the right of citizens to redress injustice and speak to their elected representatives—quickly surfaced as a key issue.

By law, the Wisconsin capitol must remain open if members of the public want to take part in legislative business. Democrats in the assembly, in order to prevent a fast-track vote on Walker's union-busting bill, were maintaining a twenty-four-hour hearing on the legislation. Concerned citizens, knowing the Republicans were eager to limit public access and end the hearing, began to sleep overnight in the capitol in order to be available for the hearing and to make sure the building stayed open to the public. The effort, dubbed a "sleepover, Madison-style," continued for almost a month as the capitol rotunda was renamed "the People's Popular Assembly."

Establishing their own rules of behavior, the protesters called for quiet after the capitol doors closed at 11:00 P.M. If you were in, you could stay in. If you were outside, you had to wait until entrances reopened in the morning. On a cold Monday in mid-February, I rushed to the capitol around 8:00 P.M., sleeping bag, photography equipment, and snacks in hand. Like most people, I spent my first several hours walking around in amazement at such a unique experience in popular democracy. Young mothers with their infants, gray-haired clergy, students with laptop computers—it was a cross section of dedicated Wisconsinites. Around 11:00 P.M., as quiet descended, I was lucky to find a spot to sleep in a sympathetic legislator's office. Like just about everyone else, I slept poorly and intermittently. Four hours later, I gave up any hope of sleep. I grabbed my camera and walked around to document a scene I knew I would never again experience.

As I walked around the rotunda, silence dominated. Some sleepers had come prepared with earplugs and eye masks. Others had elaborate setups complete with inflatable mattresses. Some huddled close to each other, the cold of the granite and marble floors seeping up through thin blankets. Just about everyone had a homemade sign or two. I laughed to myself at some of the signs—such as the retro, hippie-like picture of Scott Walker complete with pig nose and the caption "It's All About . . . Me!!!" There were also no-nonsense rules of conduct posted throughout the capitol, such as "Welcome to the democratic process! Please pick up after yourself."

At one point, I noticed a security guard in the middle of the rotunda, gazing upward at the inside of the dome—an architectural wonder of awe-inspiring beauty. He was trying to take a picture, but there was little light available. I offered him use of my tripod. In return, he snapped a picture of me. We whispered our thanks to each other.

Continuing my journey around the rotunda, I came upon firefighters gathered around the statue of Fightin' Bob La Follette. An iconic hero in Wisconsin who fought the corporate titans of his day (in particular, lumber and railroad barons), Fightin' Bob was an early-twentieth-century Wisconsin governor, senator, and presidential candidate under the Progressive Party. He is reverently remembered as a populist leader who helped establish Wisconsin's progressive tradition and belief in public institutions as a bedrock of democracy. Throughout the demonstrations, protesters proudly had their picture taken at the Fightin' Bob statue. On that particular night, scores of firefighters were quietly sleeping in the shadow of La Follette's bust, their hats, boots, and firefighting gear neatly stacked nearby.

Firefighters from throughout the state took part in the protests in a show of solidarity and mutual concern for Wisconsin's future. No pronouncement was ever formally made, but everyone knew that the firefighters had first dibs on gathering around the Fightin' Bob statue. It was the demonstrators' way of recognizing that, at this moment in history, the firefighters had moved beyond protecting the public against fire and natural disasters and, in the spirit of Fightin' Bob, were protecting citizens against a man-made misfortune.

*   *   *

On Wednesday, March 9, day twenty-three of the round-the-clock protests, the Senate Republicans pulled an unexpected parliamentary maneuver. They eliminated fiscal measures from the union-busting bill, which meant Democratic support was not needed to reach the votes required for bills with spending provisions. Without any public hearings and only two hours of public notice, the Senate passed the measure. The next day, as protesters chanted "Shame, shame, shame," the Republican-dominated assembly also approved the bill.

Republicans had hoped that passage of the antiunion bill would end the protesting. Once again they underestimated the depth of the people's anger. That Saturday, the largest crowd yet descended on Madison, with estimates ranging up to 250,000 people. Reflecting Wisconsin's long tradition of a farm-labor alliance, a "tractorcade" of farmers traveled to Madison to lead the day's protests. The Democratic state senators who had left the state, dubbed "Wisconsin's Fab Fourteen," returned to a hero's welcome.

Rather than being disheartened by the Republicans' maneuvering, the crowd sent a message. The sleeping giant of popular outrage, now awakened, was preparing for the long haul. Walker might have won round one, but the fight was far from over. Most immediately, energy focused on petitions to recall Senate Republicans, with promises to recall Governor Walker after the legal requirement was met of a year in office.

Three months later, on June 4, 2011, Mary Arms proudly carries an "I Love My Public Schools" placard as she crosses Milwaukee's Sixteenth Street Viaduct. Next to her, longtime friend Betty Martin carries a sign that links Milwaukee's Open Housing movement of the 1960s and Walker's attacks on public education, asking: "1967, Fair Housing After 200 Nights. 2011, How Long for Education Rights?"

The viaduct is the same bridge that Arms and Martin crossed forty-four years earlier during Milwaukee's civil rights era, to be greeted by thousands of angry whites shouting racial epithets and, in some cases, hurling rocks and beer bottles.

Arms, Martin, and others from the NAACP Youth Council of the 1960s grabbed their protest signs that June day in 2011 to lead a multiracial group of activists protesting the governor's agenda. The presence of the Youth

Council sent an unequivocal message: the right to a quality public education is a fundamental civil right and must be defended at all costs. "People used to ask us during Open Housing, 'How long you guys going to march?'" Arms recalls. "'Until we get what we want,' we'd reply. And that's the spirit we need today."

When Arms and Martin walked across the Sixteenth Street Viaduct in 2011, they were in the forefront of a multiracial display that is not necessarily the norm in Milwaukee. African Americans, whites, and Latinos, young children and gray-haired veterans, ministers and teachers joined in common cause under the slogan "We Are One Milwaukee and Our Kids Count."

Vel Phillips, the African American Common Council member who spearheaded the open housing legislation in the 1960s, was grand marshal of the march. When she crossed the viaduct, she joined hands with Michael Bonds, the African American president of the Milwaukee school board. Gregory Thornton, the district's African American superintendent, spoke to the crowd. Elected officials joined ministers, activists, parents, teachers, and students in the march, which began and ended at public schools. The grassroots group Voces de la Frontera provided translation and brought hundreds of people to defend bilingual education and the rights of undocumented students. The crowd was an unusual and heartening multicultural gathering in a city known for its segregation and divisions.

In an interview in her dining room in the fall of 2011, Arms talked about the significance of both open housing and public education.[20] An "I Love My Public Schools" placard from the protest that June is still on display, propped up against the wall.

Arms shows the same positive spirit she had as a teenage member of the NAACP Youth Council. She explains that she learned at a young age not to be afraid of political turmoil. Born in 1950 in Belzoni, Mississippi, Arms moved with her family to Milwaukee when she was two, but she returned to Belzoni every summer for much of her youth. Civil rights icons were a part of Arms's daily life when she visited her relatives, often stopping by her grandfather's or uncle's home. "We were supposed to stay with Granny and help with gardening and things," she says. "But I also remember all these people, you know, like Fannie Lou Hamer, Medgar Evers. And my grandfather wasn't afraid to house the Freedom Bus Riders at his farm."

Arms first met civil rights leader Father James Groppi while attending one of the Milwaukee Freedom Schools in 1964. She joined the NAACP Youth Council during the Open Housing movement's protests a few years later. After that seminal struggle, the decades quickly sped by as Arms raised five children and helped with her twelve grandchildren. Her health could be better, and she eagerly awaits the day she can retire from her office job at a local hospital. When Peggy Rozga, Groppi's widow, asked her to take part in the June 4, 2011, demonstration as part of a contingent of 1960s activists, she had no doubt she would attend. "Too many people act like they're afraid, that protesting is a thing of the past. But the injustices are still going on, and people like Walker are still getting away with things. And you can't let them."

Reflecting on decades of history, Arms does not have any easy answers. She's not on the inside of political deliberations on how best to counter Governor Walker and the Republican agenda, and she is not committed to one particular tactic over another. She is proud to have been a foot soldier in struggles spanning a half century, well aware that it is the people on the ground who keep a movement alive. She knows there will be ups and downs as the struggle unfolds.

As a foot soldier, Arms says, she has learned one essential lesson: "You just got to keep on, make sure you keep that fire going. There's always something you can do. Always."

NOTES

Introduction

1. National Center for Education Statistics, *The Nation's Report Card: Reading 2009* (NCES 2010-458), 55. Institute of Education Sciences, U.S. Department of Education, Washington, DC.

2. "Black Men Hit Hard by Unemployment in Milwaukee," *Washington Post*, December 24, 2009.

3. 2009 figures: Marc Levine, "The Crisis Deepens: Black Male Joblessness in Milwaukee 2009," Working Paper, Center for Economic Development, University of Wisconsin–Milwaukee, October 2010, 2. 2010 figures: Marc Levine, "Race and Male Employment in the Wake of the Great Recession," Working Paper, Center for Economic Development, University of Wisconsin–Milwaukee, January 2012, 2.

4. "The 10 Most Segregated Urban Areas in America," salon.com, March 29, 2011.

5. Personal correspondence from Marc Levine, founding director of Center for Economic Development, University of Wisconsin–Milwaukee, October 7, 2011. The figure refers to black men ages twenty-five to fifty-four.

6. Thomas J. Sugrue, *Sweet Land of Liberty* (New York: Random House, 2009), xix, citing Lewis Mumford Center for Comparative Urban and Regional Research, University at Albany, "Metropolitan Area Rankings: Population for All Ages: Sortable List of Dissimilarity Scores," mumfords1.dyndns.org/cen2000/WholePop/WPsort /sort_d1.html; Gary Orfield and Chungmei Lee, *Racial Transformation and the Changing Nature of Segregation* (Cambridge, MA: The Civil Rights Project at Harvard University, 2006), Table 11.

7. *Plyler v. Doe*, decided June 15, 1982, Justice William J. Brennan Jr. writing for the majority.

8. U.S. Census, 2010 Annual Survey of Public Employment and Payroll.

9. "PolitiFact Wisconsin," *Milwaukee Journal Sentinel*, February 19, 2012, via jsonline .com.

1. The Glory Days of 1957

1. As recounted by Howard Bryant, *The Last Hero: A Life of Henry Aaron* (New York: Pantheon Books, 2010), 222.

2. Ibid., 205.

3. In his autobiography, Aaron notes how the Wisconsin *CIO News* commented on the irony of the news developments, "just as I had. It wrote, 'Milwaukee's dusky Hank Aaron blasted the Braves into the World Series only a few hours after an insane mob of white supremacists took the Stars and Stripes in Little Rock and tramped it on the ground in front of Central High School.'" Hank Aaron, with Lonnie Wheeler, *I Had a Hammer: The Hank Aaron Story* (New York: HarperCollins, 1991), 174.

4. Ibid., 173–74.

5. Peter Irons, *Jim Crow's Children* (New York: Viking, 2002), 177.

6. Ellen Levine, *Freedom's Children: Young Civil Rights Activists Tell Their Own Stories* (New York: Puffin Books, 1993), 42.

7. Taylor Branch, *Parting the Waters: America in the King Years 1954–63* (New York: Simon & Schuster, 1988), 222. Taylor also recounts how the troops not only kept out the Little Rock Nine but also barred the black service workers, leading to more than a few grumbles from white faculty who did not want to cook their own meals and sweep their own classrooms.

8. Ibid., 223.

9. Ibid.

10. Ibid., 224.

11. Melba Patillo Beals, *Warriors Don't Cry*, abridged ed. (New York: Simon Pulse, 1995), 90; Branch, *Parting the Waters*, 224.

12. Levine, *Freedom's Children*, 48.

13. http://my.barackobama.com/page/community/post_group/ObamaHQ/Chfp, Post from Obama HQ by Sam Graham-Felsen, September 25, 2007, accessed September 8, 2010.

14. Robert W. Wells, *This Is Milwaukee* (Garden City, NY: Doubleday, 1970), 238–39.

15. John Gurda, *The Making of Milwaukee* (Milwaukee: Milwaukee County Historical Society, 1999), 350.

16. Bryant, *Last Hero*, 90.

17. Wells, *This Is Milwaukee*, 239.

18. Gurda, *The Making of Milwaukee*, 351.

19. Robert D. Putnam, *Bowling Alone: The Collapse and Revival of American Community* (New York: Simon & Schuster, 2000), as quoted by John Gurda in "We Gain Something but We Lose It Too," *Milwaukee Journal Sentinel*, September 5, 2010.

20. John L. Rury, "The Changing Social Context of Urban Education," in *Seeds of Crisis: Public Schooling in Milwaukee Since 1920*, ed. John L. Rury and Frank A. Cassell (Madison: University of Wisconsin Press, 1993), 11.

21. Milwaukee Public Schools, *Our Roots Grow Deep*, 2nd ed. (Milwaukee: Board of School Directors, 1974), 21.

22. Ibid., 21, 68.

23. Ibid., 21.

24. Ibid.

25. Ibid.

26. Paul Haubrich, "Student Life in Milwaukee High Schools, 1920–1885," in Rury and Cassell, *Seeds of Crisis*, 207.

27. Rolland Callaway, *MPS, a Chronological History 1836–1986* (Milwaukee: Caritas Communications, 2008), 3: 136.

28. James G. Cibulka and Frederick I. Olson, "The Organization and Politics of the Milwaukee Public School System, 1920–1986," in Rury and Cassell, *Seeds of Crisis*, 89.

29. *Our Roots Grow Deep*, 22, 68.

30. *1986–1996 School Building and Sites Plan*, presented to the Milwaukee Board of School Directors by the School Building and Sites Commission, May 15, 1986, 27.

31. Marc V. Levine and John F. Zipp, "A City at Risk," in Rury and Cassell, *Seeds of Crisis*, 47.

32. "Beer Headed for Price Rise," *Milwaukee Journal*, August 10, 1956.

33. Bryant, *Last Hero*, 186.

34. Ibid., 103.

35. Sandy Tolan, *Me and Hank: A Boy and His Hero, Twenty-Five Years Later* (New York: Free Press, 2001), 93.

36. Aaron, *If I Had a Hammer*, 179.

37. Aaron's autobiography refers to Alfredia attending school in "Milwaukee," seeming to use the term for the metropolitan area in general. At the time of the incident, Aaron lived in Mequon. Milwaukee native Sandy Tolan, in his book *Me and Hank*, notes that the school was in Mequon. Alfredia, in Aaron's *If I Had a Hammer*, talks about walking to school.

38. Aaron, *If I Had a Hammer*, 180.

2. The 1950s: Milwaukee's Black Community Comes of Age

1. Personal interview as part of research for "Valiant Lady Vel," *Milwaukee Magazine*, January 2005.

2. "Schools' Race Policies Aired," *Milwaukee Journal*, October 12, 1953.

3. Personal anecdotes such as this, unless otherwise noted, are based on "Valiant Lady Vel," *Milwaukee Magazine*, January 2005.

4. Charles T. O'Reilly, "The Inner Core—North, A Study of Milwaukee's Negro Community," University of Wisconsin–Milwaukee, School of Social Work, December 1963, Map 2.

5. This vignette is included in "Valiant Lady Vel," *Milwaukee Magazine*, January 2005.

6. O'Reilly, "The Inner Core," i, ii, 1.

7. Ruth Zubrensky, "A Report on Past Discrimination Against African-Americans in Milwaukee, 1835–1999," Milwaukee, July 1999.

8. William R. Tisdale and Fred M. Freiberg, "Our Housing History," Testimony on a Proposed Metropolitan School Desegregation Plan, Presented to the Milwaukee School Board, March 24, 1984.

9. Gurda, *Making of Milwaukee*, 358–59; Zubrensky, "A Report on Past Discrimination."

10. John Gurda, *The Making of Milwaukee* (Milwaukee: Milwankee County Historical Society, 1999), 170, 362–63.

11. Irwin D. Rinder, Milwaukee Commission on Human Rights, "The Housing of Negroes in Milwaukee: 1955," 47.

12. "Mayor's Study Committee on Social Problems in the Inner Core Area of the City, Final Report to the Honorable Frank P. Zeidler, Mayor, City of Milwaukee, April 15, 1960," 8.

13. Ibid., 2.

14. Paul Geib, "From Mississippi to Milwaukee: A Case Study of the Southern Black Migration to Milwaukee, 1940–1970," *Journal of Negro History* 83, no. 4 (Autumn 1998): 233.

15. Ibid., 235.

16. Research by Jack Dougherty, files of the Wisconsin Black Historical Society and Museum.

17. Zubrensky, "A Report on Past Discrimination."

18. Ibid.

19. Personal interview, June 2010.

20. Jack Dougherty, *More than One Struggle* (Chapel Hill: University of North Carolina Press, 2004), 20, 22, 31.

21. Ibid., 32.

22. "Zeidler Tops McGuire by 11,712 Votes," *Milwaukee Journal*, March 7, 1956.

23. Kevin D. Smith, "From Socialism to Racism: The Politics of Class and Identity in Postwar Milwaukee," *Michigan Historical Review*, Spring 2003.

24. "Races: The Shame of Milwaukee," *Time*, April 2, 1956.

25. *Milwaukee Journal*, March 11, 1956, newspaper archives available through the Milwaukee Public Library, Central Library.

26. "Races: The Shame of Milwaukee."

27. Ibid.

28. "'Hoodlum Mob' Ad Angers Police Chief," *Milwaukee Journal*, March 29, 1956.

29. Smith, "From Socialism to Racism."

30. "The Selma of the North," a description first used during Milwaukee's open housing marches, was later the title of a book on the Milwaukee civil rights movement by Patrick D. Jones (Cambridge, MA: Harvard University Press, 2009).

3. 1964: Freedom Schools Come to Milwaukee

1. "Take This Hammer," WNET, originally produced by KQED for National Education Television (NET). Accessed via https://diva.sfsu.edu/bundles/187041, 7:59.

2. Personal interview, March 2010.

3. MUSIC leaflet, "Keep Your Children Out of School," MUSIC Records, Box 1, Folder 3, Archives/Milwaukee Area Research Center. University of Wisconsin–Milwaukee Libraries.

4. "Ald Phillips Levels Blast at Seraphim," *Milwaukee Journal*, June 25, 1964.

5. Frank A. Aukofer, *City with a Chance: A Case History of Civil Rights Revolution* (Milwaukee: Marquette University Press, 2007), 80.

6. Patrick D. Jones, *The Selma of the North: Civil Rights Insurgency in Milwaukee* (Cambridge, MA: Harvard University Press, 2009), 70.

7. "11,500 Boycott Public Schools to Protest de Facto Segregation."

8. "King Rejects Excuse in School Segregation," *Milwaukee Journal*, January 27, 1964.

9. "Suffer, Sacrifice, Die in Order to be Free," *Milwaukee Star*, February 1, 1964.

10. "11,500 Boycott Public Schools to Protest de Facto Segregation."

11. Personal interview, March 2010.

12. "Program of Activities, Primary Grades," MUSIC Records, Box 1, Folder 2, Archives/Milwaukee Area Research Center. University of Wisconsin–Milwaukee Libraries.

13. Written by Florence Howe and distributed to Freedom School teachers in Milwaukee. Florence Howe, "Mississippi's Freedom Schools: The Politics of Education," *Harvard Educational Review* 35, no. 2 (Spring 1965): 144–60. Copyright © 1965 President and Fellows of Harvard College. For more information, please visit harvardeducationalreview.org.

14. Aukofer, *City with a Chance*, 77.

15. "NAACP Rap on Schools Anticipated," *Milwaukee Sentinel*, October 22, 1963.

16. "Attitudes and Opinions of Milwaukee Public School Teachers in Central City Schools," 1965 report to the Milwaukee School Board, in possession of the author.

17. "I Spent 4 Years in an Integrated High School," *U.S. News & World Report*, November 7, 1958.

18. Jones, *Selma of the North*, 53.

19. Ibid., 60.

20. Ibid., 61.

21. "Barbee Supports LBJ on Vietnam, Raps Dissenters," *Milwaukee Sentinel*, May 22, 1967.

22. "Protest March Slated Against School Board," *Milwaukee Journal*, January 27, 1964.

23. Personal interview, April 2010.

24. Eugene Kane, "Honor Barbee's Legacy with Action of Your Own," *Milwaukee Journal*, January 5, 2003, via jsonline.com.

4. Milwaukee Loves George Wallace

1. "Shouts Back Wallace at Rally on South Side," *Milwaukee Journal*, April 2, 1964.
2. "Wallace Urges Racial 'Reality,'" *New York Times*, September 6, 1963.
3. "Shouts Back Wallace at Rally on South Side."
4. "Wisconsin Vote Hailed in South by Rights Foes," *New York Times*, April 9, 1964.
5. William F. Thompson, *The History of Wisconsin, Volume VI: Continuity and Change, 1940–1965* (Madison: State Historical Society of Wisconsin, 1988), 732–33.
6. Ibid., 730.

5. Milwaukee's Great Migration #1: Blacks Move from the South to the Inner Core

1. Nicholas Lemann, *The Promised Land: The Great Black Migration and How It Changed America* (New York: Vintage Books, 1992), 6.
2. Roy L. Hamilton, "Expectations and Realities of a Migrant Group: Black Migration from the South to Milwaukee, 1946 to 1958," master's thesis, University of Wisconsin–Milwaukee, 1981, 33.
3. Personal interview, July 2010.
4. Paul Geib, "From Mississippi to Milwaukee: A Case Study of the Southern Black Migration to Milwaukee, 1940–1970," *Journal of Negro History* 83, no. 4 (Autumn 1998): 232.
5. "Mayor's Study Committee on Social Problems in the Inner Core Area of the City," 1960, 10; Charles T. O'Reilly, "The Inner Core—North, a Study of Milwaukee's Negro Community," A Project of the School of Social Work, University of Wisconsin–Milwaukee, 1963, 11.
6. 1970 unemployment: Geib, "From Mississippi to Milwaukee," 243. Geib notes that in 1940, 36 percent of black men were in professional, skilled, or semiskilled jobs. By 1970, that percentage had risen to 66.1 percent, with most in semiskilled jobs (242). In 1940, only 141 homes in Milwaukee were occupied by black homeowners (241). By 1980 the number had risen to 15,482 (241). Figures on median income and poverty: "Only the City Can Do It; Now the Hard Part Begins," *Milwaukee Journal Sentinel*, based in part on data from "The Economic State of Milwaukee: The City and The Region, 1998," Center for Economic Development, University of Wisconsin–Milwaukee, 1998, 43–44, and Marc Levine, "The Two Milwaukees: Separate and Unequal," paper presented to Milwaukee County Task Force on Segregation and Race Relations, April 30, 2003, 12. The black poverty rate in Milwaukee was 22 percent lower than the comparable national average, and median income was 19 percent higher.
7. Geib, "From Mississippi to Milwaukee," 244–45.

6. 1965: Direct Action Targets "Intact Busing"

1. Following the protests, there were instances in which African American students were allowed to stay at the receiving school for lunch, with the first such reported

instance in 1964, according to "Racial Isolation in the Public Schools, A Report of the United States Commission on Civil Rights, 1967," 57.

2. MUSIC document on intact busing, citing the Milwaukee School Board Finance Committee Minutes, 8-28-57 (at 45), Archives/Milwaukee Area Research Center, University of Wisconsin–Milwaukee Libraries.

3. For a detailed analysis of busing for modernization or overcrowding from 1958 to 1974, see *Amos et al. v Board of School Directors of the City of Milwaukee et al.*, decided January 19, 1976, by U.S. District Judge John W. Reynolds Jr., 48–52.

4. "Racial Isolation in the Public Schools," 57.

5. Bob Peterson, "Neighborhood Schools, Busing and the Struggle for Equality," *Rethinking Schools* 12, no. 3 (Spring 1998). See also Judge Reynolds's decision, 50.

6. "Racial Isolation in the Public Schools," 57.

7. This account is based on "11 Demonstrators Seized for Blocking School Buses," *Milwaukee Journal*, May 24, 1965.

8. "Pickets' Trial Set June 2 in School Bus Incident," *Milwaukee Sentinel*, May 25, 1965.

9. "13 Disrupt School Board Committee," *Milwaukee Sentinel*, May 25, 1965.

10. Patrick D. Jones, *The Selma of the North: Civil Rights Insurgency in Milwaukee* (Cambridge, MA: Harvard University Press, 2009), 102.

11. Taylor Branch, *At Canaan's Edge: America In the King Years 1965–68* (New York: Simon & Schuster, 2007), 50.

12. Ibid., 49–52.

13. Jones, *Selma of the North*, 107.

14. Ibid., 92.

15. Ibid., 88.

16. "New Group Arranges Talk by Author Griffin," *Milwaukee Journal*, January 26, 1965.

17. "Priest Defends Actions Which Led to Arrest," *Milwaukee Journal*, June 7, 1965.

18. Jones, *Selma of the North*, 102.

19. Ibid., 76.

20. Frank A. Aukofer, *City with a Chance: A Case History of Civil Rights Revolution* (Milwaukee: Marquette University Press, 2007), 102.

21. Ibid., 97.

22. Jones, *Selma of the North*, 113–15.

23. Ibid., 122.

24. "Guard Restrains White Hecklers," *Milwaukee Journal*, August 29, 1966.

25. "Tension Joins March to Wauwatosa," *Milwaukee Journal*, August 29, 1966.

7. 1967–68: Open Housing Moves to Center Stage

1. Patrick D. Jones, *The Selma of the North: Civil Rights Insurgency in Milwaukee* (Cambridge, MA: Harvard University Press, 2009), 169–70.

2. Frank A. Aukofer, *City with a Chance: A Case History of Civil Rights Revolution* (Milwaukee: Marquette University Press, 2007), 159.

3. Ibid., 163.

4. Ibid., 184.

5. Audio tape, WTMJ Special Report on School Boycotts and De Facto Segregation in Milwaukee, University of Wisconsin–Milwaukee archives, October 18, 1965. Available online through the UWM "The March on Milwaukee Civil Rights History Project," www4.uwm.edu/libraries/digilib/march/index.cfm.

6. Jones, *Selma of the North*, 242.

7. "War Foes Raid Office Here, Seize, Burn Draft Records," *Milwaukee Sentinel*, September 25, 1968, and "Draft Office Here Raided, Protesters Burn Records," *Milwaukee Journal*, September 25, 1968.

8. *Brown* and *Milliken*: The U.S. Supreme Court Advances and Retreats

1. Richard Kluger, *Simple Justice* (New York: Alfred A. Knopf, 1976), 700.

2. Ibid., 708.

3. Derrick A. Bell, *Silent Covenants:* Brown v. Board of Education *and the Unfulfilled Hopes for Racial Reform* (New York: Oxford University Press, 2004), 3.

4. Peter Irons, *Jim Crow's Children, The Broken Promise of the Brown Decision* (New York: Viking, 2002), 12.

5. Ibid., 1.

6. Ibid., 12–13.

7. Ibid., 173, 177.

8. Ibid., 222–23.

9. Thomas J. Sugrue, *Sweet Land of Liberty* (New York: Random House, 2009), 465.

10. Ibid., 467.

11. Ibid., 451.

12. Ibid., 450.

13. Ibid., 482–83.

14. Irons, *Jim Crow's Children*, 241.

15. Ibid., 242.

16. Sugrue, *Sweet Land of Liberty*, 487.

17. Ibid., 538.

9. January 19, 1976: The Court Rules—Milwaukee's Schools Are Segregated

1. "Suit Here Charges School Segregation," *Milwaukee Journal*, June 18, 1965. The paper cites Barbee as saying it was the first suit in the nation with white parents as plaintiffs.

2. *Amos et al. v. Board of School Directors of the City of Milwaukee et al.*, decided January 19, 1976, by Federal District Court Judge John W. Reynolds Jr., 105.

staff bulletin, September 21, 1987.

Murrin Tried Out Territory," *Milwaukee Sentinel*, July 2, 1975.

McMurrin, personal writings, sent to author.

ett, "A Plan for Increasing Educational Opportunities," 86.

k, *Against the Wind*, 310.

nent by Special Master John A. Gronouski, June 9, 1976, to Judge Reynolds,
rt of the Special Master's Second Progress Report. A copy of the document is
e possession of the author.

k, *Against the Wind*, 317, quoting the *Milwaukee Courier*, July 17, 1976.

ember 7, 1976: The Buses Roll and Desegregation Begins

nal interview, April 2010.

McNally, "Taking Liberties," *Shepherd Express*, October 28, 1999.

ool Integration Goes Well, But . . ." editorial, *Milwaukee Sentinel*, September
76.

Dahlk, *Against the Wind: African Americans and the Schools in Milwaukee,
–2002* (Milwaukee: Marquette University Press, 2010), 315, quoting *Milwau-
ournal* statistics.

e Murphy and John Pawasarat, "Why It Failed: School Desegregation 10
s Later," *Milwaukee Magazine*, September 1986.

gration Ideas Run the Spectrum," *Milwaukee Journal*, November 15, 1976.

d A. Bennett, "A Plan for Increasing Educational Opportunities and Improv-
Racial Balance in Milwaukee," in *School Desegregation Plans that Work*, ed.
les V. Willie (Westport, CT: Greenwood Press, 1984), 88.

hite Benefit' Was Driving Force of Busing," *Milwaukee Journal Sentinel*, Octo-
9, 1999.

gration Gets a D," *Milwaukee Journal*, April 24, 1977.

n a forthcoming memoir by Bob Peterson, "The Making of an Activist."

; also Dahlk, *Against the Wind*, 575.

Least the Kids Get Back to Class," *Milwaukee Journal* editorial, May 10,
.

lk, *Against the Wind*, 576.

ika is a pseudonym.

ghborhood Schools, Busing, and the Struggle for Equality," *Rethinking Schools
o. 3 (Spring 1998).

onal interview, March 2010.

phy and Pawasarat, "Why It Failed."

egration Issue Far from Settled," *Milwaukee Journal*, February 28, 1979.

tlement OK'd Despite Objections," *Milwaukee Journal*, February 28, 1979.

yd Barbee's Battle," *Milwaukee Journal Sentinel*, October 27, 1996.

3. Barbee's main assistant in the early years was Maril
   and dedicated activist. Moreheuser worked nonstop o
   ing a subsistence-level salary based on small donatio
   Before the trial began, Moreheuser moved to New Jers
   national acclaim for her groundbreaking work on equ

4. "Most Side with Board on Bussing," *Milwaukee Senti*

5. *Amos* decision, 129.

6. Lois Quinn, Michael Barndt, and Diane Pollard, "R
   Desegregation and Government Housing Programs
   prepared for the National Institute of Education, 198(

7. David A. Bennett, "A Plan for Increasing Educational
   ing Racial Balance in Milwaukee," in *School Desegre*
   Charles V. Willie (Westport, CT: Greenwood Press, 1

8. "'Makes My Blood Boil,'" *Milwaukee Sentinel*, Januaı

9. Bill Dahlk, *Against the Wind: African Americans an*
   1963–2002 (Milwaukee: Marquette University Press,
   waukee Journal, January 20, 25, 1976.

10. "Schools Defended as Victim, Not Criminal," *Milwauk*

11. "Parochial School Haven Ruled Out," *Milwaukee Sen*

12. Catholic Interracial Council, "Segregation in Milwa
    Schools," *Equity and Excellence in Education* 5 (1967)
    as *Integrated Education* in 1967], 20–21.

13. Dahlk, *Against the Wind*, 306, quoting the *Milwauke*

14. "Reactions Vary Widely to Reynolds' Ruling," *Mil*
    Women" page, January 20, 1976.

15. President Richard Nixon, "Special Message to the Co
    Opportunities and School Busing," March 17, 1972.

16. President Gerald Ford, "The President's News Confer

17. Peter Irons, *Jim Crow's Children: The Broken Promise*
    York: Viking, 2002), 252.

18. Ibid.

19. "Violence Mars Busing in Boston," *New York Times*, ‹

20. Irons, *Jim Crow's Children*, 256.

21. Ibid., 257.

22. "Wallace Sounds Busing Refrain," *Milwaukee Journa*

23. Personal phone interview, June 2010.

24. "Our New Superintendent," *Milwaukee Journal* edito:

25. Marilee C. Risk, *The Executive Educator*, from the pei
    Bruce Murphy and John Pawasarat, "Why It Failed: S‹
    Later," *Milwaukee Magazine*, September 1986.

26.
27.
28.
29.
30.
31.

32.

10.
1.
2.
3.

4.

5.

6.
7.

8.

9.
10.
11.
12.

13.
14.
15.

16.
17.
18.
19.
20.

21. "The Milwaukee School Desegregation Case," William H. Lynch, 1986, from Lynch's personal files.

22. "'White Benefit' Was Driving Force of Busing."

23. Murphy and Pawasarat, "Why It Failed."

24. Ibid.

25. Ibid.

11. 1981: Police Brutality Moves to Center Stage

1. "Witnesses Say Lacy Was Pinned," *Milwaukee Journal*, September 19, 1981.

2. "No Blows Struck, Officers Say," *Milwaukee Journal*, July 11, 1981; "Jury Faces Puzzling Task," *Milwaukee Journal*, October 13, 1981; "Officials Prepare to Arrest 3 Officers," *Milwaukee Journal*, October 15, 1981.

3. "Fright May Have Caused Man's Death After His Arrest," *Milwaukee Sentinel*, July 11, 1981.

4. "Milwaukee's Cops Under Fire," *Newsweek*, February 15, 1982.

5. "Racial Isolation in Milwaukee Public Schools, A Final Report to the U.S. Commission on Civil Rights," May 1967, 35.

6. "Milwaukee's Cops Under Fire."

7. "Milwaukee Policemen's Trial May Be Delayed," *New York Times*, UPI report, October 18, 1981.

8. *Chicago Tribune*, August 16, 1981, quoted in Laura R. Woliver, "A Measure of Justice: Police Conduct and Black Civil Rights: The Coalition for Justice for Ernest Lacy," *Western Political Quarterly* 43, no. 2 (June 1990).

9. Woliver, "Measure of Justice," 418.

10. Ibid., 426.

11. "A Farewell to 'the Good People,'" *Milwaukee Journal*, May 2, 1984.

12. "Serial Murder Case Exposes Deep Milwaukee Tensions," *New York Times*, August 2, 1991.

13. Ibid.

14. Details are based on the ruling of the United States Court of Appeals, Seventh Circuit, *United States of America v. Bartlett, Sprengler and Masarik*, decided June 8, 2009, decision by Chief Judge Frank H. Easterbrook.

15. Ibid.

16. "1981 Police Beating Holds Grim Lessons. Prosecutors in Jude Case Will Face Obstacles," *Milwaukee Journal Sentinel*, February 28, 2005, via jsonline.com.

17. "The Jude Case: A Case of Credibility? Witnesses May Have Undermined 'Code of Silence' Arguments," *Milwaukee Journal Sentinel*, April 16, 2006, via jsonline.com.

18. "Milwaukee Police Looked into 'Punishers' Group," *Milwaukee Journal Sentinel*, January 6, 2011.

12. Milwaukee's Great Migration #2: Whites Move to the Suburbs

1. Douglas S. Massey and Nancy A. Denton, *American Apartheid: Segregation and the Making of the Underclass* (Cambridge: MA, Harvard University Press, 1993), 8.
2. Personal interview, February 2011.
3. Charles T. O'Reilly, "The Inner Core—North, A Study of Milwaukee's Negro Community," The University of Wisconsin—Milwaukee, School of Social Work, December 1963, Map 2.
4. John Gurda, *The Making of Milwaukee* (Milwaukee: Milwaukee County Historical Society, 1999), 335.
5. R.L. McNeely and M.R. Kinlow, *Milwaukee Today: A Racial Gap Study*, Milwaukee Urban League, 1987, 48.
6. Statement on Metropolitan School Desegregation, A Report to the U.S. Commission on Civil Rights, 1977, 23, quoting FHA manual provisions for 1935 and subsequent years.
7. Massey and Denton, *American Apartheid*, 55.
8. Ibid., 96.
9. Jay Gilmer, *Milwaukee Journal*, January 22, 1995, quoting a 1988 *Atlanta Journal-Constitution* report, reinforced by a study by the *Washington Post* and read into the *Congressional Record* of February 23, 1989.
10. "Lending Gap for Minorities Rises with Pay," *Milwaukee Journal*, January 12, 1995, via jsonline.com.
11. "Embracing Diversity, Housing in Southeastern Wisconsin," Public Policy Forum, February 2002, 5.
12. John L. Rury, "The Changing Social Context of Urban Education," in *Seeds of Crisis: Public Schooling in Milwaukee Since 1920*, ed. John L. Rury and Frank A. Cassell (Madison: University of Wisconsin Press, 1993), 14.
13. The 2010 Census listed 89.6 percent who classified themselves as "white" when listing just one race, and 91.6 percent who considered themselves "white" either alone or in combination with one or more other races.
14. Poverty rate based on the 2005–9 American Community Survey 5-Year Estimates of the U.S. Census.
15. "Poverty Numbers Spike in Milwaukee," *Milwaukee Journal Sentinel*, September 21, 2011, via jsonline.com.
16. "New Berlin Accused of Racial Bias," *Milwaukee Journal Sentinel*, June 24, 2011, based on data from the lawsuit.

13. The 1980s: The Rust Belt and Reaganomics

1. "MPS Mired in 'Distressed' City, Poverty Thwarts Schools," *Milwaukee Journal Sentinel*, January 8, 1998, reporting on an *Education Week* story quoting Myron Orfield, author of "Metropolitics: A Regional Agenda for Community and Stability."

2. John Gurda, *The Making of Milwaukee* (Milwaukee: Milwaukee County Historical Society, 1999), 415–17.

3. Marc Levine, "The Crisis of Black Male Joblessness in Milwaukee: Trends, Explanations and Policy Options," Working Paper, Center for Economic Development, University of Wisconsin–Milwaukee, March 2007, 35.

4. "Hit by a Global Train," *Milwaukee Journal Sentinel*, December 4, 2004.

5. Ibid. The article also cites the similar flip in poverty statistics.

6. Marc Levine, "The Crisis Deepens: Black Male Joblessness in Milwaukee, 2009," Working Paper, Center for Economic Development, University of Wisconsin–Milwaukee, October 2010.

7. Marc V. Levine and John F. Zipp, "A City at Risk: The Changing Social and Economic Context of Public Schooling in Milwaukee," in *Seeds of Crisis: Public Schooling in Milwaukee Since 1920*, ed. John L. Rury and Frank A. Cassell (Madison: University of Wisconsin Press, 1993), 56.

8. William Julius Wilson, *The Truly Disadvantaged* (Chicago: University of Chicago Press, 1987).

9. William Julius Wilson, *When Work Disappears* (New York: Vintage Books, 1997), xiii.

10. Because of Ken's history of drug use, Thompson is a pseudonym.

11. Wisconsin Department of Natural Resources, fact sheet on "Milwaukee's 30th Street Industrial Corridor Project," accessed March 21, 2011, http://dnr.wi.gov/org/aw/rr/rbrownfields/corridor.htm.

12. Barbara Miner, "The Stealth Depression in Black America," *The Progressive*, January 2005.

13. Michael Lind, *Up from Conservatism: Why the Right Is Wrong for America* (New York: Free Press, 1996), 3.

14. "Reagan Campaigns at Mississippi Fair," *New York Times*, August 4, 1980.

15. Bob Herbert, "Righting Reagan's Wrongs?" *New York Times*, November 13, 2007.

16. Kenneth O'Reilly, *Nixon's Piano: Presidents and Racial Politics from Washington to Clinton* (New York: Free Press, 1995), 351.

17. Ibid., 370.

18. "Quotation of the Day," *New York Times*, November 20, 1981.

19. Wilson, *When Work Disappears*, 49.

20. Personal correspondence from Levine, October 7, 2011.

14. Desegregation: Forward and Backward in the 1980s

1. Personal interview, February 2011.

2. Chapter 220 technically refers to state-funded intradistrict integration initiatives within MPS and the interdistrict program between MPS and the suburb. The public at large, however, does not make those distinctions and uses the term *Chapter 220* to refer to the MPS/suburban transfers.

3. Personal interview, October 2011.

4. "Conta Stirs Up a Hornet's Nest," *Milwaukee Journal*, January 14, 1975.

5. Personal interview, June 2011.

6. Metropolitan Integration Research Center, "Reorganization of Local School District: A Wisconsin Tradition," March 1984, 2, quoting a 1983 report by Dr. Herbert Grover, state superintendent.

7. William R. Tisdale and Fred M. Freiberg, "Our Housing History," Testimony on a Proposed Metropolitan School Desegregation Plan, Presented to the Milwaukee School Board, March 24, 1984.

8. "Rule of Lawyers: No Room for Citizens at This Trial," *Milwaukee Journal*, April 29, 1987.

9. R.L. McNeely and M.R. Kinlow, "Milwaukee Today a Racial Gap Study," Milwaukee Urban League, 1987, 42, using 1980 Census figures.

10. Letter from Charles S. McNeer, president of the Greater Milwaukee Committee, to John Peterburs, secretary–business manager of the Milwaukee Public Schools, January 28, 1986, Personal files of Mary Bills.

11. 1984 testimony before the MPS board representing Concerned Citizens for Quality Education of Black Children, copy of testimony from the personal files of Mary Bills.

12. Letter from Goyke, December 19, 1984, to suburban school districts; copy of letter is in the possession of the author.

13. Personal interview, May 2010.

14. McNeely and Kinlow, "Milwaukee Today," 48.

15. "An Evaluation of the Chapter 220 Program," State of Wisconsin Legislative Audit Bureau, 1994, 16.

16. "Interdistrict Chapter 220: Changing Goals and Perspectives," Public Policy Forum, 1999, i.

17. "An Evaluation of the Chapter 220 Program," 4.

18. "Impact of School Desegregation in Milwaukee Public Schools on Quality Education for Minorities . . . 15 Years Later," Wisconsin Advisory Committee to the United States Commission on Civil Rights, August 1992, 31.

19. Peter Murrell Jr., "Superintendent's Stance on Separate District Assailed," *Rethinking Schools* 2, no. 3 (March/April 1988).

20. "Blacks Push School Plan," *Milwaukee Journal*, August 11, 1987.

21. "Fuller Defends Plan for Inner City District," *Milwaukee Sentinel*, August 15, 1987.

22. Bill Dahlk, *Against the Wind: African Americans and the Schools in Milwaukee, 1963–2002* (Milwaukee: Marquette University Press, 2010), 349.

23. "Blacks, Whites Criticize School Resegregation Idea," *Milwaukee Journal*, August 12, 1987.

24. Chester Sheard, "NAACP Aide Calls Black School District 'Urban Apartheid,'" *Milwaukee Sentinel*, September 27, 1987; "Blacks, Whites Criticize School Resegregation Idea."

25. "Thompson Backs Inner City District," *Milwaukee Sentinel*, September 2, 1987.
26. Tom Bamberger, "The Education of Howard Fuller," *Milwaukee Magazine*, July 1988.
27. Dahlk, *Against the Wind*, 416.
28. "NAACP Lawyer Condemns Black School District," *Milwaukee Journal*, February 22, 1988.
29. "Black District Clears One Hurdle," *Milwaukee Journal*, March 18, 1988.
30. Jonathan Coleman, *Long Way to Go: Black and White in America* (New York: Atlantic Monthly Press, 1997), 377.

15. Latino Students: Moving Beyond Black and White
1. Rolland Callaway, *MPS, a Chronological History, 1836–1986*, 1:70.
2. Ibid., 1:238.
3. Tony Baez, Ricardo R. Fernandez, and Judith T. Guskin, *Desegregation and Hispanic Students: A Community Perspective* (Washington, DC: National Clearinghouse for Bilingual Education, 1980).
4. Ibid., 80.
5. Callaway, *MPS, a Chronological History*, 4:77.
6. "Public Schooling in the Milwaukee Metropolitan Area," 1988, Public Policy Forum, 9.
7. I was involved with various parent committees at Fratney, where I had the good fortune to work with Bob Peterson. We married in 1993 and together we raised my daughters Caitlin and Mahalia. In the spring of 2011, Bob was elected president of the Milwaukee teachers union.

16. Money: The Root of All Solutions
1. "Shared cost" figures are monies spent on an "ordinary" student in each district and do not include federal and state monies to help compensate for extraordinary needs such as special education or English language needs (with such funds rarely sufficient to cover the extra costs). As the number rises of students with extraordinary needs, money is often taken from the dollars meant for education of an "ordinary" student.
2. Michael Barndt and Joel McNally, "The Return to Separate and Unequal," *Rethinking Schools* report, Spring 2001.
3. In recent years, funding discussions have focused on "revenue limits per pupil." Under Wisconsin law, all school districts are subject to the revenue limit—the amount of money that a district can raise for basic student needs using both state aid and local property taxes. (In addition, districts are eligible for state and federal "categorical" funds to fund specific programs such as special education and bilingual education. Overall, state aid accounted for 44.3 percent of school district revenue in Wisconsin in 2008–9, with local property taxes providing 39.9 percent.)

Milwaukee's revenue limit per pupil in 2009–10 was $46 above the state average of $10,107, and far below almost all nearby suburban districts. Twenty suburban districts had a limit above Milwaukee, and three below. The Maple Dale–Indian Hill district to the north of Milwaukee had a revenue limit per pupil that was $6,683 more than Milwaukee's. For a school of four hundred students, this amounts to $2.673 million.

Shorewood, a district that abuts the City of Milwaukee, is a more typical suburb. Its revenue limit per pupil was $12,041—$1,888 more than Milwaukee's. For a school of four hundred pupils, that amounts to roughly $750,000 more, or the cost of seven or eight teachers.

4. Data provided by Lynn Krebs, who at the time was coordinator of Advanced Placement for the Milwaukee Public Schools.

5. Tanika is a pseudonym.

6. Figures based on data from the Wisconsin Department of Public Instruction. Figures available through the WINSS database at http://data.dpi.state.wi.us/data.

7. Personal interview, June 2010.

17. 1990: Vouchers Pass, Abandonment Begins

1. Ann Bastian, "Lessons from the Voucher War," in *Selling Out Our Schools*, ed. Robert Lowe and Barbara Miner (Milwaukee: Rethinking Schools, 1996), 21.

2. Greg Anrig, "An Idea Whose Time Has Gone," *Washington Monthly*, April 2008.

3. "'Choice' School in Turmoil Because of Staff Cuts, Changes," *Milwaukee Journal*, November 23, 1990.

4. In the more than twenty years of voucher schools receiving public funds, it wasn't until 2010 that the schools were required to have students take the state's standardized tests and report the data to the DPI.

5. The University School was not eligible for the voucher program at that time, because it was not in the city of Milwaukee. Judge Evans's ruling, however, pertains to private schools in general.

6. "University School Wins Speech Dispute," *Milwaukee Journal Sentinel*, September 1, 1995, via jsonline.com.

7. John J. Miller, "Strategic Investment in Ideas: How Two Foundations Reshaped America," Philanthropy Roundtable, Washington, D.C., 2003, 40. The report was based on Bradley and Olin Foundation annual reports, and interviews and assistance from foundation employees and grantees.

8. "Money Talks: Michael Joyce and the Bradley Foundation May Be the Voice of GOP's Future—for Millions of Reasons," *Chicago Tribune*, March 4, 1993.

9. Miller, "Strategic Investment in Ideas," 36.

10. Joyce later left the Bush administration, and died in 2006 at the age of sixty-three from what the *Milwaukee Journal Sentinel* described as "a long battle with liver

illness." See "Foundation Chief Nurtured Conservative Movement," *Milwaukee Journal Sentinel*, February 26, 2006, via jsonline.com.

11. John Gurda, *The Bradley Legacy: Lynde and Harry Bradley, Their Company, and Their Foundation* (Milwaukee: Lynde and Harry Bradley Foundation, 1992), 116.

12. Miller, "Strategic Investment in Ideas," 38–39.

13. Ibid., 7.

14. "From Local Roots, Bradley Foundation Builds Conservative Empire," *Milwaukee Journal Sentinel*, November 19, 2011, via jsonline.com.

15. Barbara Miner, "The Power and the Money: Bradley Foundation Bankrolls Conservative Agenda," *Rethinking Schools* 8, no. 3 (Spring 1994).

16. As quoted in *False Choices: Vouchers, Public Schools, and Our Children's Future*, a Rethinking Schools Special Report, Fall 2001.

17. Miner, "The Power and the Money."

18. Ibid., citing *Milwaukee Magazine*.

19. NPR, *All Things Considered* interview with David Brock, July 2, 2001. See Internet-based archive, www.npr.org/programs/atc/features/2001/jul/010702.brock.html.

20. Clint Bolick, "Clinton's Quota Queens," *Wall Street Journal*, April 30, 1993.

21. "Foundation Chief Nurtured Conservative Movement," *Milwaukee Journal Sentinel*, February 26, 2006, via jsonline.com.

22. Barbara Miner, "Bradley Foundation Bankrolls Conservative Agenda," in *Selling Out Our Schools*, ed. Robert Lowe and Barbara Miner (Milwaukee: Rethinking Schools, 1996).

23. Charles Murray and Richard J. Herrnstein, *The Bell Curve: Intelligence and Class Structure in American Life* (New York: Free Press, 1994), 436.

24. Miner, "The Power and the Money."

25. Barbara Miner, "*The Bell Curve*: Stealth Book of the 1990s?" *Rethinking Schools* 12, no. 4 (Summer 1998), citing the December 1997 issue of *National Review*.

26. Milton Friedman, "The Role of Government in Education," in *Economics and the Public Interest*, ed. Robert A. Solo (New Brunswick, NJ: Rutgers University Press, 1955).

27. Clint Bolick, *Voucher Wars: Waging the Legal Battle over School Choice* (Washington, DC: Cato Institute, 2003), 5.

28. Robert Lowe, "The Illusion of 'Choice,'" *Rethinking Schools* 6, no. 3 (March/April 1992).

29. Miller, "Strategic Investment in Ideas," 41.

30. Tommy G. Thompson, *Power to the People: An American State at Work* (New York: HarperCollins, 1996), 91.

31. Miller, "Strategic Investment in Ideas," 40.

32. Bennett also served as the so-called drug czar under George H.W. Bush, and once told Larry King that he believed it was a "morally plausible" position to behead drug dealers. June 15, 1989, appearance on *Larry King Live*.

33. Miner, "The Power and the Money," citing Milwaukee's *Business Journal*.

34. Thompson, *Power to the People*, 93.

35. Mikel Holt, *Not Yet "Free at Last": The Unfinished Business of the Civil Rights Movement, Our Battle for School Choice* (Oakland, CA: Institute for Contemporary Studies, 2000), 57.

36. Ibid., 58.

37. Alex Molnar, "Educational Vouchers: A Review of the Research," Center for Education Research, Analysis and Innovation, University of Wisconsin–Milwaukee, October 1999.

38. Personal interview, February 2011.

39. "Grover Says Paper's Editorial Made an Unfair Comparison. The *Wall Street Journal* Likens Him to Wallace Over School Choice Stance," *Milwaukee Journal*, June 29, 1990, via jsonline.com.

40. "Academy Quits School Choice, Parents Told Children at Juanita Virgil Are Re-enrolling in Public Schools," *Milwaukee Journal*, January 7, 1991.

41. Lowe, "The Illusion of 'Choice.'" Figures are full-time equivalent, from the Wisconsin Department of Public Instruction that oversees the voucher program.

42. John F. Witte, "Second Year Report, Milwaukee Parental Choice Program," University of Wisconsin–Madison, December 1992, 20.

43. The Teamsters have about 1.4 million members; see www.teamster.org/content /fast-facts. The National Education Association has 3.2 million members; see www .nea.org/home/1594.htm. The American Federation of Teachers has 1.5 million members; see www.aft.org/about.

18. Voucher Crossfire: Fighting for the Soul of Public Education

1. Benjamin R. Barber, *An Aristocracy of Everyone: The Politics of Education and the Future of America* (New York: Ballantine Books, 1992) 263.

2. Barber, *A Passion for Democracy* (Princeton, NJ: Princeton University Press, 1998), 175.

3. Barber, *Aristocracy of Everyone*, 9.

4. John Dewey, *Democracy and Education* (New York: Macmillan, 1916), chap. vii.

5. "Why We Are Publishing *Selling Out Our Schools*," in *Selling Out Our Schools: Vouchers, Markets, and the Future of Public Education*, ed. Robert Lowe and Barbara Miner (Milwaukee: Rethinking Schools, 1996).

6. The state student antidiscrimination statute specifically allows school boards to operate "one or more schools that enroll only one sex or provide one or more courses that enroll only one sex if the school board makes available to the opposite sex, under the same policies and criteria of admission, schools or courses that are comparable to each such school or course."

7. Figures are for 2010. See *Public Policy Forum Research Brief* 99, no. 2 (February 2011).

8. *Edwards v. Aguillard*, decided June 19, 1987, Justice William J. Brennan Jr., writing for the majority.

9. Frances Patterson, an assistant professor at Valdosta State University in Georgia, surveyed the content of religious-based textbooks used in as many as ten thousand evangelical and fundamentalist Christian schools. "Abortion and homosexuality are strongly condemned [in the textbooks]," she wrote in *Rethinking Schools* 16, no. 2 (Winter 2001–2). "The coverage of abortion begins in elementary school materials and increases in both detail and vehemence through the grades. Language such as 'innocent babies,' 'grisly procedure,' 'legalized murder,' and 'slaughter of unborn babies' is common. Abortion is also explicitly linked to other sinful conduct, including homosexuality, which, in turn, is linked to egregious criminal conduct." One of the publishers surveyed was A Beka Book. In a 2005 survey of private voucher schools, the *Milwaukee Journal Sentinel* reported that at least two schools used curriculum materials from A Beka Book.

10. *Coulee Catholic Schools v. Labor and Industry Review Commission, Department of Workforce Development and Wendy Ostlund, Respondents-Respondents*, decided July 21, 2009, decision by Justice Michael J. Gableman.

11. John Norquist, event transcript, New York City Conference on School Choice, Manhattan Institute for Policy Research, December 13, 2000, www.manhattan institute.org/html/nyc_school_choice4.htm.

12. Warren Furutani, "Vouchers: A Battle for the Soul of Public Education," in *Selling Out Our Schools, Vouchers, Markets, and the Future of Public Education*, ed. Robert Lowe and Barbara Miner (Milwaukee: Rethinking Schools, 1996).

19. Multicultural Crossfire: Redefining the Public School Curriculum

1. Henry Louis Gates Jr., "Multiculturalism: A Conversation Among Different Voices," in *Rethinking Schools: An Agenda for Change*, ed. D. Levine et al. (New York: The New Press, 1995), 8. Gates made the comments while chair of the Afro-American Studies Department at Harvard.

2. Personal interview, February 2011.

3. Hawthorne Faison, named acting superintendent immediately after McMurrin's departure, was the first African American to head MPS, but he did so on a temporary basis during the search for a new superintendent.

4. Bill Dahlk, *Against the Wind: African Americans and the Schools in Milwaukee, 1963–2002* (Milwaukee: Marquette University Press, 2010), 465.

5. Jason De Parle, *American Dream: Three Women, Ten Kids, and a Nation's Drive to End Welfare* (New York: Penguin Books, 2005), 61. High-poverty tracts are defined as those where two-thirds of the residents are poor.

6. "Peterkin Looks Good, but Can't Do It Alone," *Milwaukee Journal* editorial, May 10, 1988.

7. Curtis Lawrence, "Milwaukee: A Case Study," *Rethinking Schools* 15, no. 1 (Fall 2000).

8. Ibid.

9. Dahlk, *Against the Wind*, 505, quoting "Ghetto Blasters," *New Republic*, April 15, 1991.

10. "Promise Exits with Peterkin," *Milwaukee Journal*, November 21, 1990.

11. Stan Karp, "Trouble over the Rainbow," *Rethinking Schools* 7, no. 3 (Spring 1993).

12. Ibid.

13. "Texas Conservatives Win Curriculum Change," *New York Times*, March 12, 2010.

14. "California to Require Gay History in Schools," *New York Times*, July 14, 2011.

20. 1993–95: White Voters Reject New Schools for Black Children, and Things Fall Apart

1. "The Feb. 16 MPS Referendum," *Rethinking Schools* 7, no. 3 (Spring 1993).

2. "Mayor Has Cheaper MPS Building Plan," *Milwaukee Sentinel*, October 28, 1992.

3. "Mayor Sees End of Urban Schools, Says Voucher, Choice System Preferred, *Milwaukee Sentinel*, January 2, 1991, quoting from John Norquist, "No More Tin Cups," *WI Interest* 1, no. 1 (1992), published by the Wisconsin Policy Research Institute.

4. Bill Dahlk, *Against the Wind: African Americans and the Schools in Milwaukee, 1963–2002* (Milwaukee: Marquette University Press, 2010), 566.

5. Quoted in "The Feb. 16 MPS Referendum."

6. "The Feb. 16 MPS Referendum," quoting statistics from the Milwaukee Election Commission.

7. Ibid.; Associated Press, "Testifies Against Police Partner," *New York Times*, October 18, 1981.

8. "Fatigued 'First Biker's' Stadium Tax Comments Struck Out," *Milwaukee Journal Sentinel*, September 7, 1995.

9. "Miller Park Sales Tax Ending Between 2015, '18," *Milwaukee Journal Sentinel*, January 2, 2010.

10. Jason DeParle, *American Dream: Three Women, Ten Kids, and a Nation's Drive to End Welfare* (New York: Penguin Books, 2005), 16.

11. John J. Miller, "Strategic Investment in Ideas: How Two Foundations Reshaped America," Philanthropy Roundtable, Washington, DC, 2003, 50.

12. Charles Murray and Richard J. Herrnstein, *The Bell Curve: Intelligence and Class Structure in American Life* (New York: Free Press, 1994), 548.

13. Ellen Bravo, *Taking on the Big Boys: Or Why Feminism is Good for Families, Business and the Nation* (New York: Feminist Press, 2007), 175, citing *Christian Century*, July 17, 1996.

14. De Parle, *American Dream*, 162.

15. Data based on MPS District Report Cards, available through MPS at http://www2.milwaukee.k12.wi.us/acctrep/mpsrc.html.

16. "Teacher Union Seeks Foul Deal," *Milwaukee Journal*, March 24, 1993.

17. Delbert K. Clear, "The Milwaukee Teachers' Education Association," March 20, 1990, 61, paper made available courtesy of the Milwaukee Teachers' Education Association.
18. Personal interview, September 2011.
19. "Teachers Union Elects Vocal Critic," *Milwaukee Journal Sentinel*, April 28, 1997, via jsonline.com.
20. Copeland was elected to two consecutive terms as union president, the maximum allowed. She was in her second term as union vice president when she died of cancer in 2005.
21. "Community Voice or Captive of the Right? The Black Alliance for Educational Options," People for the American Way Foundation, Special Report, July 2003, 14, n. 21. The report estimates more than $1.7 million from Bradley in the institute's early years, from 1996 to June 2001.

21. 1995: Vouchers for Religious Schools, Abandonment Advances

1. Sara Mosle, "Talking to the Teacher," *New York Times Magazine*, September 12, 1999.
2. Personal email from Behrendt, spring 2009.
3. Milwaukee Parental Choice Program, MPCP Facts and Figures for 1998–99, Department of Public Instruction fact sheet. The 6,000 figure includes all voucher students, some of whom were in kindergarten and were not full-time. The number of FTE voucher students that year was 5,761.
4. "Are Voucher Schools Putting the Squeeze on MPS," *Public Policy Forum Research Brief* 95, no. 1 (February 2007).
5. Figure based on data in Catholic Interracial Council, "Segregation in Milwaukee's Catholic Elementary Schools," *Equity and Excellence in Education* 5 (1967) [the publication was known as *Integrated Education* in 1967].
6. Correspondence from the personal files of Mary Bills.
7. Mordecai Lee, "Why the Wisconsin Legislature Approved Vouchers for Religious Schools," *Rethinking Schools* 10, no. 4 (Summer 1996). Lee also led the Wisconsin Coalition for Public Education, formed to defeat the voucher expansion.
8. Barbara Miner, "Wisconsin Debates Religious Vouchers," *Rethinking Schools* 9, no. 3 (Spring 1995).
9. "Expansion of Choice Supported," *Milwaukee Sentinel*, February 18, 1995.
10. Lee, "Why the Wisconsin Legislature Approved Vouchers."
11. "DPI Bans Single-Sex Schools in Choice Plan," *Milwaukee Journal Sentinel*, July 26, 1998.
12. "Single-Sex Schools OK in Choice Plan, DPI Now Says," *Milwaukee Journal Sentinel*, July 31, 1998.
13. Dan McGroarty, a Bradley Fellow at the Institute for Contemporary Studies and author of *Break These Chains: The Battle for School Choice*, was one of many conservatives who, before differences surfaced, called Williams the "mother of school choice."

14. "Rift Seen in Support of Choice. Williams Shifts Gears Away from Businesses," *Milwaukee Journal Sentinel*, September 10, 1995, via jsonline.com.

15. Personal interview, summer 2010.

16. Bruce Murphy, "The Rise and Fall of Polly Williams," *Milwaukee Magazine*, June 2001.

17. Ibid.

18. Ibid.

19. Ibid.

20. Howard Fuller declined to be interviewed for this book.

21. Bruce Murphy, "Everybody's Savior," *Milwaukee Magazine*, January 1994.

22. The best overview of Howard Fuller's childhood and early career is in the cover story feature by Tom Bamberger, "Who Is Howard Fuller and What Does He Want?" *Milwaukee Magazine*, July 1988.

23. Howard Fuller, press release from the Black Alliance for Educational Options, October 22, 2008.

24. Institute for the Transformation of Learning website, www.marquette.edu/educa tion/centers_clinics/institute-for-the-transformation-of-learning.shtml.

25. Bradley Foundation Annual Reports.

26. Information on funding from 2001 to 2008 is from the Media Matters Action Network, http://mediamattersaction.org/transparency/organization/black_Alliance_for _Educational_Options/funders?year=-. The Bradley funding is based on the foundation's annual reports. The information on the additional $900,000 in start-up funding from the Walton Family Foundation is from "Community Voice or Captive of the Right? The Black Alliance for Educational Options," People for the American Way Foundation, July 2003, 6, citing the conservative weekly *Human Events*.

27. "Community Voice or Captive of the Right?" 2.

28. Barbara Miner, "Supreme Court Debates Vouchers," *Rethinking Schools* 16, no. 3 (Spring 2002).

29. Ibid.

30. This ungrammatical name has caused ongoing confusion but was indeed the school's official name at the time. The school later changed its name to Alex's Academics of Excellence.

31. "Judge Sentences Choice School's CEO, a Convicted Rapist, for Tax Fraud," *Milwaukee Journal Sentinel*, May 4, 2000, via jsonline.com.

32. Sarah Carr, "Who Cleans Up Problem Choice Schools?" *Milwaukee Journal Sentinel*, September 15, 2003.

33. "A Directory of Milwaukee's Voucher Schools," summaries of a special report on visits to 106 of the 115 schools, original URL www.jsonline,com/news,metro /aug05/352269.asp, posted August 31, 2005. Nine of the schools refused to allow reporters to visit.

34. "Harambee Ex-official Guilty. Former Financial Chief for School Convicted of Taking Up to $750,000," *Milwaukee Journal Sentinel*, August 20, 2005, via jsonline.com.

35. "Teachers Paid from Sale of Mercedes. Car Is Only Asset Worth Much from Failed Mandella School," *Milwaukee Journal Sentinel*, December 17, 2005, via jsonline.com.

36. Milwaukee Parental Choice Program, Wisconsin Briefs from the Legislative Reference Bureau, October 2006, Brief 06-15.

37. Howard Fuller's comments can be seen at http://wn.com/Waiting_for_Superman _panel_discussion_clip_2, Panel at KIPP Summit, 2 of 9.

38. "Summary of 2009 Wisconsin Act 28 as It Relates to the Milwaukee Parental Choice Program," Wisconsin Department of Public Instruction.

39. "Are Voucher Schools Putting the Squeeze on MPS?" *Public Policy Forum Research Brief* 95, no. 1 (February 2007).

40. MPS Facilities Master Plan, Demographic Report of the Milwaukee Board of School Directors, February 1992, prepared by Houlihan and Associates, Inc., 27.

41. Wisconsin Department of Public Instruction, 2010 Private School Enrollment, available as Excel spreadsheet: http://www.dpi.wi.gov/lbstat/privdata.html.

42. "Milwaukee Parental Choice Program Facts and Figures for 2010–2011 as of November 2010," Wisconsin Department of Public Instruction.

43. *Public Policy Forum Research Brief* 99, no. 2 (February 2011): 2.

22. 1999: (Re)Segregation Déjà Vu—Neighborhood Schools and Open Enrollment

1. "MPS Budget Would Eliminate 260 Teaching Positions," *Milwaukee Journal Sentinel*, April 29, 2010, via jsonline.com.

2. Personal memo by Elijah Mueller, in author's personal files. See also "The Emperors Are Exposed," *Shepherd Express*, March 30, 2000.

3. "Board Member Regrets Comment About Laptops," *Milwaukee Journal Sentinel*, February 16, 1999, via jsonline.com.

4. A 1999 report found that Wisconsin had the second-highest increase in segregated schools from 1980 to 1996 (with the data driven by Milwaukee, the state's largest district with the highest percentage of African Americans). See Gary Orfield and John T. Yun, "Resegregation in American Schools," The Civil Rights Project, Harvard University, June 1999, 19.

5. Bob Peterson and Larry Miller, "Forward to the Past?" *Rethinking Schools* 15, no. 1 (Fall 2000).

6. Bob Peterson, "Neighborhood Schools, Busing and the Struggle for Equality," *Rethinking Schools* 12, no. 3 (Spring 1998).

7. "The Implications of Eliminating Busing: Considerations at the End of an Era," November 1999, Public Policy Forum, i.

8. "School's Plan Wins Board's Approval 8–0, Vote Marks 'End of Forced Busing,'" *Milwaukee Journal Sentinel*, August 25, 2000.

9. "The Implications of Eliminating Busing," ii.

10. MPS District Report Card, 2009–2010, 9, 10.

11. Department of Public Instruction WINSS data analysis, http://data.dpi.state.wi.us /data.

12. Data available through the state Department of Public Instruction's WINSS data-base, available at http://data.dpi.state.wi.us/data.

13. Barbara Miner, "MPS Revamps Admissions Policies for High Schools," *Rethinking Schools* 11, no. 1 (Fall 1995).

14. "Big Bucks Being Spent on School Race," *Milwaukee Journal*, March 31, 1991.

15. Bob Peterson, "Milwaukee: Who Won and Why," *Rethinking Schools* 13, no. 4 (Summer 1999).

16. 2000 U.S. Census data. Also available through the Carfree Census database at www.bikesatwork.com/carfree/census-lookup.php?state_select=ALL_STATES &lower_pop=250000&upper_pop=999999999&sort_num=5&show_rows=25 &first_row=0.

17. "Some Places' Integration Seats Vanish. Aid Formula Makes Big Players Prefer Open Enrollment to 220," *Milwaukee Journal Sentinel*, December 26, 2010, via jsonline.com.

18. "MPS Watches Kids Hop Border," *Milwaukee Journal Sentinel*, February 6, 2011. Statistics on Chapter 220 in 2000: "Chapter 220 Plan Aims to Cut Busing," *Milwaukee Journal Sentinel*, October 4, 2000.

19. "Charter School Fund Drive Launched," *Milwaukee Journal Sentinel*, October 13, 1998. See also "City Agrees Charter Schools Are Public, but Dispute Goes On," *Milwaukee Journal Sentinel*, October 20, 1998, via jsonline.com.

20. There is no report by either UWM or the city compiling overall figures. Data for charters can be gathered on a school-by-school basis using the state Department of Public Instruction database. In 2010, most of the UWM charters had one-third to one-half of MPS's almost 20 percent special ed enrollment, with a few in the double digits. None approached the MPS average, except for a three-year-old to second grade school geared toward disabled children. City charters tended to have a higher percentage of special ed, but still below the MPS average.

21. Personal interview, June 2010.

22. See, for instance, the ERIC Clearinghouse on Disabilities and Gifted Education, ERIC Digest E609, Public Charter Schools and Students with Disabilities, at www .ericdigests.org/2002-2/public.htm.

23. Joe Nathan, "Progressives Should Support Charter Schools," *Rethinking Schools* 11, no. 2 (Winter 1996–97).

24. Much of this analysis rests on the introduction I co-wrote for the book *Keeping the Promise: The Debate over Charter Schools* (Milwaukee: Rethinking Schools, in col-laboration with Center for Community Change, 2008).

25. Gary Orfield, "Foreword," in Erica Frankenberg, Genevieve Siegel Hawley, and Jia Wang, *Choice Without Equity: Charter School Segregation and the Need for Civil Rights Standards* (Los Angeles: Civil Rights Project/Proyecto Derechos Civiles, UCLA Graduate School of Education & Information Studies, 2010), 1–2, available at www.civilrightsproject.ucla.edu.

26. *The Condition of Education 2011*, Indicator 3, Charter School Enrollment. S. Aud, W. Hussar, G. Kena, K. Bianco, L. Frohlich, J. Kemp, and K. Tahan, *The Condition of Education 2011* (NCES 2011-033), U.S. Department of Education, National Center for Education Statistics (Washington, DC: U.S. Government Printing Office, 2011).

27. Alex Molnar, Gary Miron, and Jessica L. Urschel, "Profiles of For-Profit Education Management Organizations," National Education Policy Center, School of Education, University of Colorado at Boulder, December 2010.

28. EdisonLearning, www.edisonlearning.com/about-edisonlearning.

29. "The Best School $75 Million Can Buy," *New York Times*, July 8, 2011.

23. Milwaukee's Great Migration #3: Global Immigrants Make Milwaukee Their Home

1. Because Denis does not have legal immigration papers, his last name has been changed. Information based on personal interview, September 2011.

2. In addition to bilingual programs at twenty elementary and middle schools, four high schools offer bilingual Spanish/English programs. Two-way bilingual programs, in which roughly half the students speak English as their home language and half speak Spanish, are offered at two elementary schools and one middle school. Immersion programs providing English-speaking students a chance to immerse themselves in learning a second language are offered at six MPS schools, focusing on French, German, Spanish, and Italian. A program in Mandarin Chinese is also being developed. Stand-alone English as a Second Language programs are offered at fifteen MPS schools.

3. The vignettes of Manny Molina and Chris Her-Xiong are based on Barbara Miner, "Local Color," *Milwaukee Magazine*, November 2009.

24. 2002–10: No Child Left Behind. Really?

1. Personal interview, March 2010.

2. Diane Ravitch, "Room for Debate: A Running Commentary on the News," *New York Times* online, March 6, 2011.

3. Harvey Kantor and Robert Lowe, "Reflections on History and Quality Education," *Educational Researcher* 33 (June–July 2004): 477.

4. Barbara Miner, "Seed Money for Conservatives," *Rethinking Schools* 19, no. 4 (Summer 2004), citing a National Public Radio interview on May 25, 2001.

5. James D. Anderson, "The Historical Context for Understanding the Test Score Gap," *Journal of Public Management & Social Policy* 10, no. 1 (Summer 2004): 11.

6. Robert Lowe, "Diane Ravitch Revisited," *Urban Review,* June 8, 2011, DOI: 10.1007/ s11256-011-0180-3, citing data from the National Assessment of Educational Progress, National Center for Education Statistics (2010).

7. Diane Ravitch, "What Works Best: Help or Punishment?" Bridging Differences blog, *Education Week,* May 17, 2011.

8. MPS District Improvement Plan 2010–11, September 9, 2010, Milwaukee Public Schools, Department of District and School Improvement.

9. Data based on the 2002–3 District Report Card, available through the MPS Division of Assessment and Accountability.

10. Data accessed October 3, 2011, at www.thedailybeast.com/newsweek/features/2010 /americas-best-high-schools/list.html. Riverside University High School and Milwaukee School of Languages were also consistently listed amount the nation's top schools.

11. The Louisville case was *Meredith v. Jefferson County Board of Education.* The Seattle case was *Parents Involved in Community Schools v. Seattle School District No. 1.*

12. "Justices Question School Diversity Plans," Associated Press, December 4, 2006, as printed in the *Washington Post.*

13. "Supreme Court Votes to Limit the Use of Race in Integration Plans," *New York Times,* June 29, 2007.

14. Ibid.

15. Superintendent Gregory Thornton, blog, March 31, 2011, available at: http://super intendentthornton.blogspot.com.

16. Complaint filed June 6, 2011, with the U.S. Department of Justice, Civil Rights Division. Complaint accessed on October 3, 2011, at www.aclu.org/files/assets/ complaint_to_doj_re_milwaukee_voucher_program_final.pdf.

17. Ibid.

18. Ibid.

19. "City Is No. 9 in Poverty Clusters; Study Links Milwaukee, New Orleans," *Milwaukee Journal Sentinel,* October 12, 2005, via jsonline.com.

20. "Milwaukee Tops Segregation Study," *Milwaukee Journal Sentinel,* December 15, 2010, via jsonline.com. Data based on the 2005–9 American Community Survey of the U.S. Census.

21. Marc Levine, "The Crisis of Black Male Joblessness in Milwaukee," Working Paper, Center for Economic Development, University of Wisconsin–Milwaukee, March 2007. The Levine paper cites John Pawasarat, "Barriers to Employment: Prison Time," Milwaukee Employment and Training Institute, University of Wisconsin–Milwaukee, 2007, 4–5. In 2001, Wisconsin led the country in black incarceration rates, with an estimated 4,058 black prison and jail inmates per 100,000 residents—a figure putting Wisconsin far ahead of its closest competitors,

Iowa and Texas. Overall, Wisconsin's incarceration rate for blacks was more than ten times the rate for whites.

22. "For Milwaukee's Children, an Early Grave," *Milwaukee Journal Sentinel*, January 22, 2011, via jsonline.com.

25. The Heartland Rises Up, and a New Era of Protest Begins

1. Firefighters and police were exempted from Walker's legislation.

2. "Charles Woodson, Green Bay Packers See Connection Between Wisconsin Unions' Plight and Their Own," *New York Daily News*, February 20, 2011.

3. Tuesday was the first day of protests involving thousands of people from across the state, and was the beginning of the capitol sleepover. Hundreds of students and faculty from the University of Wisconsin had protested on Monday in a Valentine's Day "Don't Break My Heart" protest. For a timeline of events: www.presstv.ir/usdetail/168712.html or http://host.madison.com/wsj/news/local/govt-and-politics/article_28e93294-4136-11e0-9680-001cc4c002e0.html or www.thedailypage.com/isthmus/article.php?article=32447.

4. The 98,000 members included teachers, support staff from secretaries to bus drivers, active retired members, and university students studying to be educators. The American Federation of Teachers–Wisconsin had 17,000 members. Overall, K–12 and higher education accounted for 229,141 full- and part-time employees in Wisconsin—a significant percentage of the 384,869 full- and part-time government employees in the state. WEAC data accessed at www.weac.org/About_WEAC/Fact_Sheet.aspx. AFT data accessed www.aft-wisconsin.org/?zone=/unionactive/view_page.cfm&page=About20AFT2DW. Government employee data based on the 2010 Annual Survey of Public Employment and Payroll of the U.S. Census Bureau.

5. William Cronon, "Wisconsin's Radical Break," *New York Times*, March 21, 2011.

6. "Wisconsin Is 'Ground Zero' for Battle Over Union," *USA Today*, updated February 28, 2011.

7. Katrina vanden Heuvel, "Wisconsin: Ground Zero in the Fight for Democracy," *The Nation* blog, February 24, 2011, and *Washington Post*, February 22, 2011.

8. "From Local Roots, Bradley Foundation Builds Conservative Empire," *Milwaukee Journal Sentinel*, November 19, 2011, via jsonline.com.

9. Transcript of prank Koch-Walker conversation, *Wisconsin State Journal*, posted February 23, 2011. Walker believed the interview was with billionaire conservative donor David Koch, although it was with blogger Ian Murphy.

10. The study is available through the Center on Budget and Policy Priorities, "New School Year Brings Steep Cuts in State Funding for Schools," www.cbpp.org/cms/index.cfm?fa=view&id=3569&emailView=1, updated October 7, 2011.

11. State Superintendent Tony Evers, testimony to the Joint Committee in Finance, March 31, 2011.

12. Data on the overall results: "Choice Schools Not Outperforming MPS," *Milwaukee Journal Sentinel*, March 29, 2011. Data on the non-special-ed results, "Test results spark debate over best way to measure achievement," *Milwaukee Journal Sentinel*, April 7, 2011, via jsonline.com.

13. "Choice Pupils Shuffle. High Turnover Impedes Study of Academic Gains," *Milwaukee Journal Sentinel*, August 13, 2010, via jsonline.com.

14. Patrick McIlheran, "No Worse, and Maybe Improving," *Milwaukee Journal Sentinel*, April 11, 2010.

15. O. Ricardo Pimentel, "Yes, You All Were Duped by Choice," *Milwaukee Journal Sentinel*, March 8, 2011.

16. Wisconsin Department of Public Instruction, news release, June 16, 2011, "Assembly Budget Has Potential to Expand Vouchers Statewide." Also, Wisconsin Department of Public Instruction, news release, June 3, 2011, "Evers Statement: Committee Expands Vouchers While Cutting Public School Funding."

17. "Summary of 2011 Wisconsin Act 32 Final 2011–13 Budget with Vetoes," Wisconsin Department of Public Instruction, June 2011.

18. "Advocates of Privatized Education Want to End Public Schools," *Star-Ledger*, July 11, 2011, via nj.com.

19. "Selling Out Public Schools," Wisconsin Center for Investigative Journalism, *Capital Times*, September 21, 2011, via http://host.madison.com.

20. Personal interview, September 2011.

INDEX

Rogers, Aaron, 250
Roosevelt, Franklin D., 22
Roosevelt, Theodore, 254
Roth, Stephen J., 75
Roy, Angelique, 140
Rozga, Margaret "Peggy," 117, 265
rust belt, 100, 110, 114–22
Ruth, Babe, 3, 4

Sadaukai, Owusu (Fuller), 208
St. Mark's AME Church, 30
Samolyk, Vicki, 149–50
San Antonio v. Rodriguez, 146
Sa'Rai and Zigler Upper Excellerated
    Academy, 214
Scaife family philanthropy, 163
Scalia, Antonin, 210–11
Schlaefer, Father Austin, 52
Schlitz beer, 13, 115
Seale, Bobby, 179
Seattle, desegregation in, 244
Selective Service, draft files burned,
    66–67
Selma, Alabama, "Bloody Sunday," 51–53
Sensenbrenner, F. James, 78, 127
Seppeh, David, 213
September 11 attacks, 237
Seraphim, Christ, 30
Serbian immigrants, 20
Shagaloff, June, 34
sharecropper system, 44, 45–46
Simon, William E., 161
Sinicki, Chris, 224
slavery, 73, 151
Small, Sandra, 224
Socialist Party, 24, 26, 27–28
Social Security, 156, 240
Sonnenberg, Michael, 224
Souter, David H., 211
South Boston, 80–81, 84
Stalin, Joseph, 28
Stanford, Greg, 194
Steinman, Edward, 141
Stengel, Casey, 3, 4
Stevens, John Paul, 245
Stollenwerk, John, 200
Story, Harold, 34, 35
Student Nonviolent Coordinating
    Committee (SNCC), 33

Sturdivant, Tom, 3–4
Sugrue, Thomas, 74, 75
Supreme Court, U.S.: *Brown v. Board of
    Education*, 4, 5, 6, 29, 33, 67, 71–74,
    75, 76, 130, 141, 167, 173, 210, 244;
    on church/state separation, 210–11;
    desegregation overturned by, 244–45;
    Green v. New Kent County, 74; on
    housing covenants, 111; *Lau v. Nichols*,
    141, 142; *Milliken v. Bradley*, 71, 74–75;
    Milwaukee school desegregation case,
    78–79, 97–98, 99; *Plessy v. Ferguson*, 73,
    75; *San Antonio v. Rodriguez*, 146; on
    special education, 245–47; on the
    teaching of evolution, 175; on voucher
    schools, 203, 241
Swan, Monroe, 46–47, 79, 204

Taylor, Tenasha, 160
Taylor, Theadoll, 226
Teamsters Union, 170, 284n43
Tea Party, 165, 176, 200–201, 260
Tenorio, Rita, 144, 145
Texas, law and order in, 248
Texas Board of Education, 187
Thomas, Clarence, 164
Thompson, Bruce, 217, 218–19, 222
Thompson, Ken, 118–19
Thompson, Tommy, 136, 168, 169,
    190–92, 194, 200–201, 202, 219, 226;
    Power to the People, 167
Thornton, Gregory, 247, 264
Tubman, Harriet, 185
Turner, Jason, 192

Ullrich, Jeannie, 124–26
*United States of America v. Bartlett,
    Sprengler and Masarik*, 277n14
University of Virginia, 172
University of Wisconsin–Milwaukee,
    228
Urban League, 22, 23, 86
UW-Madison Teaching Assistants'
    Association, 251

Vieau, Jacques, 140
Vietnam War, antiwar protests, 38, 66–67,
    161
Vincent, Harold, 11, 48, 50–51

CELEBRATING INDEPENDENT PUBLISHING

Thank you for reading this book published by The New Press. The New Press is a nonprofit, public interest publisher. New Press books and authors play a crucial role in sparking conversations about the key political and social issues of our day.

We hope you enjoyed this book and that you will stay in touch with The New Press. Here are a few ways to stay up to date with our books, events, and the issues we cover:

- Sign up at www.thenewpress.com/subscribe to receive updates on New Press authors and issues and to be notified about local events
- Like us on Facebook: www.facebook.com/newpressbooks
- Follow us on Twitter: www.twitter.com/thenewpress

Please consider buying New Press books for yourself; for friends and family; or to donate to schools, libraries, community centers, prison libraries, and other organizations involved with the issues our authors write about.

The New Press is a 501(c)(3) nonprofit organization. You can also support our work with a tax-deductible gift by visiting www.thenewpress.com /donate.